MANPOWER and TRAINING for CORRECTIONS

MANPOWER and TRAINING for CORRECTIONS

Proceedings of an Arden House Conference

June 24-26, 1964

CHARLES S. PRIGMORE, PH.D., *Editor*

CO-SPONSORS:

American Correctional Association
American Sociological Association (Criminology Section)
Council on Social Work Education
National Council on Crime and Delinquency
Western Interstate Commission for Higher Education

COUNCIL ON SOCIAL WORK EDUCATION
345 EAST 46TH STREET • NEW YORK, N. Y. 10017

LIBRARY OF CONGRESS CATALOG NUMBER 65-25759
No. 65-96-1

PRINTED IN THE UNITED STATES OF AMERICA BY
SOWERS PRINTING CO., LEBANON, PENNSYLVANIA

Foreword

THE COUNCIL ON SOCIAL WORK EDUCATION has always had a keen interest in the field of corrections. In 1960, with the help of a grant from the Ford Foundation, the Council established a special project to develop and enhance social work education for correctional practice. The overall objectives of this project were to increase the number of social workers entering the correctional field and to introduce correctional content and perspectives into the generic curriculum of schools of social work.

This task of expanding both the quantity and quality of social work education for corrections required that the relationship of social work education to the many professions and groups who share responsibility for correctional rehabilitation be specified. The identification of correctional manpower resources available for effective multidisciplinary collaboration became one of a series of crucial issues as the Council, together with schools, began to identify resources for field work instruction and to recruit students and faculty interested in corrections.

The Conference described in this book was one of a series of activities undertaken by the Council on Social Work Education in cooperation with other interested agencies to assess correctional manpower needs and resources. As the roster of participants reveals, the Arden House Conference brought together the many diversified groups traditionally involved in correctional rehabilitation. In so doing, it reaffirmed the viewpoint of its sponsors that corrections is a field of practice which requires the utilization of many specialized skills, pursued by multiple professional and semi-professional groups in cooperation with one another.

It is our hope that the interdisciplinary communication and collaboration initiated at the Arden House Conference will be continued under the direction of an agency that can unite the many groups in a cooperative national program for corrections.

The Council is proud to have played a key role in helping to promote the interest and establish the means to bring this cooperation about. The Council will continue to work together with appropriate groups in enhancing correctional practice. It will continue to give special attention to the preparation of social work personnel for practice in corrections as well as in all other traditional and new settings desiring and requiring social workers.

The Council is most appreciative of the help of the American Correctional Association, the National Council on Crime and Delinquency, the American Sociological Association, and the Western Interstate Commission for Higher Education which joined the Council in sponsoring the Arden House Conference. We gratefully acknowledge the contribution of the Ford Foundation in financing this Conference and in supporting the Council's interest and activities in the field of corrections.

We extend our thanks to Milton Rector, who chaired the Council's Committee on Corrections as well as the Arden House Conference; to the members of the Council's Advisory Committee on the Corrections Project whose names appear in the appendix; to Charles Prigmore for his work in planning the Conference and compiling the papers for this book; to Lionel Koppman for editing the material for publication; and to Constance Coates for assisting in the various stages of the preparation of the book.

We hope the book will be of interest and value to many.

ARNULF M. PINS
Associate Executive Director

November 1, 1965

Preface

AMONG THE MOST SIGNIFICANT STRUGGLES of our time is the effort to provide social justice to all people—equal protection of the law, equal opportunity in education and employment, and equal opportunity in recreation, housing, worship, and use of public accommodations.

Equal protection of the law, or equal justice, has been a claim of our society since its inception, and it is true that for those citizens who can afford its costs our system of civil and criminal justice guarantees every man, woman, and child his or her "day in court." It costs money to employ well qualified counsel, prepare appeals, take advantage of bail bond provisions, and otherwise utilize the excellent safeguards in our laws. Unfortunately, it is true that the jail is often the poor man's bail bond, an inexperienced attorney the poor man's counsel, the state training school the poor boy's psychiatrist, and an untrained parole officer his counselor and social worker.

In the past decades, a number of steps have been taken by some national organizations to reduce these inequities and, at the same time, reduce the threat of crime and delinquency. But sound criminal or family court laws, better organized probation or parole departments, good systems of institutions, and diagnostic centers will only ensure equality of treatment for offenders and safety for the public if they are well staffed.

Personnel throughout *all* these correctional programs must be well selected and well qualified. They must be capable of effecting change in the attitudes and behavior of offenders and potential offenders, thus improving the services and programs for prevention and treatment of crime and delinquency.

Well qualified correctional employees are not born but made. They are not found on every street corner, but must be sought out and prepared for their arduous but rewarding careers. When recruited, they must find the satisfactions and tenure of a career in the service of other people. Without these employees, laws, institutions, and services are but a hollow promise at best.

The need for trained staff has greatly increased in the past decade because of the general population growth, a continuing rise in delinquency and crime, and an increasing demand on the part of the public that the problem be dealt with effectively. At the same time, the existing manpower supply in corrections is being tapped for anti-poverty programs and training centers, mental health programs, mental retardation services, and social problem prevention campaigns. Personnel essential to correctional rehabilitation include teachers, social workers, psychologists, psychiatrists, lawyers, sociologists, management and training specialists, and thousands of nonprofessional but equally important persons with special skills in designing prevention programs. The situation has become so acute that it is impossible to staff new or existing programs adequately in most jurisdictions.

It is no longer possible for the correctional field to rely on makeshift solutions or hope for a miracle. Planned, coordinated action to provide adequate manpower, and to improve salaries and working conditions in order to hold qualified staff, is now urgent and mandatory. The time for action is *now*.

The whole field of corrections is grateful to the Council on Social Work Education for initiating and giving leadership to the special activities which have led to this significant Conference. Special thanks are also expressed to the American Correctional Association, the American Sociological Association, the National Council on Crime and Delinquency, and the Western Interstate Commission for Higher Education for their co-sponsorship of the Conference and their help in its planning and conduct.

It is my earnest hope that the Arden House Conference on Manpower and Training for Corrections of 1964 has set the stage for the alleviation of these critical correctional manpower problems. I am confident that correctional personnel throughout America concur in this conviction, and that they will wholeheartedly support the Joint Commission on Correctional Manpower and Training and implement the other Arden House Conference decisions.

MILTON G. RECTOR, *Chairman*
Arden House Conference on Manpower
and Training for Corrections

Contents

APPENDIXES

Decisions of the Conference

PRIORITY MANPOWER AND TRAINING NEEDS

Recruitment

1. A broad recruitment campaign should be launched to attract more as well as higher quality personnel to perform correctional tasks.

2. The recruitment campaign should focus on the recruitment of personnel at all levels.

Pre-Entry Preparation

1. When tasks are identified for which graduate professional education is necessary, the field of corrections should collaborate with the professional schools, graduate schools, and educational and other professional associations to develop and improve guidelines for curricula.

2. When tasks are identified for which graduate professional education is not necessary, systematic exploration of undergraduate preparation for these tasks should be undertaken, and steps taken to develop, with colleges and universities, appropriate guidelines.

3. When tasks are identified for which traditional college-level training is not indicated or necessary, systematic exploration of other effective kinds of preparation for such tasks should be undertaken.

4. Stipends and scholarships currently available for graduate professional, undergraduate, and other preparation for corrections should be identified, and reports prepared for use of agencies, schools, and prospective applicants.

Post-Entry Education and Training

1. The role of in-service training should be clarified and related to professional education and to specific agency or institution needs.

2. A comprehensive assessment and evaluation of current in-service training programs should be undertaken.

3. New and experimental approaches to in-service training should continue to be sought through creative action research programs and staff development experiments.

4. Joint university-agency efforts to integrate the practice of working with individuals, groups, and communities should be expanded.

5. Further studies of the impact of administrative structure and policy upon manpower utilization should be encouraged.

6. A comprehensive monograph on training should be developed, setting forth the basic goals and nature of in-service training for correctional and related services.

7. Instructional guides should be developed for in-service training, short-term institutes, and workshops for all groups of correctional personnel. These guides should be made available to educational institutions, correctional agencies, and merit systems.

8. Centers for in-service training should be established and expanded for correctional systems. Such centers may be developed on a local, state, regional, and national basis depending upon the size of the various correctional systems involved. These centers should have broad-gauge training approaches which will increase understanding and cooperation between agencies and institutions identified with corrections, social welfare, and mental health.

9. A program of exchange of faculty and practitioners for varying periods of time should be launched. Such a program would serve to relate professional education more closely to practice than it has been in the past, and it would serve to give practitioners a better grasp of recent advances in research and curriculum. It would facilitate joint educational-practice experimentation and demonstration.

10. Expanded in-service training programs involving top and middle management should be designed and promoted. Such programs should include information about the kinds of tasks persons with various levels of education and training can be expected to perform.

11. Specific program areas in which correctional and related agencies can qualify for training grants, field instruction, and internship training should be identified and utilized.

Financing

1. The adequacy of existing stipends in the correctional field requires study. Such factors as the marital status and financial obligations of recipients should be considered to insure maximum flexibility.

2. The number of present stipends should be increased, and new resources sought. Stipends are needed for professional and graduate education, work-study programs, enriched in-service training, and faculty-practitioner exchange programs.

3. Increased consultation should be provided to correctional agencies, professional schools, and other educational institutions by appropriate groups, in order to expand the utilization of existing stipend programs.

4. Particular emphasis should be given to the search for funds for recruitment and development of qualified field instructors.

5. Funds should be sought to systematize and expand programs of in-service training for all groups of correctional and related personnel.

EMPLOYING AGENCIES AND INSTITUTIONS

Salaries

1. Federal, state, and local governments should provide and maintain salary levels for correctional work consistent with the required educational background and skills, as evidenced by comparison with other fields.

2. Salary levels should be high enough to hold competent staff and to attract a greater share of able young people to educational programs leading to work in the correctional field. Salary levels should take into account the hazards of, and the patience and the breadth of experience needed for, service in the correctional field.

3. Private agencies providing services in the correctional field should also be encouraged to establish and maintain salary levels in keeping with the requirements and levels in other fields.

4. Completion of specialized education which increases job effectiveness or other evidence of growth and competence in service should be rewarded by salary increases and other recognition outside the annual increment provisions.

5. Compensation systems for correctional personnel should provide sufficiently broad ranges of pay and levels of job classifications to insure a meaningful number and size of salary increases in order to maintain incentive.

Civil Service

1. Traditional civil service guarantees should be extended to government employees working in this field.

2. Civil service law or regulations should permit a wide choice to appointing authorities in selecting from a list of eligibles, perhaps one out of five, in order to allow a broader range of candidates.

3. Race, religion, national origin, or residence should not be part of civil service qualifications.

4. Evaluation of personal qualifications through the use of an oral examination should be part of the examination procedure or the appointment process.

5. Utilization of positions which are exempt from qualifications should be decreased. Administrators in charge of correctional services should be under civil service or meet comparable requirements of education, experience, and background for appointment.

6. More professional positions should be established with qualifications such that more personnel can serve as field instructors and internship supervisors. New professionals will then have supervisors with backgrounds such that the new professionals can pass qualifying examinations and professional boards.

7. Rapid changes in the correctional field make mandatory an increase in the number of training and research personnel to facilitate staff development and introduction of new ideas.

Education and Training

1. Government at all levels should provide leadership in all areas related to correctional manpower and training.

2. Continuing education and training for administrators should receive top priority because training is the responsibility of "command."

3. Administrators in corrections should be drawn from personnel of many occupations, experienced and trained in the correctional field. Therefore, provision should be made for potential administrators from all groups to acquire administrative training and experience.

4. More systematic and better planned post-entry training programs are needed to enhance the competence of correctional staff.

5. The use of the trainee position for career entrance into corrections should be utilized, provided there is a built-in system of opportunities for further professional graduate education as well as for in-service training.

6. Correctional systems should develop centers for staff training or arrange for use of community education for this purpose. State government should provide such services for small courts, institutions, parole staffs, and other agencies unable to afford training resources.

7. Stipends for educational expenses, and leave with pay, where appropriate, should be established for post-entry education, and directed

particularly at first-line supervisors and middle management in systems without fully qualified staffs.

8. It is the responsibility of correctional agencies, in cooperation with schools, to expand field placements and internships for students in various disciplines and professions. These placements should have the proper supervision to assure that the experience is of maximum training value and stipends adequate to attract qualified students should be provided, both for summer and academic-year programs.

9. Government at all levels, especially the federal government, should continue to expand financial support and grants for demonstration, experimentation, and evaluative research.

10. When any new or expanded governmental activity is launched in the field of corrections, stipends and field placement facilities should be established in order to attract and educate personnel for the new venture.

11. Correctional agencies should develop job classifications and agency policies designed to make maximum use of special training and special skills of staff members.

12. Since corrections is a vital service, affecting all citizens of our country, it is the obligation of all schools to make their appropriate contribution to correctional education and training.

Research

1. Research and development staff must be an integral part of any correctional administration. The increasingly rapid rate of change in the conditions of human life, the growth of knowledge and skill in the behavioral and social sciences, the shifts in the causes of crime as societal changes occur, the consequent innovation and experimentation in corrections, and the growing public demand for objective evidence of the effectiveness of correctional treatment make this mandatory.

2. For research to be of practical value in guiding and evaluating correctional policies and practices, two prerequisites are that correctional officials have some understanding of the fundamentals of research methodology, and that research personnel be trained and experienced in the operations of the correctional agencies which they serve.

3. In order to promote and facilitate this training of correctional researchers and administrators for mutual understanding, correctional agencies and universities should collaborate to provide internships in correctional agencies for university students interested in correctional research, as well as to provide stipends for the graduate education of those correctional staff who demonstrate aptitude for and commitment to correctional research.

4. Arrangements for continuing communication should be established among directors of correctional agencies, their research staffs, and university officials, to coordinate their mutual efforts to advance that scientific knowledge which enhances the effectiveness of corrections.

5. One component of this coordination should be collaborative research to determine the factors which limit the utilization of research in corrections, to the end that this utilization may be augmented wherever it is found to be deficient.

6. Interstate and local cooperation of correctional research agencies should be fostered to coordinate their efforts for maximum efficiency and for comparison of their findings. Existing commissions, boards and other structures created for this purpose should be used wherever possible.

7. The proposed Joint Commission is urged to investigate the current practice of the utilization of correctional facilities, resources, and manpower for treatment, detention, and management of mentally ill or mentally disturbed persons, adult or juvenile, who are not criminal offenders.

Financing

Federal, state, and local governments should appropriate all necessary sums of money in accordance with such governmental role and obligation, to effectuate each and every one of the proposals heretofore enumerated and recommended, and to accomplish the purposes to which such proposals are directed.

NATIONAL CORRECTIONAL ORGANIZATIONS

Coordination of Effort

1. A massive and centrally focused action program on correctional manpower and training requires that the national correctional organizations develop close liaison and coordination among themselves and with related professional associations, to support and promote a wide variety of educational and training programs for personnel in the correctional field.

2. The national correctional organizations should maintain liaison with local, state, and regional correctional organizations, as well as with

correctional organizations in other countries and with international organizations, in order to assure the effectiveness of a massive action program.

Expansion of Membership

The national correctional organizations should be encouraged to expand their memberships, since a broader membership base will bring together in staff development programs the rank and file of personnel dealing directly with offenders and will facilitate communication and cohesion throughout the correctional field.

Recruitment

The appropriate national organizations should jointly plan continuing activities to give leadership, and to aid the leadership programs of others, in manpower recruiting and training in the following ways:

a. Through their promotional and professional publications.
b. Through such organized public interpretation efforts as corrections career day speaker bureaus, national conferences and institutes, and speaker's kits for school and community speaker programs—i.e., debating teams and toastmaster clubs.
c. Through research, studies, and technical consultation to test and upgrade practices, organization of services, and utilization of personnel and services.
d. Through committees on the development of standards and committees for personnel and practice.
e. Through sponsoring legislation and social action to increase legislative and public support for professionally educated and trained personnel and for the kind of correctional administration and organizations which can compete favorably with other fields which recruit qualified career personnel.
f. Through the promotion of in-service training and staff development, including field placements, educational leave, scholarships, and stipends, as a responsibility of correctional administration.
g. Through the promotion of the concept of comprehensive planning for community, county, state, and federal correctional services, public and private, to insure maximum inter-agency cooperation and priority setting in practice training and utilization of professionally educated personnel.
h. Through encouraging public and school libraries, including high school and college libraries, to include appropriate material with recruitment value.

Education and Training

1. The national correctional organizations should give priority to the need for professional education for tasks which require such preparation. Alternatives to such professional education should be recognized as alternatives to be utilized until the supply of appropriately qualified personnel is adequate.
2. The national correctional organizations should review the existing facilities and consider as a priority task the encouragement and promotion of student placement facilities and internships for the range of disciplines and professions involved in corrections. Such facilities should also include supervised laboratory opportunities for demonstration, experimentation, and research.
3. The national correctional organizations should work with the professional education associations and schools in reviewing existing guidelines for the training of correctional personnel and in developing interpretive statements for the use of correctional personnel.
4. The prestige of the national correctional organizations should be employed in obtaining legislative and administrative support of programs and budgets for the education and training of correctional personnel.
5. The national correctional organizations should work with appropriate educational associations and schools toward the ongoing improvement of education and training for correctional personnel, including the incorporation in curricula of content of an interdisciplinary nature.
6. The national correctional organizations should undertake and support comprehensive and long-range studies covering manpower, education, and training in the correctional field, and the entire problem of crime and delinquency prevention and control.

NATIONAL PROFESSIONAL ORGANIZATIONS

Basic Obligations of the National Professional Organizations

Many professional organizations represent disciplines which share the responsibility for articulating and attaining the social goals of correctional activity. These organizations must recognize a continuing obligation for studying, evaluating, and improving their professional contributions to the correctional field. Such responsibility should be carried out in special recognition of corrections as an emerging sphere of human knowledge composed of segments of all the behavioral and social sciences, including law.

Establishing the Status of Corrections

The professional organizations share with the corrections field the responsibility for the establishment of qualifications essential for both professional and nonprofessional positions in the field. This responsibility extends to the development of educational, experience, and personality criteria for correctional personnel and to the ongoing staff development of their practitioners in the correctional field. Each professional organization should work in a partnership arrangement with other professions involved and with the correctional field, including the national correctional organizations, with a view towards professionalization of corrections.

Research Obligations

The professional associations should share with universities and the field of corrections the responsibility for research, demonstration, and experimentation in regard to the tasks, techniques, services, laws, and other aspects of correctional work that affect the professional practice of their practitioners and the contributions of the profession to correctional objectives. The professional associations have a corollary obligation to publish findings and theories in the professional literature.

Liaison Responsibilities

Liaison should be encouraged between the professional organizations on the national level and the various local, state, and regional organizations established by the respective professions. Primary responsibility rests with the national professional organizations to develop and sustain a richer communication at the international level.

Community Education

The professional organizations should assume a large measure of the responsibility for community education, social policy formulation, and social action in regard to social problems including crime and delinquency. The national professional organizations should encourage the formation and cooperation of lay and civic groups in the field of corrections.

Professional Education

Each profession should identify the kinds of basic education, supervision, in-service training, and continuing education, if any, recommended for various practitioner tasks in corrections with preparation in that particular profession. In particular, each professional organization should:

a. Orient its own professional curriculum in terms of the significance which corrections has assumed in our society; and

b. Explore the possibility of contributing to the development of a professional educational curriculum for corrections in terms of the particular specialty which its discipline can offer to corrections.

NATIONAL PROFESSIONAL EDUCATION ASSOCIATIONS

The national associations concerned with professional education in such disciplines as law, social work, medicine, education, and theology are in key positions with respect to the objectives of this Conference. These organizations should lead the way in implementing the following proposals for action:

Communication

1. Improved communication should be developed between professional education associations and the field of corrections.
2. Communication should be increased among the various national professional education associations related to the field of corrections.
3. Information about programs and curricula for personnel in the field of corrections should be exchanged among the professional education associations and made available to the field for study and review.
4. As a means of enhancing education for corrections the national education associations should promote liaison with and among other national, regional, state, and local education organizations established by the respective professions.

Curriculum Development and Expansion of Educational Resources

1. Study and evaluation of the qualitative and quantitative aspects of training programs at all levels should be carried out in relation to the preparation of personnel for the correctional field. Academic, community, and clinical aspects of criminology and corrections should be incorporated in professional and other school curricula.
2. Professional education associations should consider the appropriateness of education at both the graduate and undergraduate levels for specific tasks in the correctional fields.
3. Efforts should be made to improve curricula, expand and improve faculties, expand student bodies, and expand field placements and internships at both graduate and undergraduate levels, so that personnel

are most effectively prepared for professional and other positions in the correctional fields.

4. Efforts must be made to expand the capacity of existing professional schools, and to establish new programs and/or schools, to meet the increasing need for trained personnel in correctional services. This responsibility will require the full cooperation of the correctional field in creating suitable facilities and environments for teaching and research.

5. Professionally sound practices for field placements and internships should be developed, and information about them published and circulated by the professional education associations.

6. The national professional education associations should give due attention to the need for developing and improving standards to the end that corrections will be recognized as a field for professional practice based upon academic and clinical disciplines.

CORRECTIONAL POLICY-MAKERS AND ADMINISTRATORS

The correctional administrator must maintain and conserve his organization on the one hand while stimulating and facilitating needed changes on the other. The following statement describes the characteristics of an effective correctional administrator or policy-maker and at times suggests ways in which the field might move toward those ideal characteristics. The problem of how to implement these points is the basic task which remains for the proposed Joint Commission.

The term "administrator" is defined as a formally appointed decision maker, while the term "policy-maker" deals with a much more heterogeneous group including legislators, members of boards and commissions, the judiciary, and the administrators themselves.

Role of Administrators

Correctional policy-makers and administrators should recognize the key role they play in improving programs for the treatment and prevention of crime and delinquency. They should provide leadership in systematically evaluating and refining present programs and in developing new programs. This points up the need of administrators for a broad preparation which would permit them to relate effectively to the entire field of corrections and to other related fields.

Selection of Administrators

Correctional administrators should be selected on the basis of education, experience, and personal qualities. Administrators and policy-makers should: (a) organize a vigorous program of recruitment and development of effective administrators; (b) endorse and follow the merit system principle in implementing that program; (c) encourage and utilize the results of research on organization and management functions in the correctional field.

Relationships with Various Fields and the Public

1. Correctional administrators and policy-makers should act in terms of the needs of the entire field of corrections, not merely in terms of the needs of their own organizations, so that a consistent and comprehensive approach to the management of crime and delinquency can be developed. They should also act in terms of their relationships with other systems, such as education, social welfare, mental health, and law, in order that effective coordination may be achieved between corrections and those related fields.

2. Correctional policy-makers and administrators should take the initiative in improving the image of corrections. Targets of such efforts should include the general public, special interest groups, universities, and related disciplines and occupations.

3. Correctional administrators and policy-makers should organize efforts to bridge the gap between operating agencies, on the one hand, and related university departments and academic disciplines on the other, toward the end of developing a closer partnership in research and educational activities.

Relationships with Employees

1. Correctional administrators should assume leadership in increasing job satisfaction on the part of personnel at all levels, keeping in mind that meaningful work and stimulating relationships are at least as important as financial returns.

2. Correctional administrators should recognize the importance of the first-line supervisor and of middle management personnel since the top administrators of the future will come primarily from this group. Programs for advanced training of persons in these roles should be developed in all aspects of correctional work.

Education and Training

Imaginative programs of education and training should be developed for correctional administrators and policy-makers, providing them with information on research findings and program innovations, helping them to understand the nature of their roles and their organizations, and assisting in the development of effective strategies through which their objectives may be achieved.

PRIVATE FOUNDATIONS

Research and Demonstration

1. The field of corrections should foster awareness on the part of private foundations of the far-reaching effects of crime and delinquency problems and the urgent necessity for accelerated funding of research, experimental projects, and demonstration projects in the area of corrections by both public and private agencies.

2. The field of corrections should encourage private foundations to provide funds for a variety of recognized undertakings by public and private agencies which cannot appropriately be financed by public funds or for which public funds are not available.

3. Private foundations should be urged to give priority to developing the manpower needed to staff these projects, rather than expecting to secure the necessary personnel from the already meager correctional manpower pool.

4. Private foundations, as well as all agencies and individuals providing funds for experimental and demonstration projects in the area of corrections, including those in training and education, should be urged to insure the inclusion of evaluational research designs, the dissemination of the findings to the proper publics, and the incorporation of these findings at the earliest possible date into the educational and training program.

Relationship of Corrections to Private Foundations

1. Persons in corrections should be alerted to the possibility of assistance from private foundations and should be mindful of this vast potential for the support of worthwhile projects, particularly those that will awaken the community to the need for programs to curb effectively delinquency and crime.

2. There should be an identification of foundations, which as a matter of policy or practice currently are receptive to correctional projects. This information should be disseminated to all persons or agencies active or interested in this field.

Education and Training

Private foundations should be urged to provide financial aid for scholarships, stipends, training programs, work-study programs, and other partial or full subsidies that would encourage careers in the area of corrections.

JOINT COMMISSION ON MANPOWER AND TRAINING

Many of the action proposals being considered by the Arden House Conference on Manpower and Training for Corrections cannot be undertaken by existing organizations alone for a variety of reasons. Many of these proposals require a degree of unity and cohesiveness in the field of corrections which will take staff time and concentrated effort to attain. Other activities lie closer to the objectives of the existing organizations or have higher priority. Funds and staff time in existing organizations are lacking. Some proposals require studies, coordinated recruitment campaigns, liaison with many organizations. Again, much concentrated effort will be needed. For all these reasons a Joint Commission whose interests and activities will be in the area of correctional manpower and training should be established.

The Establishment of a Joint Commission

A Joint Commission on Correctional Manpower and Training should be established for a three-year period.

Tasks

This Joint Commission should:

a. Identify the goals of corrections.
b. Identify the several tasks to be performed to achieve these goals.
c. Identify the knowledge, skills, and other qualifications needed to perform the tasks.
d. Identify the preparation necessary to achieve these skills.
e. Identify the disciplines which should contribute to, and the professions which should take responsibility for, the preparation of correctional personnel.
f. Take an inventory of present correctional jobs and project future needs.
g. Inventory and identify existing and needed resources for training.

h. Promote vigorous recruitment activities by the various professions.
i. Promote the development of added training resources.
j. Take such other action as in its opinion will further the cause of correctional manpower and training.

Membership

The membership of the Joint Commission should be composed of representatives of the various national and regional organizations related to the correctional field and members-at-large from the communications media, business, industry, labor, and other key groups in the nation.

Financing

The Joint Commission should be financed by public and voluntary funds.

The Interim Committee

The five sponsoring organizations are hereby authorized by the Arden House Conference on Manpower and Training for Corrections to establish an interim committee composed of representatives of these sponsoring organizations and others as appropriate, to implement the formation of the Joint Commission.

Roster of Delegates

AMERICAN BAR ASSOCIATION
Mr. James V. Bennett
Mr. Rufus King

AMERICAN BAR FOUNDATION
Mr. William B. Eldridge
Mr. Donald W. McIntyre, Jr.

AMERICAN CORRECTIONAL ASSOCIATION
Dr. Peter Lejins

AMERICAN CORRECTIONAL CHAPLAINS' ASSOCIATION
Dr. Marlin Butts

AMERICAN JUDICATURE SOCIETY
Mr. Allen Levinthal

AMERICAN ORTHOPSYCHIATRIC ASSOCIATION
Mr. Abraham Novick
Dr. Samuel Susselman

AMERICAN PSYCHIATRIC ASSOCIATION
Dr. Richard Lonsdorf
Dr. Harvey Bluestone

AMERICAN PSYCHOLOGICAL ASSOCIATION
Mr. J. Douglas Grant
Dr. Saleem A. Shah

AMERICAN PUBLIC WELFARE ASSOCIATION
Mr. Shad J. Hoffman
Mr. Richard Farrow

AMERICAN SOCIETY OF CRIMINOLOGY
Dr. Walter Reckless

AMERICAN SOCIETY FOR PUBLIC ADMINISTRATION
Dr. Elmer K. Nelson

AMERICAN SOCIOLOGICAL ASSOCIATION *(Criminology Section)*
Dr. Daniel Glaser
Dr. Walter Reckless

ASSOCIATION OF AMERICAN LAW SCHOOLS
Professor Gerhard O. W. Mueller

ASSOCIATION OF CORRECTIONAL ADMINISTRATORS
Mr. Benjamin Weinberg

ASSOCIATION OF CORRECTIONAL PSYCHOLOGISTS
Dr. Saleem A. Shah

ASSOCIATION OF PAROLING AUTHORITIES
Mr. Paul J. Gernert

CANADIAN CORRECTIONS ASSOCIATION
Father Noel Mailloux, O.P.
Mr. W. T. McGrath

CORRECTIONAL EDUCATION ASSOCIATION
Mr. Price Chenault

CORRECTIONAL INDUSTRIES ASSOCIATION
Mr. Joseph Moore

CORRECTIONAL SERVICE FEDERATION, U.S.A.
Mr. Allan C. Hubanks

COUNCIL OF STATE GOVERNMENTS
Mr. William L. Frederick

COUNCIL ON SOCIAL WORK EDUCATION
Dean Charles B. Brink
Dr. Arnulf M. Pins

FEDERAL PROBATION OFFICERS ASSOCIATION
Mr. George W. Howard
Mr. Albert Wahl

MEDICAL CORRECTIONAL ASSOCIATION
Dr. Fabian L. Rouke

NATIONAL ASSOCIATION OF MENTAL HEALTH
Dr. Joseph Kadish
Hon. Jerome Robinson

NATIONAL ASSOCIATION OF MUNICIPAL JUDGES
Dr. Joseph Lohman

NATIONAL ASSOCIATION OF SOCIAL WORKERS *(Council on Social Work in Correctional Services)*
Mr. William V. Chudd
Mrs. Bernice A. Tajima

NATIONAL ASSOCIATION OF TRAINING SCHOOLS AND JUVENILE AGENCIES
Mr. Abraham Novick
Mr. Lawrence D. Penny

NATIONAL COMMISSION FOR SOCIAL WORK CAREERS *(co-sponsored by NASW and CSWE)*
Miss Leah Parker
Dean Joseph L. Vigilante

NATIONAL CONFERENCE OF PUBLIC YOUTH AGENCIES
Mr. Eugene P. Schwartz

NATIONAL CONFERENCE OF STATE TRIAL JUDGES
Hon. William A. Grimes
Hon. Albert Oppido

NATIONAL CONFERENCE OF SUPERINTENDENTS OF TRAINING SCHOOLS AND REFORMATORIES
Mr. William D. Clark
Mr. Benjamin J. Hill

NATIONAL COUNCIL OF JUVENILE COURT JUDGES
Hon. Paul K. Connolly
Mr. Lawrence Higgins

NATIONAL COUNCIL ON CRIME AND DELINQUENCY
Mr. Milton G. Rector
Mr. Carl M. Loeb, Jr.

NATIONAL EDUCATION ASSOCIATION
Dr. William Kvaraceus
Professor Howard B. Gill

NATIONAL INSTITUTE OF MENTAL HEALTH
Dr. Raymond Balester
Dr. David C. Twain
Dr. Milton Wittman

NATIONAL JAIL ASSOCIATION
Mr. W. S. Brent

NATIONAL LEGAL AID & DEFENDER ASSOCIATION
Mr. Junius L. Allison
Mr. Edward Q. Carr, Jr.

NATIONAL SOCIAL WELFARE ASSEMBLY, INC.
Mrs. Harold Harvey
Mrs. Louise N. Mumm

NATIONAL URBAN LEAGUE
Mr. Charles Eason

NEW ENGLAND BOARD OF HIGHER EDUCATION
Hon. Charles H. Bechtold
Dr. Martin Lichterman

OSBORNE ASSOCIATION
Dr. E. Preston Sharp
Mr. John Conrad

PAROLE & PROBATION COMPACT ADMINISTRATORS ASSOCIATION
Mr. George Elder

PRESIDENT'S COMMITTEE ON JUVENILE DELINQUENCY AND YOUTH CRIME
Mr. Bernard Russell
Dr. Denis Szabo

PROFESSIONAL COUNCIL OF N.C.C.D.
Mr. Ben S. Meeker
Mr. Leighton W. Dudley

SALVATION ARMY
Brigadier Victor Dimond

SOCIETY FOR THE STUDY OF SOCIAL PROBLEMS
Dr. Walter Friedlander
Dr. Frank E. Hartung

SOUTHERN REGIONAL EDUCATION BOARD
Dr. Cyril J. Ruilman
Dr. Harry B. Williams

SOCIAL DEFENSE SECTION, UNITED NATIONS
Miss Irene Melup
Mr. Edward Galway

U.S. DEPARTMENT OF HEALTH, EDUCATION, AND WELFARE
(Children's Bureau)
Mr. Merritt C. Gilman
Mr. Gerald Wittman

U.S. DEPARTMENT OF HEALTH, EDUCATION, AND WELFARE
(Office of Education)
Dr. Dwight R. Crum

U.S. DEPARTMENT OF HEALTH, EDUCATION AND WELFARE
(Task Force on Social Work Education and Manpower)
Mr. Merritt C. Gilman

U.S. DEPARTMENT OF LABOR
Mr. Charles Green

VOLUNTEERS OF AMERICA
Colonel John J. Ford

WARDENS ASSOCIATION OF AMERICA
Mr. John Gavin

WESTERN INTERSTATE COMMISSION FOR HIGHER EDUCATION
Dr. Robert T. Hewitt
Dr. Garrett Heyns

WOMEN'S CORRECTIONAL ASSOCIATION
Mrs. Elizabeth McCubbin

RESOURCE AGENCIES:

ADMINISTRATIVE OFFICE OF THE U.S. COURTS
Mr. Victor H. Evjen
Mr. Louis J. Sharp

U.S. BUREAU OF PRISONS
Mr. John J. Galvin
Mr. James E. Murphy

U.S. CIVIL SERVICE COMMISSION
Mr. Raymond Jacobson

U.S. DEPARTMENT OF HEALTH, EDUCATION, AND WELFARE
(Vocational Rehabilitation Administration)
Miss Marian McVeigh

ADMINISTRATIVE STAFF:

William T. Adams
Scotia B. Knouff
Frank Loveland
Harold Patton
Dr. Charles S. Prigmore
(Conference Secretary)
Hugh P. Reed
Dr. Sophia M. Robison

CHAIRMAN OF PLENARY SESSIONS:
William Gaul, Counsel
For the Special Subcommittee on Education
Committee on Education & Labor
United States House of Representatives

Contributors of Papers

CHARLES S. PRIGMORE, PH.D., *Executive Director*
Joint Commission on Correctional Manpower and Training, Washington, D.C.

TOM C. CLARK, *Associate Justice,* United States Supreme Court

DANIEL GLASER, PH.D., *Head, Department of Sociology*
University of Illinois, Urbana, Illinois

JOHN P. CONRAD, *Deputy Chief, Planning & Development*
California Department of Corrections, Sacramento, California

DONALD R. CRESSEY, PH.D., *Dean, College of Arts and Sciences*
University of California, Santa Barbara, California

JOHN M. MARTIN, PH.D., *Associate Professor in Sociology*
Fordham University, New York, New York

MILTON WITTMAN, D.S.W., *Chief, Social Work Section*
Training and Manpower Resources Branch
National Institute of Mental Health, Bethesda, Maryland

JOSEPH W. EATON, PH.D., *Professor of Sociology and Social Work*
Graduate School of Social Work
University of Pittsburgh, Pittsburgh, Pennsylvania

MENACHEM AMIR, PH.D., *Research Associate*
Szold Institute of Behavioral Sciences, Jerusalem, Israel.

ERNEST F. WITTE, PH.D., *Dean, School of Social Work*
San Diego State College, San Diego, California

BEN S. MEEKER, *Chief U.S. Probation Officer and Director*
Northern District of Illinois, Federal Probation Training Center, Chicago, Ill.

H. G. MOELLER, *Deputy Assistant Director*
Division of Inmate Training and Treatment, Bureau of Prisons,
U.S. Department of Justice

JOSEPH P. ANDERSON, ACSW, *Executive Director*
National Association of Social Workers, New York, New York

JUNIUS L. ALLISON, LL.D., *Executive Director*
National Legal Aid and Defender Association, Chicago, Illinois

DANIEL BLAIN, M.D., Pennsylvania Hospital, Philadelphia, Pennsylvania
Chairman, Manpower Commission
American Psychiatric Association

LLOYD W. MCCORKLE, *Commissioner, Division of Corrections and Parole*
New Jersey State Department of Institutions and Agencies

ALBERT C. WAGNER, *Director, Division of Corrections and Parole*
New Jersey State Department of Institutions and Agencies

CLYDE E. SULLIVAN, PH.D., *Co-Principal Investigator, SERVE Program*
Social Restoration Research Center, New York, New York

LEONARD S. COTTRELL JR., PH.D., *Social Psychologist and Secretary*
Russell Sage Foundation, New York, New York

MERRITT C. GILMAN, *Chief of the Training Branch*
Division of Juvenile Delinquency Services
Children's Bureau, U.S. Department of Health, Education and Welfare

MANPOWER and TRAINING for CORRECTIONS

Background of the Conference

by CHARLES S. PRIGMORE

IN RECENT YEARS, it has become apparent that the correctional field has not been able to move with the vigor of other and newer fields toward decisive accomplishments in diminishing crime and delinquency. A complex of interlocking factors seems to be responsible for this disturbing lack of progress:

1. No agreement exists on the goals, purposes, or aims of the correctional field. What does society expect of the roughly 100,000 people who till this vineyard in America of the 1960's? What do correctional leaders themselves see as the goals toward which their efforts are directed? The literature abounds in discussions of treatment, rehabilitation, reeducation, punishment, deterrence, and prevention of recurrence. But no clear-cut agreement has emerged, either within the field itself or in society as a whole.

2. No consensus has been developed regarding the definition and parameters of the field. Corrections has variously been seen as a subordinate aspect of the law, criminal justice, law enforcement, mental health, medicine, vocational rehabilitation, child welfare, public welfare, education, religion, ethics, political science, and public administration. Arguments can be, and have been, adduced to support each of these positions. Rather than being respected as an independent field in its own right, the correctional field has, at times, been used as a battleground for these and other partisan interests.

3. No systematic and objective clarification of tasks based on research findings and a rational consensus as to goals and parameters has been undertaken. Rather, the tasks have usually evolved as the result of pressures from impinging disciplines, professions, or fields. Thus, a given correctional institution may employ a part-time doctor, a group of teachers, a social worker, custodial personnel, cooks, and farm personnel without any systematic consideration of what competence is required for the tasks and how various professional and nonprofessional personnel are related to institutional objectives.

4. Few objective studies, surveys, demonstration projects, experiments, or research projects *aimed at the non-biased improvement of correctional practice or correctional theory* have been launched in corrections. More often, opportunities for research or demonstration in the correctional field are used to verify or extend thinking relative to one discipline or profession. The sociologist looks for the impact of social structures, the psychoanalytically oriented psychiatrist looks for the outpouring of uncontrolled id impulses, the social worker looks for breakdowns in primary family interaction, the lawyer looks for the interaction of social control and individual rights, and so forth.

5. Few resources exist to interest or help people to prepare for correctional work as a career. Although individual courses in criminology, penology, social problems, and deviant behavior are to be found in most colleges and universities, they are incorporated into curricula aimed at research and teaching in sociology or psychology, or are taught at the general, introductory level. Usually little mention is made of correctional careers, and that mention frequently is critical and discourages students from considering a career in corrections.

The few undergraduate and graduate concentrations in criminology are, understandably, research-oriented, and turn out few people with interest or skills in correctional practice. The few undergraduate and graduate curricula established as majors in corrections tend to confuse corrections as a field with corrections as a profession.

Only a handful of educational stipends or scholarships developed specifically for corrections are granted by correctional organizations. The stipends used for corrections come largely from other fields such as mental health, child welfare, or vocational rehabilitation.

The primary need—that of identification of corrections as a field with its own career patterns, recruitment devices, and educational stipends—has been unrecognized by many leaders in the field itself.

6. Finally, the complex of low salaries, staff incompetence, political domination, public apathy or opposition, routinization of activities, and widespread cynicism has defeated any attempt at long-range overhaul of the correctional structure.

The Advisory Committee to the Corrections Project of the Council on Social Work Education recognized early in 1963 that any real effort to increase the number of social workers entering and remaining in the correctional field would have to encompass an interdisciplinary program of national action to correct these defects and problems in the field of corrections. It would be necessary, in short, to unite and solidify the field in a massive campaign of national legislation, public interpretation, research, demonstration, and action.

Preparatory Meeting

The sponsoring organizations asked twelve theoreticians and practical correctional administrators to prepare position papers on various aspects of correctional manpower and training. These experts included people from a range of disciplines, including psychiatry, psychology, public administration, sociology, law, and social work. Others were asked to write comments on these papers.

After these papers were prepared, copies were sent to about sixty-five leaders in the correctional field. They were invited to a four-day preparatory meeting in New York City from February 10 to 13, 1964 to discuss the papers and to try to arrive at a consensus regarding problems and needs and possible strategies for solution.

Although most of the position papers were prepared by correctional theorists and planners in order to provide a basis for eventual practical action, the sponsors wanted to involve men on the "firing line" of correctional practice. Therefore, most of the people invited to the preparatory meeting had long histories of practical experience behind them.

This Preliminary Meeting occupied four days packed with discussion and debate, but gradually it became evident that there were definite grounds for consensus. They are:

1. Corrections is a multidisciplinary field. No one profession, discipline, or school of thought should have priority or dominance. All disciplines and professions should be encouraged and aided to initiate and support education and training for the correctional field.

2. Planning and reorganizing the total correctional effort is a key need. The "one-to-one" approach to helping offenders is not by itself the most efficient means, whether the "one-to-one" approach is handled by sociologists or social workers, or whether the theoretical formulations on which the therapeutic approach is based are derived from social psychology or psychoanalysis. Ways need to be developed for intervening at the societal level, affecting values and norms, social structures, and social institutions.

3. An attempt should be made to analyze and structure correctional tasks in the light of an emerging awareness of newer approaches to prevention and control of crime and delinquency. Then, on the basis of a rational and systematic study of tasks, it can be decided what pre-service educational preparation and what in-service training are required for each task.

4. A new profession of correctional officer seems to be emerging that may eventually require the establishment of specialized professional schools and curricula.

5. There is a need to find ways to prepare future correctional administrators and decision-makers to be statesmen and knowledgeable leaders in their handling of correctional manpower issues.

6. In the interim, until a systematic study of correctional tasks can be conducted and the new profession of correctional officer emerge, it appears that something should be done to provide better educational development of direct-service personnel whose impact on offenders is obviously greater than any other group. These direct-service personnel include correctional officers, job supervisors, and others in direct day-to-day contact with offenders.

These are only a few of the topics on which basic agreement was developed at the preparatory meeting.

Developing Action Proposals

Subsequently, about a dozen correctional administrators were asked to prepare a preliminary draft of action proposals, based on the position papers and on discussion in the preparatory meeting. These career men in direct correctional practice were chosen for their perspective and practical judgment.

At this point, sixty-one national organizations were invited to send two delegates each to the Arden House Conference on Manpower and Training for Corrections, to be held at Harriman, New York, from June 24 to June 26, 1964, and to study the action proposals. The organizations were asked to send delegates prepared to reflect the thinking of the organization they represented. The preliminary draft of the action proposals was sent out two and one-half months in advance of the Arden House Conference in order to allow full opportunity for study.

All sixty-one organizations agreed to participate in the Arden House Conference. Two or three organizations preferred, for various reasons, to call their delegates "observers." Four or five had to be convinced that the Conference was not a "front" for any one profession.

Between February and June 1964, the Arden House Conference was the subject of enormous interest in correctional and criminological circles. The sponsors and Conference secretary were deluged with requests from organizations asking to be represented and requests from individuals to come as participants, observers, or speakers. The decision that this should be an action conference, not a discussion conference, was maintained firmly, however. Since action normally requires organizational activity, only organizational delegates were permitted to participate.

The premise here was that while position papers and the preparatory meeting formulated the ideas and the correctional leaders prepared the workable proposals, the Arden House Conference would have organizational delegates who would develop strategies that would be organizationally implemented.

The Conference

Associate Justice Tom Clark of the United States Supreme Court gave the opening address and charge to the Arden House Conference.

Congressman Robert Giaimo, a member of the Appropriations Committee of the United States House of Representatives, agreed to chair the plenary sessions at Arden House where the amendments to the action proposals would be made. These had already been revised by delegates in eight committees. Due to illness, it was necessary for Congressman Giaimo to send a substitute, Mr. William Gaul, Counsel for the House Subcommittee on Education of the Committee on Education and Labor.

The eight committees were each asked to make an intensive study of one of the eight sections of the preliminary draft of action proposals. Each committee chairman obtained recommendations for revision from committee members (and committee members were encouraged to submit suggestions for revisions to the other committees). Each committee met for several hours prior to the opening of the plenary sessions as well as each morning of the Conference.

In the plenary sessions, each committee in turn had 15 minutes to present its revisions on the draft proposals. Many motions for revision or amendment from the floor were also received. Subsequently, each committee was responsible for incorporating the revisions voted on in plenary session.

It was determined that after the Arden House Conference, the final decisions for action were to be edited, printed, and sent to the sixty-one national organizations for ratification as a "blueprint for action."

The specific procedures followed at the Arden House Conference are described to show the democratic and representative process involved in decision-making. There was full and free participation in the genesis, development, revision, endorsement, and ratification of this "blueprint for action in correctional manpower and training."

Throughout the entire program of events leading up to and following the Arden House Conference, all correctional personnel were encouraged through a variety of ways to write for copies of the preliminary draft of the action proposals. In addition, the 125 members of the Professional Council of the National Council on Crime and Delinquency were each sent a copy of the preliminary draft of action proposals and asked to comment upon them.

A Glance Into the Future

Mr. Justice Clark ended his charge to the Arden House Conference with the words: "Let the voice of this Conference be heard through the corridors of every home in this land. . . . All is ready, bugler. Blow the charge."

The 90 delegates at the Arden House Conference have indicated their readiness to accept Mr. Justice Clark's charge by unanimously adopting a series of far-reaching recommendations. Can the members of the national organizations do less? If all involved and interested in corrections familiarize themselves with the action decisions of the Conference and begin working toward their implementation, a new and dynamic field of corrections will soon be achieved. Much has already happened.* The vigorous discussions and far-reaching decisions of the Arden House Conference have set the stage. More needs to be accomplished.

* *See* Epilogue, pp. 246-251.

The Charge to the Conference

by Associate Justice Tom C. Clark
Supreme Court of the United States

At the outset, let me say that I am a "probationer" in the field of corrections. I know nothing about it, and, furthermore, I admit it. Perhaps when I was the Attorney General, I had some preliminary indoctrination through my old friend, the capable Director of the Federal Bureau of Prisons. He exposed me as a visitor, not a violator, to some six or eight of his institutions, including the National Training School in Alcatraz. Therefore, unlike most judges, I have at least been behind bars.

I shall always remember my annual visit to the Training School where I invited any boy who wished to confer with me privately to come to an office that Mr. Bennett provided at the institution. You should have heard some of their stories! Likewise, I visited Alcatraz and listened to complaints of inmates. I learned on my visit to Alcatraz the truth of Oscar Wilde's lines:

> The vilest deeds like poison weeds
> Bloom well in prison air.
> It is only what is good in man
> That wastes and withers there.
> Pale anguish keeps the heavy gate
> And the warder is despair.

I bring your noble service the plaudits of my "Brothers on the Court." We wish you well in your endeavor to modernize the field of corrections. We know of no more important activity in the administration of criminal justice in America. It has been too long delayed. And I bring my personal apologies for not giving the science of corrections a more significant role in my personal curriculum. I have no excuse. Just as the bar as a whole has not truly recognized its importance and its great potentiality in our national life, neither have we. The responsibility of the bench, the bar, and the law schools is extensive in this regard and directly identifiable.

Corrections is as much an integral part of our system of justice as are investigative procedures and judicial processes. As my fellow lawyer, Junius Allison, has pointed out in his interesting and most instructive paper, most of the 350,000 inmates of state and federal institutions "have legal questions which call for the service of lawyers." Practically none of the state prison systems, I am told, has facilities that afford such service, and even in the enlightened Federal Bureau of Prisons, lawyers are badly needed. From an examination of the merits of the 1,500 *in forma pauperis* cases we considered in the Supreme Court this past term, legal advice to the applicants might well have resulted in a large percentage of cases not being filed.

As a "probationer," I do not have sufficient knowledge of corrections to ascribe any reasons for this situation. With deference to those working in the field, I believe that it would be most helpful if its dimensions could be more clearly defined, its purposes announced, and the necessary means to accomplish them identified. I well remember that when I was active on juvenile problems, there was little agreement on objectives or means among those working in the field. What were the objectives: prevention, rehabilitation, correction, or what? Accomplished through what: disciplinary measures, education, juvenile opportunity, or how? There was no uniform answer. Jealousies existed among groups; there was no agreement on overall purposes, boundaries, tasks, or division of labor between professions, much less the remedies to be followed. It was somewhat: "Tit for tat; if you kill my dog, I'll kill your cat."

I do not know what your situation is today. I do note that the March-April, 1964 number of the *American Journal of Correction* says the field of corrections is a "smorgasbord" of theories and panaceas. "Our institutional programs," it continues, "our probation and parole systems, our private agency developments, our personnel policies, our budgetary fluctuations all reflect the variety of theories, and of approaches to corrections. Each town, city, state, and region shows differences related to the varying combinations of these influences and pressures. But confusion abounds in all quarters."[1] In addition to this significant statement of the *Journal,* the papers prepared and circulated to those attending this Conference indicate that at the least, corrections needs a more definitive, cohesive, unified, and attractive image for the public as well as for those who work in its vineyard.

The field of judicial administration faced similar problems. Some seven years ago, I attempted to bring the various groups in the field

---

[1] Charles S. Prigmore, "The Arden House Conference, 1964," *American Journal of Correction,* Vol. 26, No. 4 (March-April, 1964), p. 29.

together into a joint national effort. In this I failed. However, in 1961, the American Bar Association and several similar groups—such as the American Judicature Society and the Institute of Judicial Administration—invited me to chair a Joint Committee for Effective Justice. I agreed, and as a result we brought together into a national program some twenty organizations working in judicial administration. We adopted an action program with the end purpose of modernizing procedural techniques in the trial of cases and the selection, tenure, compensation, and discipline of judges. To finance a three-year program, we secured a grant of $350,000 from the Kellogg Foundation, supplemented by an equal amount expended by various legal associations in facilities and services.

This is our third year. We will have conducted by the end of this year more than fifty seminars of three days each, which will have reached all of the 3,000 trial judges of general jurisdiction in the fifty states. Our three-year experience in these seminars has brought about a unity of action that is phenomenal. As a result, we have obtained an additional $300,000 grant from the Kellogg Foundation to conduct a College for Trial Judges, continue our selection and tenure programs, and conduct research activities. The college will operate an annual session of a month's duration, the first beginning the first week of next July at the University of Colorado at Boulder.

Finally, we have arrived at a consensus among all of the organizations actively engaged in the judicial administration field on a permanent, continuous, national program for the improvement of the administration of justice. I am happy to announce that our charter for continued, cooperative, national action was agreed upon by all of the organizations and will be signed in New York City in August. This interprofessional effort on a national scale is an example which you in corrections might well emulate. I join in the hope expressed by the *American Journal of Correction* that "some day soon . . . the field of corrections will have also defined its objectives, tasks, and training sufficiently to present a relatively united front to the nation. . . ."[2]

To transform this hope into reality you must first have unity—a unity of purpose and a unity of action. The old power struggle among groups —resulting only in division—must be abandoned. This is a *sine qua non* for two reasons: First, because unified definitive action is essential to the presentation of a national program to the public, to the Congress, and to the legislatures of the several states. Eventual success depends upon their understanding and cooperation. You cannot present a "smorgasbord" of theories and panaceas. It, therefore, behooves you

[2] *Op cit.*

to take inventory and come up with a blueprint for a joint American corrections program. Second, you must have financial backing. This you can obtain only if you can present a united front—a joint venture—operating as one house, but through many mansions.

After you agree on a symphony of action, the next step is to fashion a united program. You must agree on your target—the objective—the correction of antisocial behavior. The "bull's eye" is the individual, but he is surrounded by society in general, and we must keep in mind the whole target, not just its center. Next, you must research the historical background of the field of corrections; its present-day operation, the variety of its types, and the lack of coordination both of purpose and implementation; its old and new philosophies as related to the basic question of punishment versus treatment; the effect of these respective philosophies on society as a whole, their reflection upon the mores of our social structure, and the value of each in the improvement of our democratic culture. You must then redefine the science of corrections, its boundaries and present-day responsibilities; the place of the public, semipublic, and private agencies in the picture; the problems of staffing and training both managerial personnel and custodial employees; the place of the bureaucrat and the professional in the hierarchy, and the elimination of conflicts between them so that they work in perfect partnership; the exchange of skills, techniques, knowledge, and attitudes between selected personnel of the various state systems and the Federal Bureau of Prisons through regional seminars; the use of university facilities and the coordination of peripheral professions in the development and staffing of the program; the establishment, through the bar, of legal aid stations in every institution; the development of a public conscience toward the problems of corrections, through citizen action programs and the consequent evolvement of a correct public image of the profession and of its practitioners; and, finally, the organization of a National College for Scientific Corrections to act as coordinator, researcher, teacher, and idea man, where continuous training programs may be developed and carried out for the 100,000 people engaged in the corrections field.

Some might say that such a program borders on fantasy. But its boundaries are no larger than those we set in judicial administration; they are much smaller than those attained by the Peace Corps. Those who undertake the search for justice cannot take it by storm, for justice is swayed by slow advances. By working together and sharing in a common effort, you will acquire a common understanding that will overcome any differences. Your cause is great. The demoralization of any citizen directly affects the public welfare. The state, therefore, suffers, for the whole is no greater than the sum of its parts, and the neglect or sacrifice of any individual weakens the state. There is the great moral truth, as enunciated by the first Chief Justice of the United States, "that justice is the same whether due from one man to a million or from a million to one man." Through your work, the edifice of justice may stand in more perfect symmetry—greater than ever.

You have a most appealing objective. Indeed, your national purpose is one of the sayings of Jesus in St. Matthew: "I was in prison and ye came unto me."[3] Tonight 350,000 inmates repeat that call. Perhaps many are undeserving, but all are entitled to consideration. The most that they know is that the walls and bars of their prisons are strong; their friends few; their every day like a year. And, as Jesus said to those who so comforted in His day: "In as much as you have done it unto one of the least of these my brethren, ye have done it unto me."

Let us wait no longer. Let the voice of this Conference be heard through the corridors of every home in this land. I know that you look forward to the chance to do your share in the shaping of this destiny. I am sure that the same hush that comes to soldiers awaiting entry into battle will envelop you. Theirs is a solemn pledge: "We will not falter—we will not fail. We will be victorious if we live, and if we die we will leave our dauntless spirit in those who follow and they will not turn back. All is ready, bugler—blow the charge!"

[3] Matthew XXV:36.

The Prospect for Corrections

by DANIEL GLASER

IN CRIME AND CORRECTIONS, as in technology and society, the most dependable prediction one can make is that things will change. Not only is the world changing, but it is changing at a more rapid rate than ever before. To anticipate the future and deal with it effectively, we cannot stop after analyzing the status quo. Emergent trends must be understood, not as disconnected events, but in the perspective of continuing historical processes.

OUR HERITAGE FROM THE PAST

The record of man's approach to criminals can conveniently be summarized as a succession of three R's: Revenge, Restraint, and Reformation. While these themes occurred in this order, none of the later themes ever completely replaced its predecessor. These shifts of correctional interest reflect changes in overall societal values. A quick glance at history may help us see the developmental stage which corrections is entering.

With the growth of democracy in the Western world in the eighteenth and nineteenth centuries, there was a reaction against the previous practice of imposing penalties on the basis of whether the offender and his victim were noblemen or commoners. The notion that all men have natural rights and the capacity to reason led to the imposition of identical penalties for identical offenses, and we have by no means completely abandoned this idea; however, the same respect for human potentialities inspired a preference for confinement, rather than capital punishment, as a penalty. Accordingly, imprisonment became the predominant penalty for felonies in most of the Western world during the nineteenth century, and prisons were largely modeled on pioneering insitutions in the United States.

Initially, concern with equal penalties through imprisonment reflected an earlier interest in revenge against criminals; however, interest in reform, rather than just restraint, continually grew. Therefore, religion, work, education, and psychotherapy were successively emphasized as means of changing criminals during their confinement.

Because human beings reform at different rates and under different conditions, the revenge-oriented objective of identical imprisonment for all who commit the same offense was incompatible with reformation. Concern with changing offenders led to diversity in the nature and duration of their treatment. This variation is decreasingly based on the offenses, and increasingly based on the personal traits of offenders, their change while in custody, and the presumed prognosis of their future. Interest in this personal information on criminals altered procedures and manpower in corrections throughout the twentieth century. This trend is still continuing, but other developments seem likely to change its course.

Deferral and Division of Correctional Decisions

Concern with reformation resulted in two striking trends of judicial and correctional procedure: deferral of correctional decision on individual offenders, and division of decision-making responsibilities among more persons. An awareness of these trends is of vital importance for any projection of correctional manpower needs.

From the earliest times to the beginning of the twentieth century, a criminal's fate was almost always decided as soon as he was sentenced. If the court imposed imprisonment, it not only specified the exact duration for the penalty, but it even designated the institution to be used and the program to be followed there, such as "solitary confinement" or "hard labor." This concentration of authority in the sentencing judge or jury, and its expression at the end of the trial, diminished only with the spread of probation and parole, and with the delegation of more authority to prison administrators to make classifications.

With probation, sentencing is deferred until after the offender can be observed in the free community. In addition, the judge's role in sentencing is shared with probation officers, as his advisors. Parole further defers part of the sentencing decision, and it transfers part of the responsibility for this decision from the court to the parole board, which may then seek aid for its decision from the prison staff and others. If the board grants parole, it further defers decision on the duration of the sentence, and it solicits assistance from parole supervisory staff in making its decision on the end of parole.

The twentieth-century formalization of classification procedures within correctional institutions took from the courts their former role in determining the place and condition of an offender's incarceration. While only courts or parole boards may send a man to prison, institutional staff personnel increasingly determine what happens to him when he gets there.

Specialized reception and diagnostic units, and autonomous institutional classification authority, are a consequence of this development.

These deferral and division trends, in all their forms, have been based on the assumption that available knowledge about an offender increases in direct proportion to the length of time he is observed and the number of persons who observe him. The validity of this assumption depends on the ability of the persons making the observations. Growth in the requirement that judicial and correctional personnel be trained in the behavioral sciences has been primarily a function of increase in probation, parole, and classification services. Future increased needs of trained personnel are also likely to reflect deferral and distribution of decision-making, but these goals increasingly are achieved through two new features of correctional practice distinctive of the second half of the twentieth century: dispersion of treatment roles, and graduation of release. These further raise the level of training required in correctional work.

Dispersion of Treatment Roles

Instead of a hiatus between treatment and custodial staff, all correctional institution employees today increasingly share diagnostic, treatment, and prognostic responsibilities. Following earlier trends in mental hospitals, many correctional institutions have increased the involvement of line staff personnel in classification and casework. They are moving toward what mental health agencies have called a completely therapeutic community. This dispersion of treatment roles in corrections, however, still has diverse forms, most of which are considered experimental. The following are some scattered examples:

a. In prisons of California, District of Columbia, and some other jurisdictions, staff employees in all positions in the institutions conduct inmate counseling groups. Thus, custodial officers, industrial shop foremen, teachers, and other staff personnel formally share the counseling function.

b. In the federal prisons at El Reno, Oklahoma, and Englewood, Colorado, the traditional classification committee of top officials has been replaced by several teams of lower-ranked personnel. Each team is served by a custodial staff member designated "Liaison Officer" whose task is to interview every line officer in direct contact with an inmate whom the team is considering. This custodial staff member reports his findings to the team. By having several teams instead of one committee, reclassification is more frequent, and more staff are involved in classification. The liaison procedures extend this involvement in classification decisions even to staff members not on the separate teams.

c. In many correctional camps—for example, the Federal Youth Camp at Tucson, Arizona—each employee is assigned as an advisor to a fraction of the inmate population, and inmates are instructed to discuss all their problems with their advisor. Thus, all staff work with and add to the limited number of trained casework specialists available for such institutions.

d. In the New York Training School for Girls, the National Training School for Boys, and other institutions, some caseworkers have their caseloads concentrated in a single inmate residential unit, and they locate their office there rather than in a central administration building. This coordinates their observation, supervision, and counseling more closely with that of the cottage parents or other line staff.

e. Selected custodial officers in several federal prisons have been designated "Casework Aides" to assist the regular caseworkers in many tasks. This is a position in which custodial personnel are rotated, and it is treated as augmenting their qualifications for promotion.

The new staff tasks and procedures increase the special training requirements and expand the qualifications desirable for all institutional personnel. They also suggest the possibility of caseworkers serving as teachers of line personnel. This means that caseworkers should have more advanced education, especially as more line staff personnel acquire higher learning.

It has been the experience in some mental hospitals—for example, such as those in Kansas—that as a therapeutic orientation is given to all staff whom patients encounter, and as other aspects of institutional programs are improved, patients can be released more quickly and with a higher rate of successful post-release adjustment. Such improvements in the efficacy of institutional treatment and increases in the rate of post-release adjustment, however, have also required changes in post-hospital programs and the development of new types of community treatment agencies. These make release from institutions and return to home life less abrupt experiences than they had been before. Similar changes are necessary in post-prison programs; some of these changes have already begun.

Graduation of Release

Graduation of release has long existed in correctional institutions, in a form not coupled with entry into the free community. It occurs at variable custody levels, especially with pre-release honor units; however, the latter seldom place inmates in jobs or homes where they may stay after release. From this standpoint, a more graduated release is provided by pre-release furloughs, particularly those increasingly given to facilitate search for a parole job, but these do not alter a traditional institutional stay as drastically as do other recent correctional developments.

In North Carolina, where the central prison is supplemented by some forty scattered camps and other institutions, graduation of release is accomplished from existing edifices, for they are near release communities. Under a "Work Release" program, selected inmates are granted permission to seek employment with private employers outside the prison, after they serve 15 percent of their sentence. They leave the prison daily to go to work, and return after they are through working. From their earnings, they reimburse the prison administration for their transportation to and from work, pay other expenses, aid their dependents, and save for the time when they are released. This extends to prisons the Huber Law principles developed for jails in Wisconsin and adopted by jails elsewhere.

Although several state prison systems already have copied the North Carolina Work Release Program, only a few other states have long-term correctional institutions located near the communities where most of their inmates can find satisfactory post-release homes and jobs. Graduation of the release process in most penal systems, therefore, requires new institutions, located in major cities. The emerging pattern for the establishment of such institutions is well illustrated in the four federal prison "Release Guidance Centers," in the California Youth Authority's "Community Treatment Centers," and in the Provo, Utah, and Essexfield, New Jersey, experimental centers for juvenile probationers.

The federal centers in New York and Chicago are located in wings of YMCA hotels, while those in Detroit and Los Angeles occupy former private residential structures. Federal prisoners are transferred to these centers approximately four months before they begin their parole. After arriving there, they are counseled on how to apply for jobs, and, after a day or two, they seek employment. If hired, they begin their work immediately, returning to the release center only at night. At first, they are allowed visitors at the center; after a while, they get passes to visit their prospective homes and places of recreation. Some residents of these centers, and most of those in California, Utah, and New Jersey establishments, attend school rather than seek employment, or participate in combination work-and-school programs.

The California centers receive youth directly from juvenile institution reception centers. As are the federal establishments, these centers are intermediate between traditional incarceration and parole. The Provo and Essexfield centers receive youth on probation who live at home but who must report to the centers daily; in other words, they are intermediate between traditional probation and incarceration. In all cases, the new establishments represent something distinctly between usual modes of correctional confinement and customary methods of supervision in the free community.

Counseling, both on a group and on an individual basis, is done daily with residents of all the new graduated release centers. One staff member at each federal center is a specialist in employment counseling, dealing with problems of "selling one's self" to procure employment, and with achieving success and satisfaction in holding a job. The center residents also discuss in counseling sessions their family problems, recreational interests, relationships at the centers, budgeting of expenses, and other problems. Budgeting becomes especially significant when the residents receive income from their outside employment. Those at the federal centers are required to open a savings account, and they generally accumulate appreciable savings by the time their parole begins.

Their future parole supervision officer gradually joins in the counseling relationships and, by the time the parole date arrives, he is their primary counselor. The distinctive feature of counseling in all these centers is that the problems and situations discussed are those which the residents are experiencing at the time the counseling is done. This contrasts sharply with discussions of remote or hypothetical issues, or merely of problems at the institution, in counseling at prisons, at training schools, or at full-time residential counseling centers.

Graduated release centers have a valuable diagnostic function for parole boards or courts, apart from their rehabilitation services. If an offender is likely to have further difficulty in the free community, this should be more readily apparent when he is observed many hours daily while he is partially free at his release destination than when he is observed while he is in prison or when he reports to a parole or probation office a few times each month.

If someone in a graduated release institution fails to keep his job, is persistently undependable, drunk or disorderly on returning to the center, or reveals criminal tendencies, he can be transferred to a regular penal institution. His full release from the center can be deferred until his behavior makes it advisable. Federal prisoners sent to the pre-release guidance centers four months before their parole date but who were returned to prison and had their parole date deferred did not necessarily reflect failure on the part of the guidance centers; in fact, it could be considered that because of the centers, diagnostic gains were made, since these men had erroneously been deemed ready for parole on the basis of their behavior in a conventional prison. Moreover, when a resident at a pre-release center absconds, it is known and can be acted upon almost immediately; in contrast, several weeks often elapse before supervisory staff learn of a regular probationer or parolee absconding.

A mushrooming of graduated release institutions seems imminent. One official of a large state told me that twenty-four small pre-release centers would cost much less to establish than a proposed twelve-million-dollar prison, and would relieve the state's immediate prison congestion problems. The state officials are seriously considering such centers as an economic alternative to traditional penal construction. With a monetary argument added to rehabilitation and diagnostic arguments, and with sufficient experience now accumulated to establish that these centers carry no risks, it seems likely that legislatures will generally support the creation of such centers wherever there is pressure for prison expansion.

The new graduated release centers demand much more of staff than do traditional institutions. They have both a higher ratio of staff personnel to inmates, and higher quality of staff, on the average, than do most regular prisons. At the experimental centers, most of the staff thus far have been college graduates, but they have had to be further trained on the job. The demands that staff engage in continuous counseling with offenders in a free community, at the same time maintaining some control over them, and that staff be alert to diagnose imminent case problems are challenges for which new types of training will have to be developed.

Massive Prevention Efforts

Crime prevention, as an alternative to dealing with crimes after they occur, has long been an ideal, but the means advocated for crime prevention have been most diverse. In the first third of this century, child guidance clinics and public playground programs were emphasized. In the second third of the century, these were supplemented with programs for detached workers with street gangs, early detection, "reaching-out" casework, remedial reading, school counseling, prevention-oriented police work, and jobs for youth.

Prevention programs in the last third of this century are likely to be distinguished by their massive dimensions, their integration through new types of theory, and some consequent new procedures. These new procedures include homework centers, peer tutors, special school programs to raise levels of aspiration, monetary incentives, and political action as a constructive outlet for residents of deprived communities. These are not all entirely new, and other old types of programs continue, but the dimensions are vaster than ever before.

The prototype for the most massive undertakings is Mobilization for Youth in New York City. It is now being imitated in communities across the country. A principal financial and ideological stimulus to this expansion has been the President's Committee on Juvenile Delinquency and Youth Crime, following pioneer action by the National Institutes for Health, the Ford Foundation, and various enterprising local agencies and individuals.

These programs may seem tangential to corrections, but they are far from irrelevant. In the first place, many new prevention agencies work closely with correctional authorities in assisting offenders released to the neighborhoods where prevention activity is centered. In the second place, where these prevention programs have been initiated they are major competitors of correctional agencies in the recruitment of trained personnel. Thirdly, many prevention and treatment programs should be integrated. Some new correctional agencies, such as the graduated release centers for juvenile probationers, may well be administered jointly with prevention programs. For all these reasons, any planning for correctional manpower needs should certainly take into account the probable spread of massive prevention programs.

Diversion of Correctional Cases to Non-Correctional Agencies

Wherever there is little interest in punishing a criminal, and his basic difficulties seem to be matters normally dealt with by specialized non-correctional agencies, concern with reformation suggests that, despite his offense, he be referred to these agencies. Such referral seems especially appropriate if the offender is not considered dangerous, or if the non-correctional agency has adequate facilities for restraining and securely confining those whose release would seriously jeopardize others. There are many types of non-correctional agencies to which delinquent and criminal cases increasingly are diverted.

Only a small proportion of people legally classifiable as mentally retarded are committed to institutions for the mentally retarded. Those who are sent to such institutions are differentiated from those of similar mentality who are not removed from the free community by the fact that they were considered social problems, because of delinquency, adult misdemeanant behavior, or dependency. Variations in police, court, or administrative policy, however, seem to account for the fact that the delinquency, vagrancy, or disorderly conduct of some feeble-minded persons results in their commitment to institutions for the mentally retarded, while similar behavior by other persons of the same low mentality leads to their incarceration in correctional institutions.

Since the late President Kennedy stimulated a sharply increased governmental investment in programs and facilities for the mentally retarded, it seems likely that these establishments will handle a larger proportion of persons charged with offenses whose illegal behavior is due, in large part, to mental deficiency. This should reduce the number of rather hopeless "revolving door" commitments of feeble-minded persons to jails, state farms, and houses of correction on such charges as vagrancy and disorderly conduct. The non-correctional institutions have many more adequate resources than the correctional agencies for training mentally retarded persons, and, ultimately, for placing them in sheltered circumstances in the free community, where they may become self-supporting.

The relationship of alcohol to much persistent criminality is well established. Drunkenness itself is a major basis for commitment to jail, while considerable petty theft, forgery, assault, and diverse other crimes are closely linked with inebriety. Of course, the cure of alcoholism is not easily achieved, but mere incarceration is probably the least effective remedy for the disease. Specialized farms, homes, and hospitals for alcoholics, often operated in close coordination with Alcoholics Anonymous, offer more suitable programs for chronic drunkards than do jails and police lock-ups. As city, county, and state governments expand their treatment services for alcoholics, there should be a reduction in such expensive and futile temporizing with the alcoholic problem as the nightly arrest of hundreds of drunks or the recommitment of parolees to prison when their violation is not felonious conduct but persistent drinking.

Some crime clearly is due to sheer economic destitution, even though it may also have other causes. As automation increases the number of Americans who are chronically unemployed, illegal behavior due to destitution is likely to grow. This may occur particularly among the transient unemployed, among persons failing to utilize available welfare aid because of pride, panic, or ignorance, and among individuals ineligible for many forms of assistance due to their recent release from prison. In many communities, it may now theoretically be true that public and private welfare programs make it unnecessary for anyone to starve or freeze. Nevertheless, expert social work is still required to bring some people in need into contact with immediately available assistance. When staffs of courts and other agencies dealing with criminals provide such social work, many correctional commitments may prove unnecessary.

Possibly the most extensive diversion of correctional cases to non-correctional agencies will occur with the growth of civil commitments for drug addiction to state hospitals. New York and California, the two states where addiction is believed to be most extensive, have in the past few years enacted laws which permit such commitments. These laws have begun to be implemented. Several other states and the federal government have similar legislation under consideration. This trend reflects a growing view of drug addiction as a disease rather than as a crime, and increased skepticism as to the effectiveness of prison sentences as our only solution to drug possession.

Development of these various possibilities of diverting correctional cases to non-correctional agencies means that personnel in courts and correctional agencies must be better trained in identifying cases which can properly be transferred to non-correctional institutions, and in the procedures for effecting such transfer. Social work education is specifically oriented to this task. Increase in such education of correctional staffs should lead to the referral of offenders to agencies best suited to meet their primary needs, either as an alternative or as a supplement to correctional placements.

Whether or not the McNaghten rule for deciding that someone who committed a crime is not guilty by virtue of insanity is replaced by the controversial Durham rule, it seems evident that judicial application of the concept of criminal insanity is broadening. This will send more people accused of crimes to mental hospitals and clinics. Actually, increased emphasis in corrections on treatment instead of on punishment, and decreased determinateness in criminal sentences, may greatly diminish the differences between programs of correctional and non-correctional agencies. This increases both the authority and the responsibility of staff in all "people processing" institutions. Increased professional education, therefore, becomes a critical need for this staff, not just to augment their treatment skills but also to help inculcate the ethical norms which should distinguish the helping professions.

THE TREATMENT ETHIC AND CIVIL RIGHTS

A basic right of United States citizens is that their liberties may not be restricted without the due process of law. This requirement governs the actions of judges and juries, and makes the courts available to citizens for their protection against improper treatment by police or correctional personnel.

Until recent years, correctional actions seldom were the basis for successfully invoking the right to due process. The law traditionally viewed the criminal as having been stripped of most of his civil rights by his conviction. Therefore, any freedom greater than solitary confinement within prison, or even the freedom of parole, could arbitrarily be withdrawn at the discretion or whim of a correctional official. This authority is reflected in the fact that every minor comfort in prison, and parole itself, is designated a privilege, rather than a right.

The progressive deferral and division of what was once the court's autonomous and final decision on the fate of a prisoner has evoked a reaction. Recent judicial decisions limit the authority of prison administrators to penalize inmates. More distinctly, they restrict the right to revoke parole without a hearing or without due cause. Right of the alleged parole violator to counsel, if he desires it, and even to provision of counsel by the state if the alleged violator is indigent, is foreshadowed.[1]

The implications of these developments for correctional practice are not yet clear, but it is evident that they will raise the level of training required by correctional decision-makers. Some have feared that they would make these officials overly legalistic, causing them to refuse to impose penalties unless they have a clear legal case and perhaps to refuse to take risks in granting paroles because they will feel unable to revoke them before new offenses are committed by parolees.

Such reaction by inaction may be expected from untrained or unconcerned correctional officials, but for others, the injection of due process considerations into correctional decision-making should only exert a slight pressure. The legal requirement, essentially, is only that officials be deliberate and reasonable in their decisions, that they at least hear and consider any objections by the offender, and that they do not exceed their authority. Implied is a requirement that reasons for major decisions be recorded, so that they can be justified later, if necessary.

In the best agencies, these standards already prevail. In corrections, as in policework and in the courts, due process requirements simply reduce the risk that the fate of an offender may be determined only by the mood of the officials at the particular time. To be prepared to justify a correctional decision, an official must know the consequences of alternative decisions. He must have some proof that the diagnosis and prognosis he has made are likely to be valid. All of this requires research, and it is in research that one finds the developments likely to be most influential in American corrections.

The Routinization of Research

Case counting, for budget planning, has always been done by correctional administrators. This has been called "research"; however, I shall confine the term "research" to analyses of the effectiveness of particular correctional programs or policies in achieving correctional goals, as well as to more abstract inquiry into the causes of criminality or the processes of correctional change. Until well into the 1950's, almost all such research in correctional agencies was either initiated by college professors independently of correctional officials or pursued by correctional staff seeking higher degrees. The latter, after earning their doctorates, often entered the academic world. Thus, research in corrections was sporadic

[1] Sanford H. Kadish, "Legal Norm and Discretion in the Police and Sentencing Process," *Harvard Law Review*, Vol. 75, No. 5 (March 1962), pp. 904-931; Sol Rubin, *et al.*, *The Law of Criminal Correction* (St. Paul, Minn.: West Publishing Co., 1963), pp. 285-296, 561-564, 687-690.

and was more oriented to academic issues than to immediate problems in corrections.

This situation started to change around 1958 in California and in the ensuing years in several other jurisdictions. In this change, legislators or others not in the field of corrections often took the lead in calling for a more substantial and consistent government investment in research. They were committed, at last, to providing rehabilitative treatment for criminals rather than merely seeking revenge or restraint, but they demanded more adequate evidence on the effectiveness of prevailing and proposed types of treatment. Accordingly, research divisions, staffed by persons with higher degrees in the behavioral sciences, became integral components in the permanent administrative organization of federal, state, and even some county and municipal correctional agencies. These government research units have also contracted with universities to conduct research and have solicited foundation financing for research in their correctional system.

Correctional research can be classified into three broad categories: exploration, monitoring, and experimentation. "Exploration" appropriately encompasses the large variety of pathfinding inquiries now sponsored or cosponsored by correctional agencies. These investigate treatment processes, post-release experiences, offender traits, staff characteristics, and many other topics. They reflect a wide range of criminological and correctional theory. The many small and diverse projects listed in the periodic reports of research units of correctional administrations suggest a new tendency for officials to call for research whenever speculation raises questions for which adequate answers are not immediately available.

Monitoring in corrections has objectives analogous to those of cost-accounting and profit-and-loss analysis in business. It is concerned with maintaining continuous information on the effectiveness of different types of programs for various types of offenders. This means a shift in correctional recording from merely counting cases on hand, received or released, to tabulating long-run adjustment patterns for particular types of offenders, after specific types of correctional experience. These monitoring statistics are as much concerned with offenders no longer in conflict with the law as with those in custody or under supervision. The results are base-expectancy rates, or long-run, follow-up statistics, such as those now routinely maintained for all offenders in California and Wisconsin, for parolees in New York and Pennsylvania, and for probationers in some counties, notably Los Angeles. For the first time, administrators can talk knowingly about the rate at which the people they release get into subsequent difficulty with the law, instead of misrepresenting as a recidivism rate the percentage of their prisoners who previously had a correctional record.

As monitoring advances to the point where it is able to answer detailed questions on recidivism rates following specific types of treatment for various categories of offender, it requires more careful maintenance of case records than is the case when these records are not used for research. Inclusion of research statisticians in correctional manpower creates pressure for better-trained staff to procure more precise and significant case information for statistical analysis and to interpret the results. As machine data-processing equipment and computers take over statistical recording and tabulation components of the monitoring task, a still higher level of sophistication is required, both in researchers and in administrators.

Experimentation is the most dramatic research development in corrections, since it can yield more conclusive evaluations of treatment services than other methods of research. Neither new nor old procedures can be evaluated with much confidence unless experimental controls are imposed to assure comparability between the cases receiving a particular treatment and those not receiving it. In correctional practice, as formerly in medical practice, there has been marked resistance to withholding a treatment from control group cases until the effectiveness of the treatment is known. Consequently, practices often have been instituted at great expense, and routinely relied upon, in complete ignorance of whether these practices did more good than harm.

Corrections is finally following in the footsteps of medicine by randomly dividing persons recommended for some types of special program into experimental and control groups. This has been done in relation to reduced caseloads on parole and probation, intensive counseling in institutions, provision of psychiatric care, release to a community treatment center, and other measures. California has taken the lead in this, with other states following in growing numbers.

The findings of correctional experiments often disappoint those who have been trying to promote their favorite remedy, but negative results indicate ways to improve programs. Most often, the results indicate that each correctional service has some advantage for specific kinds of offender but is useless or even harmful for other kinds. These findings point to the selection of appropriate remedies for particular cases, rather than the application of one illusory panacea to all problems. They may also encourage dramatic innovations, on an experimental basis, for those types of offender for whom all past methods prove ineffective. Legislators seem much more willing to support major changes in treatment when presented as limited controlled experiments than when proposed as sweeping and permanent replacement of all alternative measures.

The Tasks for Correctional Manpower in Modern Industrial Society

We have reviewed ways in which tasks of correctional manpower are shifting. Interest in punishment for its own sake is rapidly being replaced by concern with promoting change in offenders. Custodial tasks are becoming less sharply separated from treatment services, for all personnel have more treatment functions. This is consistent with prior developments in a continuous and long-term trend of increasing the deferral and distribution of decisions on the fate of an offender. Even the traditional boundaries between correctional incarceration and supervision in the community no longer are clear-cut, for new types of institutions are being established which graduate former differences between confinement and release.

Furthermore, correctional services now are being fused with activities formerly thought of as independent of corrections. Delinquency prevention programs have developed on a vaster scale than ever before; they are organized on a community basis, and are concerned with the rehabilitation of known criminals in their area as well as with preventing the creation of new criminals. More correctional cases now are diverted to non-correctional agencies. Legalistic concern that there be some protection of offenders against careless or irresponsible treatment has placed judicial checks on some correctional activity previously immune to public scrutiny. Finally, scientific research, once a monopoly of the academic world, is becoming an integral part of the administration of corrections. What are the manpower implications of these developments?

There are now more than 42,000 full-time employees in state and federal prisons, but less than 9 percent of these are assigned to education, religion, classification, parole, or medical services.[2] There are about 17,000 employees in public institutions for delinquent children, with about 62 percent of these classified as in education or treatment services.[3] There are more than 13,000 probation and parole officers.[4] We only have statistics on the educational level of juvenile probation officers. These officers presumably have as much or more schooling than any other major category of correctional employee, yet less than 10 percent have master's degrees.[5] It seems extremely safe to estimate

[2] "Personnel in State and Federal Institutions 1960," *National Prisoner Statistics,* No. 29 (Washington, D. C.: U.S. Bureau of Prisons, June 1962).

[3] "Statistics on Public Institutions for Delinquent Children, 1962," *Children's Bureau Statistical Series,* No. 70 (Washington, D. C.: U.S. Children's Bureau, 1963).

[4] *Probation and Parole Directory,* 14th ed. (New York: National Council on Crime and Delinquency, 1963).

[5] *Report to the Congress on Juvenile Delinquency* (Washington, D. C.: Children's Bureau and National Institute of Mental Health, Department of Health, Education and Welfare, 1960), pp. 26-28.

that of the total of approximately 75,000 correctional employees in the United States, the number with some college education is less than a fourth, and that less than 5 percent have reached the master's degree level. It would be interesting to have precise data on the proportions with various educational attainments in some cross-sectional sample of agencies and institutions.

If any conclusion can be drawn from the emerging trends in corrections, it is that the quantity, quality, and location of correctional manpower must change, for the tasks of corrections are being redistributed. The old differences among those institutions which keep the inmates, those which put them to work, and those which try to change them are diminishing. All staff personnel are increasingly involved in the change effort, in officially reporting their observations of each offender's experience, and in decisions on optimum individual programs and release dates. Not all correctional institution employees need be college graduates, but higher education certainly will be needed by many more than now have it.

More important, there is a need for new types of education. The emerging trends in corrections call for curricula not yet available in most social work schools, including programs of supervised experience with the new types of correctional service. Graduate schools, particularly, will have to meet the needs for people capable of conducting fruitful research and for people who are effective both in training—and in learning from—less educated line staff.

The need for more people with new types of training is particularly evident in the new correctional activities that are mushrooming in the population centers from which most delinquents and criminals come, and to which most return. In the graduated release centers, all staff are involved in the most continuous and immediately relevant counseling now found in correctional agencies. In probation and parole, field staff will be closely involved with the graduated release centers, with large-scale delinquency prevention programs, and with the widespread research now underway on intensive types of service for parolees and probationers. The prevention programs themselves will create major demands for new types of trained manpower.

As research continues and experience with the new treatment services is accumulated, the rate of change in corrections is likely to increase still further. We cannot defer recruiting and training personnel until some final state of corrections is achieved, for change is continuous, in corrections as in other aspects of modern life. This means that we must train personnel not just to meet the changing needs that we now note, but also to be capable of growing with new developments and contributing to them. This requires leaders educated in the fundamentals of behavioral science, understanding both theory and research methodology in sociology, psychology, and psychiatry, who are also efficient administrators.

It is clear that the correctional manpower needs outlined herein will not be achieved simply by schooling people to some terminal point and then employing them. Rather, there will have to be continuing education for staff at all levels, both on a part-time basis while they are employed, and occasionally on educational leaves for a protracted period.

What ways and means are feasible for supplying these many correctional manpower requirements? That is the problem for this conference. It is also a problem which will require continuous study in the future. If this conference can marshal the best information and insight available, it will provide a foundation for increasingly more adequate knowledge in the years ahead.

Remarks

by Walter C. Reckless

In the area of institutional care and treatment, I think we definitely need to focus on the staff member who is in the greatest daily contact with the inmate. In institutions for juvenile delinquents, this person is usually the cottage parent; in correctional institutions for adults, this person is usually the correction officer or the guard.

In my long experience in studying correctional institutions and training students for work in correctional institutions, it became patently clear that professional staff has very little impact directly on the inmate (with the possible exception of some very small, highly-staffed residential treatment centers). Practically all the psychologists in prisons and training schools are pencil pushers. Practically all those considered correctional social workers are devoting most or all of their time to collecting background information, contacting agencies on the outside, formulating release plans, sitting in on classification committees, and so forth. These two professional positions are very seldom wheeled in line to have a direct impact on the inmate. The guard, the cottage parent, the recreational leader, the teacher, and the shop foreman are much more likely to have direct impact.

The first-hand studies which I have conducted since 1948, both in Europe and America, indicate that inmates of juvenile institutions or adult institutions focus upon the cottage parent, the guard, the teacher, or the shop foreman as the adult staff member in the institution who knew them the best and who did the most for them. Even at our Juvenile Diagnostic Center in Columbus, which is heavily staffed with professional personnel, the children only select a professionally trained staff member in 30 percent of the instances as the person who knew them the best and helped them the most.

The facts of life seem to be that we need professional staff in a correctional institution who, on a daily basis, can discuss the approaches to the inmate with certain clusters of cottage parents or guards. We need training officers in these institutions who can stake out this role for the so-called lower staff. We need professional persons who do not look down upon staff members in lower positions but instead build up the image of these staff members so that they realize their importance in the institution.

The hope is that correctional officers and cottage parents will increasingly be selected from interested B.A. and B.S. students at colleges and universities, and that their salaries will be at such a level that they are equal to teachers' salaries. It is hoped that professors of sociology who teach criminology courses in colleges and universities can be reached in order to encourage seniors to take internships in correctional institutions and to look upon correctional work as a career service. The cultivators of the Lord's vineyard need to come from the B.A. students. The professionals who have been trained at the M.A., M.D., and Ph.D. levels must be used more effectively. Their role assignments have been fairly horrible in the past, and the result is that only the second-class social workers, the second-class psychologists, the third run of medical doctors and psychiatrists, and the fourth run of teachers will accept positions in such institutions. I believe that more effective role assignments for such staff would increase our chances of getting the first run of all these professionally trained persons. Their know-how and their approaches must filter through lower staff personnel to inmates. If it takes a revolutionary act to get rid of the pencil pushing in institutions in order for the professional staff to play a positive role in having an impact, then this is what we must work for. And the impact studies such as I have done for the last 16 years should show in 25 years hence some very tangible results through the perceptions of juvenile and adult offenders as they take a backward view at release of what happened to them during their institutional stay.

The probation and parole services have a natural role assignment which the correctional institution does not have—namely, the relationship of the officer or worker to a certain number of probationers or parolees. Here it is much easier for the worker or the officer to know that we must help positively in the adjustment of individual cases. Here it becomes a natural course of events to have supervisors in large offices, whose role assignment is to help build up the effectiveness of five, six, seven, or eight workers assigned to him. We should aim for every probation and parole worker in the United States to have a B.A. degree and be encouraged to come into probation and parole offices as interns and to discover for themselves the great possibility of making a contribution in life at this point. The salaries usually match the salaries of teachers. Here, again, we need to enlist the interest of our colleagues who are in critical positions to encourage students to focus upon probation and parole work as a career, namely, our sociology professors and instructors who teach criminology. The professional social worker and/or the professional psychologist should be used as the case supervisor. There is no reason for those in social work to say that they should monopolize all the case supervisors. Persons with M.A. degrees in psychology can do just as good a job, and it is even possible that those with M.S. degrees in adult education can do just as good a job. The role assignment here is for the case supervisor to build up the image and the effectiveness of the beginning probation and parole worker and to select from his charges a few who should return to the university for their M.S.W. degrees and their M.A. degrees in psychology.

*The Division of Correctional Labor**

by JOHN P. CONRAD

THIS CONFERENCE needs no elaborate statements to establish more firmly the extent of the changes in the structure and fabric of corrections during the last twenty years. These changes continue, and their end is not in sight. The stagnation which once was the common characteristic of agencies charged with the management of offenders is giving way to a flood of ideas. Some of these ideas stream into corrections from outside its boundaries. Some are generated from necessities bearing on the old structure. The new approaches require types and levels of service which were never contemplated by the designers of the nineteenth-century correctional models. They are still hard to incorporate in the well-worn and hard-pressed systems of today.

The common factor in the many changes which have complicated the simple old structure almost beyond recognition is professionalization. We have adopted, at first with the reluctance of the traditionalist, but increasingly with the enthusiasm of intellectual adventure, the proposition that the execution of correctional tasks is a skill which is based on a body of communicable knowledge. The school of common sense and hard knocks is still in session. Within its walls the professional and scientific recruits to this field still have much to learn; but the day of the self-taught correctional administrator or clinician is almost over, just as it has long since passed in large-scale corporate enterprise or in law or medicine. We stand to lose some not inconsiderable assets; for many years, corrections has been host to an assortment of autodidacts whose innovating enthusiasm has done much to make possible the professionalization of which I speak.

In return for this loss and others, the clear trend toward professionalization makes possible a consistently improving practice, a rationally developed level of expectations, and the kind of scientific cross-fertilization which can only occur when there is a basis for scientific communi-

---

* Mr. Conrad's position paper was submitted as background for the Arden House Conference.

cation. In this paper, I want to dissect the correctional field in a search for the elements of the new profession and the essential scientific underpinnings which must be provided. It is a search for probabilities rather than certainties; if we can learn to adjust our probabilities to the certainty of social change, the correctional field need never return to the old days of stagnation.

The Objectives of Correctional Process

I will labor the obvious no further. Let me venture now into the murk of definitions. Some of us who are engaged in the administration of corrections have been instructed by specialists in the administrative arts as to the practice of management by objectives. Without going into the value of these principles, we have at least profited from the experience to the extent that we have examined at considerable length the objectives of the correctional process. In California, we found that the basic objectives are arguable, overlapping, and four in number. Because a professional task must be related to an objective, to something which must be done, I must dwell on each objective at least enough to be sure that we all are clear as to its significance for this paper.

The first objective is *control.* Correctional institutions and agencies exist for the protection of the public. The prison or training school must safely keep its committed inmates until authorized to release them. It must not only maintain security measures for the prevention of escape; it must also maintain peace and order within its perimeter. In this country the objective of control within a correctional institution is hardly debatable. It is a primary objective from which a correctional institution cannot escape accountability. In the case of the probation or parole agency, the responsibility for control is shared with the police, the courts, and the parole boards, but in the form which these functions take in the United States and Great Britain, inescapable control obligations are attached.

The law seldom prescribes in detail the methods of control which a prison warden or a probation officer must adopt. I hold that control is most effective when it is compatible with and supportive of the second objective of *resocialization;* but whether or not I am right, it is certain that whatever is done within a correctional apparatus to treat or resocialize or simply to help its clientele, it must be done in ways which do not reduce the effectiveness of control.

I have used the term, *resocialization.*[1] I do not want to evade all the

---

[1] My use of the term "resocialization" is borrowed from the approach of Dr. Elliot Studt. Her application of the term as an element in the process of social restoration is a valuable analytic tool to which I have not done sufficient justice in this paper. In her forthcoming report on theoretical research in correctional practice a fuller explication will be found.

issues which are concealed in this word by neatly brushing them off as semantics. Semantics are important, and these semantics are far too important to attempt to settle in a paragraph or two of such a paper as this; but I see as a primary objective of the correctional apparatus the restoration of the offender to the community as a responsible member of the community. There are some difficulties with this objective. It is quite true that some offenders, though very few in number, are permanent clients of the correctional apparatus. For them the objective of resocialization must be to assist them to the greatest effectiveness they can achieve within the degree of control which they must accept. At the other end of the scale are those offenders who by accident of some situation must be committed to correctional control but who remain quite competent to resume a responsible place in the community without any programmed help. The task of resocialization for the man who has committed homicide by motor vehicle or the boy scooped up in a wave of hysteria who would normally be sent home is less difficult, less liable to failure than with the established criminal or delinquent. But it exists. In common with all other correctional clients, the situational offender has been publicly degraded and stigmatized. It is necessary to identify him as a good risk for early restoration and to offset the handicaps which his status has imposed upon him.

With all this said, the task of resocialization for the great majority of correctional clients must focus on a complex of changes, all of which must be dealt with if the task is to be successfully completed. The offender is the product of a delinquent situation. Ordinarily, we must see this situation as composed of the interaction of the offender's personality deficits with the deficiencies in the environment. The offender's personal deficit may be, for example, a low order of intelligence incapacitating him for a trained vocation. This lack has incapacitated him for any positive relationship with the legitimate opportunity structure, increasingly deficient in opportunities for unskilled youth. The result is a delinquent situation and a court action by which the boy in question is identified as an offender and various handicaps are added to his already difficult predicament. The task of the correctional system is to reduce the personal deficit, assist the youth in achieving a successful relationship with the opportunity structure, and help him resist the identification which stigmatization as an offender imposes. So defined, resocialization is a term for a wide variety of activities aimed at the restoration of the offender to the community.

In California, a third responsibility of the correctional apparatus is to conduct *research* into the causes and prevention of crime and the treatment of the criminal. Although this objective is not everywhere established in the statutes creating correctional agencies, the need for research is so widely accepted in the leadership of the correctional professions that it seems appropriate to regard research as an implicit objective where it is not legally explicit. In the senses in which research becomes a primary objective rather than a means for the improvement of control and resocialization, we are concerned with the improvement of the legal and structural aspects of the apparatus itself. Through the increase of fundamental knowledge about this particular variety of social deviation, we may ultimately expect not merely more effective control and resocialization of this or that offender but rather more effective social organization.

Lastly, and least obviously, we come to the *utilization of manpower*. We regard it as essential that offenders should be contributing members of society and that the manpower concentrated in a correctional institution should be constructively used for present purposes and conserved for the future. Such important uses as land reclamation, forest-fire fighting, and various correctional industries transform correctional institutions from total economic losses into partly self-sustaining units. Of course, we see the work which is done by inmates as contributing to their resocialization and simplifying their control, but it is also an end in itself. If the American economy can ever again reach a full-employment status, as in Sweden or the Netherlands, the utilization of inmate manpower will be seen to be an objective much more essential to society than now is the case. For the correctional administrator its importance is basic.

Basic Assumptions About Correctional Process

If I have adequately set forth the objectives of correctional process, what can we infer about the nature and structure of the apparatus which will guide us in examining the professional services needed to carry out these objectives? It is here that I come to the basic assumptions governing the dimensions of this paper. I must admit that many of these assumptions, as even the friendliest critic will agree, are controversial. For the purposes of proceeding with a coherent argument, I have had to settle on certain propositions as establishing the scope of the problem. Here they are:

1. *For the purposes of this discussion and for the foreseeable future, the structure of the correctional apparatus will include those services essential to the management of the legally identified delinquent*. These services fall into two very broad categories: the institution, and the field agency or probation and parole. Further, it is to be expected that in the United States most correctional services will be publicly administered. This assumption excluded specific consideration in this

paper of the professional requirements of crime-prevention programs. The importance of crime prevention is not to be depreciated, but within the structure in use here it is an entirely separate service, unrelated to the case concerns for the individual offender which are basic to the correctional objectives. Obviously, a successful correctional facility will contribute to the prevention of crime by changing criminals into citizens; but the correctional apparatus cannot carry out the ultimate tasks of crime prevention which, for our era at least, consist of making American cities into satisfying environments for people of all ages and degrees to live out their lives. In working toward this end, the correctional professions will participate along with city planners, architects, schoolmasters, the police, and many other community organizers. Community improvement must not be attempted in the name of crime prevention alone or neither result will be achieved.

Also excluded is specific consideration of the many valuable and innovating private agencies in the field. The worth of such enterprises as Norman House, the remarkable hostel for released prisoners in London, or Synanon, the protective community for narcotic addicts in Southern California, or the Big Brother Association, is not in dispute. These agencies are invaluable adjuncts to correctional process, but their consideration as part of the process would intolerably confuse an unwieldy enough analysis.

One final word about our examination of the structure of correctional process. What we hope to describe is an optimum structure. It is *not* utopian; it *is* achievable. The bureaucratic paralysis common to correctional systems oriented solely to control is not only unnecessary, it is dangerously obsolete. We assume that with professional management the correctional process can be rationalized. The problem for the professional engaged in corrections is to find ways of gaining this end.

2. *The optimum correctional structure will require a common understanding of its ends and means by all personnel in contact with clients.* Whether or not a high degree of professional understanding is needed to carry out a particular task, the employee must understand the multiplicity of objectives and their inter-relationship. So stated, this requirement seems self-evident, but few organizations are required to serve so many ends with means which are seemingly so incompatible. The consequence in correctional agencies is that functions are assigned primacies by officials and employees whose concerns seem to them to be located in the area of one particular objective. The endless oratory over the cleavage between custody and treatment obviously arises from uncertainty about the primacy of objectives. Merely to deplore it is not to end it. The reconciliation of objectives demands a clear conceptualization of the interrelatedness of correctional goals and the clarification of

this understanding of the tasks for all employees, particularly those in contact with clients.

3. *Regardless of educational resources outside the correctional apparatus, systematic and dynamic training programs must be provided for all classes of employees if professionalization is to be maintained.* Clergymen and physicians, no less than ordinary correctional officers, have professional problems not common to their basic disciplines but common to all correctional workers. These problems are yielding to increases in knowledge; for sustained improvement of the system and to prevent it from subsiding into the indifferentism of an indolent bureaucracy, the increases in knowledge must be made available through training to all hands.

4. *In the present state of our ignorance, research is essential to professional practice.* For centuries, correctional workers have fatuously dealt in verities which were presumed to be eternal. Modern correctional research has called into question these certainties which defeated so much of our work. We are now willing enough to settle for the uncertainties so characteristic of the world outside our walls. We must continue to be involved in research. In a field which has neither established expectations of accomplishment nor even a consensus on the standards of good practice, the process of self-study is essential. Research is indispensable protection from a lapse into cynical stagnation.

The Levels of Correctional Activity

In corrections there are four identifiable levels of activity. It is important to define them clearly in our search for the basic elements of knowledge required for practice. Each level is directly or indirectly involved in the meeting of correctional objectives. Before we demonstrate their relationships, we must continue with our exercise in definitions.

Even more than with most public organizations, the keystone of the correctional structure is administration. Because control is of the essence of the task, *administrative* activity is crucial to the success of the system. At the level of administration the tasks of leadership, planning, decision-making, and review must be carried out. Essentially, administration is a professional task, consisting as it does of the application of organized knowledge to the solution of problems. It will be considered separately here because preparation for administrative tasks includes aspects not ordinarily included in professional education.

In the context of this discussion, *scientific* activity in the correctional field is directed at the increase of useful knowledge about social deviation. Naturally, those personnel whose activities are exclusively scientific will be located in research settings. It must be expected, however, that a correctional system successfully engaged in research will enlist scientific activity in other sectors. The scientist is essential to correctional success. By his own original work and by his access to other scientists outside the system, he makes possible the increased effectiveness of correctional practice.

It is the theme of this analysis that the professionalization of corrections has transformed its practice, and can be clearly enough related to the objectives of the system so that the dimensions of a basic discipline can be prescribed. We must therefore stick closely to our definition of *professionalism* so that some necessary distinctions can be made. For the older professions, such criteria of professionalism as traditions, codes of ethics, national and regional organizations, standardized graduate training, and licensing procedures take on the importance of sharply drawn boundaries. Really none of these criteria applies uniformly, if at all, to the field of corrections. We must look for a more basic distinguishing feature.

I am therefore led to a consideration of the common denominators of the major professions. If we can isolate three of these denominators, we can make a clarification which seems to me fundamental to the professionalization of corrections. The factors common to all professions are *practice, a class of problems, and an organized body of scientific knowledge.* Thus the profession of medicine consists of standard techniques of applying the various biological sciences to the problems of human disease. The profession of engineering consists of standard techniques of applying the various physical sciences to the problems of controlling the physical environment. The profession of social work is the application of the social sciences to the problems of human maladaptation. The correctional profession, then, is the application of the relevant social sciences to the control and resocialization of the criminal.

It is important to emphasize that this definition distinguishes quite practically between the professional worker and the scientist. The scientist's training will be in his particular sector of human knowledge. He will learn what there is now known about that sector and the techniques required to increase knowledge. The professional worker, on the other hand, must know those parts of a body of knowledge which are relevant to the problems he must attempt to solve. He must also know the practice of his profession, those techniques by which knowledge is applied to the problems. If he is resourceful enough, he will collaborate with scientists and other professionals in the improvement of practice and the application of new knowledge to problems.

To define the correctional profession is not to create it. Up to the present and probably well into the future, what professional services are carried out in the correctional field have been imported from outside the field. There is no question that this process will continue. Correctional institutions will always need physicians and clergymen, just as the military service does; but unlike the Army or the Navy, correctional agencies have never generated their own profession. The distinction must be brought into bolder relief. The professional specialty of psychiatry has been generated by two sources: the mental hospital and the application of psychoanalytic theory to the treatment of neuroses. The profession of social work has been generated from three primary sources: the social welfare agency for families and children, the hospital, and the public assistance agency. The correctional apparatus has valiantly striven to import both the psychiatrist and the social worker because both seem to have relevant knowledge and techniques. Neither has materialized at all sufficiently. Though the chronic shortage of practitioners in these fields must take some of the blame, I believe that the answer must be sought elsewhere. The practice of psychiatrists as they are now trained is directed at the problems of psychosis, which is peripheral to correctional work, or at the problem of the neurotic who refers himself voluntarily for treatment. Few psychiatrists are trained for the treatment of the sociopath, the character disorder, or the psychopath, to use only a few of the terms chosen for the correctional clinic. Most have learned that such diagnoses are untreatable problems. Under the circumstances, it is little wonder that correctional psychiatrists are few and far between. By the conditions of a professional commitment, the practitioner declines problems he is not equipped to solve.

The problem of the social worker is similar. Although in public assistance, he learns much about the exercise of coercive controls, little in his training prepares him for the unwilling client of the correctional apparatus. Few social workers come to the field well prepared with techniques to make possible the added adaptations of their knowledge and skill to the correctional problem. It is reasonable to expect that experimentation and experience from other fields will someday make possible the professional practice of probation. In this way, social workers are colonizers from another domain. They find that there are ways of using their knowledge, but a great deal is useless. They must urgently seek to adapt their tools for the rough, new world in which they now work.

Are the probation officer and his twin, the parole agent, professional workers? As practice now stands, it is difficult to concede to them this status. Most have been trained on the job, few have been grounded in the social science disciplines, and the problems with which they are required to deal are not presented in a professional form. The typical probation officer with a caseload of 75 or upward—often far, far upward—is not in a position to apply orderly casework skills, if he has any. He learns to be a caseload manager, a "trouble-shooter," and what he needs to know is seldom derived from a scientific approach to the problems of social deviation. What is lacking is the conceptualization of probation practice at a professional level.

The most populated level of the correctional structure, aside from the clients themselves, is the ancillary vocation of custody. The modern correctional officer, or group supervisor, or cottage parent has evolved from a nose-following enforcer of regulations into an employee on whose influence over clients increasing reliance is placed. There are still correctional officers who can only count or subdue their charges; there are still group supervisors who can only intimidate their groups and march them from one rehabilitative experience to the next. No administrator likes to admit to their presence on his premises, and their number is declining both by attrition and by the influences of training. Custodial workers are recruited with increasingly better educational equipment, and, motivated by a civil service structure which often lends itself to more mobility than most, they tend to bring some enthusiasm and purpose to in-service training. Nevertheless, the adequate performance of custodial work requires only instruction in methods by supervisors or special trainers. It does not require the assimilation of an organized body of scientific knowledge. It is highly unlikely that this will ever be the case, although in the future development of his role the custodial worker will undoubtedly be trained for more sophisticated assignments. His success as a group counselor in advanced correctional institutions in many different countries demonstrates, among other things, that the scope of on-the-job training may well include many functions previously thought to be best reserved for professionally trained personnel.

Nevertheless, the role of the custodial worker is ancillary or technical, to be shaped as an instrument in administrative or professional practice. As an avenue to the next higher levels of correctional activity, it is not to be ignored. In the next section, I shall return to an examination of the custodial roles, looking to a reconciliation of the control and resocialization functions at the level at which this reconciliation is most urgently needed.

The Task of Correctional Control

What are the requirements of knowledge and skill needed to accomplish the task of correctional control? The essence of the task, of course, is the maintenance of certain limits on the freedom of action of the client in the interests of the protection of the public, compliance with the requirements of the court, and, sometimes, the protection of the client from other clients and from himself. It is often assumed by outsiders that in the correctional institutions, the combination of cells and locks establish these limits quite adequately, while for the probation officer contact requirements would perform the same function. It is essential to understand that these conclusions are far from the truth, not only because such a concept of control conflicts with the objectives of resocialization and the utilization of manpower, but also because the mechanical application of control devices defeats itself and leads to loss of control.

To be effective, custody or surveillance of the correctional client must be appropriate, equitable, and organized in consistency with the resocialization and manpower utilization operations of the agency. While few decisions taken in a correctional agency with respect to clients are free of major control aspects, when control is the *only* consideration the dehumanizing and punitive effects merely contribute to an increased need for more rigid control. It is significant that wherever a correctional apparatus has devoted attention to increasing the effectiveness of resocialization programs and to better utilization of manpower, the need for maximum control has markedly diminished.

Appropriate control depends on effective evaluation and a thorough understanding of the measures needed to establish the prescribed limits. This is hardly a novel proposition. Prison wardens and parole board members have always been expected to know the grim requirements of limit setting. They have also fully understood the need for effective evaluation of their charges. Usually, in the era when they were virtually without professional support, they relied heavily on an inspection of the offender's physiognomy in the expectation that a sound intuitive judgment would thereby come to them. The consequence was ordinarily in the direction of imposing superfluous control. More contemporary correctional decision-makers understand that the measures to establish control should be sufficient to its maintenance and no more. The selection of the proper degree of control depends on the professional application of knowledge to the problem of evaluation. The administrator should preferably know from experience how to make such evaluations himself, or he should at least know how to use them intelligently.

Equitable administration of control obviously requires a thorough knowledge of the criminal law and the principles underlying the civil rights of the individual, whether citizen or felon. It is not enough to know that legal counsel should be sought when needed; the administration of control should be zealous in assuring that all persons subject to it should have a sense that fairness is an active element in decision making rather than a necessary limit. Because misinformation about constitutional rights and the elements of the law is prevalent in all sections of the correctional community, it is essential that a thorough grounding in the relevant aspects of jurisprudence should be afforded to all personnel.

The organization of a correctional institution or agency is a complex task whose dimensions are sometimes almost incredible by virtue of the unreasonable size of American correctional systems. The administrator of control cannot maintain it without due regard to the other objectives of the system. He must see to it that control is consistent with resocialization and the efficient use of manpower. As the techniques of resocialization increase in effectiveness, their impact on the means of control becomes critical. For example, correctional administrators are increasingly alert to the possibilities of providing constructive roles for inmates or parolees in the maintenance of control. The ancient and dishonored resort to the informer is disavowed, but the use of group counseling and the maintenance of a therapeutic milieu provides instruments of control which are not only consistent with the objective of resocialization but also afford the offender some opportunity for autonomy as an individual and as a member of the group.

Finally, in order that the control task can be done at all, it must be organized. The theory of organization is moving so rapidly towards a new maturity that it is doubtful that any correctional agency has been able to keep abreast. However, it must be seen to be essential that measures be taken to carry out the normal organizational tasks efficiently. The recruiting, training, and supervision of staff; the preparation and defense of budget requests; the maintenance of sound communications on a bilateral basis; the allocation of line and staff operations; the provision for review and improvement of operations—all these and many more administrative tasks must be well done if correctional control is to be maintained. It is a role for which relevant training is seldom provided at the right time. The typical correctional administrator finds himself in middle life learning as best he can a new role for which neither intuition nor common sense can adequately prepare him. It is time that thought should be given to the curriculum of a school of correctional administration, aimed not at the fledgling still at the university but rather at the successful practitioner ready after years of subordinate service for elevation to the highest echelon.

We see, then, that the management of the tasks of correctional control depends on the following essential elements, to be acquired as suggested in the following table:

	Skill	*Training Source*
1.	Measures of control.	Agency in-service training.
2.	Evaluation of offender.	Graduate courses in criminology or other behavioral science.
3.	Constitutional and criminal law.	Graduate courses under auspices of school of criminology.
4.	Techniques of resocialization.	Graduate courses in psychiatry and social work conducted under the auspices of a school of criminology.
5.	Organization and training of correctional staff.	Post-graduate doctoral training in specialized professional school.

It will be seen that in this area there is an important role for the corrections-oriented school of criminology. These schools are not provided with the clinical resources or staff wherewith they can hope to train correctional resocialization specialists. They are fitted, however, to provide an undergraduate education suited to the performance of subprofessional correctional functions. As the successful entrant matures into a supervisor and broadens his responsibilities to include such resocialization aspects as group counseling and therapeutic community activity, he would be appropriately re-engaged in graduate work which would qualify him for these extensions. Finally, as the command level is approached by some, an intensive and prolonged course in correctional administration might be made available on a stipendiary basis.

The Tasks of Correctional Resocialization

In the correctional apparatus, resocialization should be an objective to which every employee in contact with clients is directly and meaningfully related. However, it will be useful to consolidate for consideration under this heading the various professional services which must be provided for this purpose. To make the analysis simpler, I shall divide these services under two headings: non-correctional and correctional.

Considering first the non-correctional services for convenience, in order to get them out of the way, we must provide correctional integration for the clergy, the physician and surgeon, the schoolmaster, the vocational trainer, the librarian, and the recreation supervisor. All of these professions are, of course, imported from outside the limits of the institution. Their representatives have a way of persisting in their correctional specialty, and many of these professionals have formed associations of their own which publish periodicals and conduct professional conferences.

The essential nature of their services is obvious. Few correctional institutions could manage without a full complement. While probation agencies naturally do not provide this broad spectrum of services, the probation administrator must understand not only the resources of the institutions he operates—such as camps and juvenile halls—but also those to which he must recommend the commitment of clients. It follows, then, that the integration of the service professional requires a plan of specialized in-service training in which his role is considered in relationship to the successful discharge of other roles. A specialized in-service training for professionals is unusual but not unknown in correctional institutions. It should not be assumed that the professional will always and with ease assume his responsibility of learning by himself what he needs to know about the setting in which he works. Many good men are lost by this assumption; many promising entrants deteriorate into hopeless mediocrity through lack of attention to this responsibility.

Because of the common denominator of professionalism it is desirable that the training of the service professional be conducted by the correctional professional, who, in turn, should be prepared specifically for this work. The maintenance of these professional services on an even inter-disciplinary keel calls for tact, discretion, and due regard to special circumstances of age, outside experience, prestige, and so forth; but with the complexity of all correctional operations dictated by the multiplicity of objectives, this investment of time and planning appears to be an essential training requirement.

So far we have considered those professions which are imported into the correctional apparatus with no appreciable change in the conditions of practice. The pastoral work of the chaplain, the clinical practice of the physician, and the educational endeavors of the teacher are essentially the same inside and outside the institution. In their dealings with the correctional client, these professionals have the advantage of clear and understandable roles which are familiar to all concerned.

The tasks of resocialization are also unfamiliar roles which are peculiar to the correctional scene. It will be a long time before these roles are clearly defined to the satisfaction of all concerned. Here we can only make a modest contribution toward that happy day. We believe that although controversy will unavoidably continue for a long time as to who should do what, the tide of confusion as to what should actually be done is receding. If we can identify these tasks, it should be possible to relate them to appropriate training. We shall make the broad classification of resocialization tasks, which is obvious enough, and then describe each task according to the skills needed to perform it. It is here that the sensitive questions of jurisdiction abound; only a process of professional evolution can solve them.

The four primary tasks of resocialization are seen as analysis, prescription, program execution, and evaluation. They are common to all phases of the correctional process, both in institutions and in the field. At present their performance is distributed among various levels and disciplines. The professionalization of the field will clearly limit the distribution considerably, but necessity and the lack of appropriately trained people will result in expedients which would not be tolerated in more abundantly staffed systems. From the prolonged use of such expedients much can be learned, as we have found, for example, in correctional ventures into group counseling and milieu treatment.

In the task of analysis, the field must make the necessary definition of the client's problem. In medicine, the corresponding function is diagnosis, a term which I shall avoid in this analysis because of its narrower significance in medical usage. In the analysis of the client and his situation, the correctional clinician is concerned in making those distinctions which will enable the apparatus to maintain the needed controls as well as to proceed with resocialization. Beyond the usual diagnostic objective of ascertaining the personal deficits of the client, the task extends to an understanding of his past, present, and probable future interaction with the environments open to him. This is now a multi-disciplinary task. Information must be gathered with some discrimination of its relevance to defining the correctional problem the client represents. The special skills of reconnaissance interviewing are, of course, essential. Additional skills in the observation of behavior, especially in the institution or in other structured situations are essential. To apply these professional skills, which are fundamental to the profession of social work, it is necessary to augment the usual education of the social worker with some intensive training in personality dynamics and in the social origins of criminal behavior. What the analysis of the correctional situation should produce is a clearly defined hypothesis relating criminal behavior to the forces within the client and his environment which produced it. It is a deceptively difficult task requiring a broad theoretical knowledge as well as the skill and intuition of a good interviewer.

In addition to the production of a discriminating social history, the analysis of the client's situation demands the administration of a battery of psychological tests to make certain determinations. Some of these tests are intended for coarse screening and may be administered with little direct professional involvement. Some, as in the case of the individually administered projective tests, will always require a professional psychologist. Where, as in most large correctional systems, the volume of work creates a need for sorting it efficiently, the social worker can act as the primary analyst, making determinations as to which cases may need further differentiation by psychological test and psychiatric study. In the present structure of the professional disciplines concerned, the task of analysis must continue to be so distributed. Whether some merger of functions into new roles may become possible through broadened training will remain for the evolution of these disciplines to determine.

Prescription is the process of relating analysis to program resources. The question of relevance of program to client problem is perhaps the muddiest in the field; but given the analysis of the client's problem through the professional procedures outlined above, someone with a broad knowledge of the resources available must offer a prescription on how to proceed. This prescription may be in the form of a recommendation to a court or parole board, or a plan for an institutional classification committee to implement. It is here that knowledge of resources, to be gained mostly from experience with the system, must be tied to knowledge of the principles which govern the effective use of these resources. For example, what are the forces within the relationship of a probation officer to his probationer which are constructive as to what classes of probationer? Or, what are the influences of long-term confinement which must be considered in a pre-sentence recommendation to various classes of offender? Most such questions require fundamental knowledge derived from the behavioral sciences. There can be little question that on these, as with so many other issues, it is essential that the correctional practitioner be well-grounded in sociology and social psychology; but beyond these academic fundamentals, his success must also depend on his ability to provide for feedback on the prescription process throughout systematic observation of results. Both system and individual must make this provision; for the individual, it forms a necessary part of his professional identity.

Program execution consists of the management of the direct and indirect influences which are to be brought to bear on the client's behavior. Three general classes of skill are required, in addition to those needed for the task of prescription. These are usually referred to as treatment: individual psychotherapy, group therapy, and therapeutic milieu management. Something should be said about each.

In the very nature of the correctional apparatus, various staff-client relationships are inevitably set up which are deliberately intended to influence client behavior. These range from the implicit influences of a custodial officer or a work supervisor over inmates in a correctional institution to the formal therapeutic approach of a psychiatrist. The relationship of a probation or a parole officer to his client will also vary from cursory surveillance to well-planned and sophisticated counseling. All these relationships are buttressed in all cases by the powerful supports of official legitimation. To the client, society firmly says: "Your contacts with this staff representative are intended for your improvement and are *ipso facto* good for you. If you choose not to avail yourself of these services, we must conclude that you do not wish to better yourself." The moral obligation on correctional administration and on the correctional practitioner to perfect these services is very great. What may pass for well-meant bumbling in non-authoritarian agencies cannot be disregarded by the client in the *correctional context*. It is essential, then, that psychotherapy be located on a continuum of influences upon the offender. All contact participants in the correctional process must be consistently trained in these concepts of therapy which are relevant to their kinds of relationships with clients. In most correctional systems, rather effective measures are taken to eliminate the grosser kinds of destructive staff influences; but this is not enough in a system which must take responsibility for all influences upon its clients, as is the case with the total institution. Contact staff must be adequately oriented as to the goals and methods of positive influence. This concept has obvious implications for training. It becomes necessary that the professional level of personnel be soundly oriented in the theoretical basis of practice and adequately prepared in the art of applying this theory through the therapeutic interview. It is further necessary that professional personnel be enabled to train staff of all levels to undertake positive and constructive relationships with clients. This does not mean that every custodial officer will be a psychotherapist, but that he will be able to structure his relationships with clients consistent with a therapeutic objective.

This also is the case with group processes. The general field of corrections has led the way in the use of lay leadership in group counseling. The demonstration that such a process is not only harmless but often is actually beneficial has overshadowed the study of methods for training the counselor to achieve predictable effectiveness. Now the regime for training anybody in effective group processes is hardly in a satisfactory state of conceptualization. Some hold that what is learned from training in individual psychotherapy may be usefully extended to cover training for group therapy. Some believe that training in group dynamics should be added; and others believe that there is no substitute for an apprenticeship under an experienced practitioner. The actual practice seems to consist of exposure to group processes accompanied by some theoretical orientation. Confidence is gained by experience and problems are solved by sharing with the supervisors and fellow practitioners.

The results can hardly be appraised because of the lack of any method for objective appraisal; but while awaiting the development of such a method, it seems that much more could be done to prepare the professional for the practice of this art, which, in turn, could be extended to enrich the contributions of lay counselors. It should not be beyond the competence of the professional schools to design a specific curriculum which would prepare students in the theory of group influences on behavior, the general practice of group therapy, and its specific application to the correctional client.

The history of milieu treatment in corrections is recent, and this is not the place to relate it or to ascribe credit for its origin and development. What must be done here is to define it, to specify the professional roles which need to be played and to present some preliminary thoughts about training for these roles. While the progress of conventional group processes has far outstripped the development of training for practice, the same can hardly be said about the use of the correctional milieu as an influence.

Let us arbitrarily define correctional milieu treatment as the use of all resources of the institution, including the offenders themselves, for therapeutic influence on all offenders. Seen thus, the task of advanced correctional practice is to develop not merely an aseptic institution in which no one will be harmed by the experience, but a therapeutic facility which will benefit all concerned. While such an objective seems almost fanciful as applied to adult recidivists, for example, its logic is more obvious with more hopeful cases; and as we more closely approach an effective basis for action with the least hopeful clients, the use of the correctional milieu for treatment gains will become equally reasonable.

What we hope to accomplish with such treatment methods is the use of the institutional community (and, in some California experiments, parole communities and half-way houses) as a means whereby an offender can achieve a new identity through learning new social roles. The skills learned by the practitioner in interviewing and group treatment continue to be relevant. Beyond this kind of skill, there is needed an understanding of communications methods in small communities, the significance of process and events, and the nature of role systems in total institutions. At present, we must limit ourselves to saying that the effective practitioner must familiarize himself with the growing literature in this new and promising field, and should be versed broadly in the behavioral sciences. It is probably too early for professional schools to be standardizing curricula, but seminars on theory and practice are urgently needed.

We come finally to the process of evaluation of the client in terms of decisions which the courts or other authorities must make about his destiny. In varying degrees, this process of evaluation has been delegated to the correctional practitioner through the device of recommendations to the decision-maker. What the practitioner must do when he is so assigned is to determine whether the events and experience which have followed the original analysis of the client's situation have sufficiently changed it to justify restoration to full status in the community or to some intermediate status requiring less social control. With greater or less degrees of formality, such evaluations go on all the time in corrections. They differ from the processes of analysis to the extent that the question, *What must we do?* differs from the question, *Is he ready for an altered control relationship?* Again, the practitioner must have a thorough knowledge of personality dynamics as they relate to criminality and of environmental influences which positively or negatively bear on criminality. The art of reconnaissance interviewing, the understanding of the treatment potentiality of correctional facilities, and the capacity for objectivity are further essentials.

Much more could no doubt be said about the nature and dimensions of correctional practice at the professional level. At this point, however, we can conclude this analysis by identifying the constituent knowledges and skills which comprise professional practice in corrections.

Interviewing, the basic art, requires some theoretical training and a long and arduous experience of supervised practice. At present, schools of psychiatry, psychology, and social work provide both ingredients of training. The techniques of training vary considerably in sophistication and intensity. The capacity of none of these disciplines is adequate to supply the need, and all must be expected to contribute substantially to the future development of practice.

Group treatment and observation now tend to be learned in in-service training, if they are systematically learned at all. As we have emphasized above, it seems urgent to enrich professional curricula with training in group processes relevant to a field which is increasingly dependent on them. Again, all three disciplines active in correctional practice should incorporate relevant training, aimed not only at promoting a general competence in group process but also a familiarity with the general problems of applying it in the correctional context.

Mastery of these arts is essential to successful correctional practice in any of the disciplines professionally engaged in corrections. Fully effective practice requires some additional skills in at least some workers. The peculiarities of mass treatment demand that some participants possess capabilities in the organization and supervision of the work of other professionals. There is a tendency, which must be regarded as natural enough, for such training to be learned on the job; after all, the production of a practitioner is a formidable enough task for a professional school. The fact of the matter is that work organization and supervision are difficult tasks in themselves, and by no means to be regarded as the natural culmination of a few years of successful practice. The bodies of knowledge to be assimilated are sufficiently large and complex to justify special curricula for practitioners about to be appointed to positions requiring this kind of competence. That such an approach to professional education will require massive readjustments in the organization of professional schools and of the agency itself does not obviate the reality of the need. We cannot much longer continue to relegate the training of correctional leadership to tradition, intuition, and sometimes an unsettling week of "sensitivity training" in the professional schools. Post-graduate training for administration and leadership is needed to meet the requirements of the correctional agencies.

To complete a structure which is fatally incomplete without it, the knowledge which various social sciences have assembled on the nature of crime and criminal must be communicated in an orderly fashion to the aspirant. For some universities, it will be feasible to design a sequence of instruction in sociology and psychology which will incorporate what needs to be known. For others, it will be expedient to reinforce the curriculum in criminology. The social and psychological factors producing criminality must be brought into a focus for training for correctional practice. The discipline of criminology does not now present the means for training aspirants for clinical work. If the older professional schools can adapt their curricula and augment their production of trained manpower to meet the special needs of prisons, training schools, and probation agencies, schools of criminology will not be able to develop the needs for clinical training. It is not easy to foresee the tremendous expansion of schools of social work and departments of psychology which would be necessary to bring about such a development; but if such professional schools cannot incorporate specialized training for corrections, it is highly probable that schools of criminology must begin to train candidates for practice.

On the Utilization of Client Manpower

The theme of hard labor has been persistently played throughout the history of penology. In prisons all over the world, solutions are sought to the problem of work. Nobody disputes that the offender should work, or that he should work hard. The difficult thing is to find any work at all for him in an industrial civilization which has little use for strong backs and even less for untrained minds.

The solution of make-work is rightly scorned by all, and is preferred only to the outright idleness which afflicts all too many correctional clients. Fortunately, some kinds of conservation and community improvement projects lend themselves readily to participation by some correctional clients. It is evident that where thoughtful attention has been given to the design of work programs for prisoners and probationers, the results have diminished the enormous human waste which goes on in most correctional operations. Such planning does not happen by serendipity. It occurs because the manpower problem is integrated with the resocialization problem and someone, ordinarily a clinically oriented administrator, has seen that social restoration is accomplished by involvement and not by dosage. Administrative and professional personnel for correctional work programs must be drawn from disciplines such as forestry, business management, and industrial engineering; but they won't even arrive and certainly won't stay unless they are given realistic roles in the employment of inmates. This objective certainly requires the sympathetic and creative participation of the professional correctional worker, fully alert to the implications of the appropriate employment of the offender to the aims of resocialization. This kind of participation requires not merely the awareness that prisoners should work and parolees must, but a substantial knowledge of the occupational world, the capacity for keeping abreast of employment trends, and some imagination about the relatedness of the limited variety of work programs available within any institution to the much broader variety outside. The specialty of vocational psychology is not exactly an over-populated profession, but it must be strategically represented throughout the correctional apparatus.

The New Role of Research

It is research which has made possible the new professional roles in corrections. In the past, now, and for the foreseeable future, most research applicable to the field will be done outside the boundaries of the apparatus in universities, institutes, and foundations. The accelerating pace of the social sciences now seems to require that the correctional agency arm itself with facilities to enable it to put research into operation. There are many ways of accomplishing this end, but in the system to which I am most accustomed, the establishment of a division of research has proved to be successful.

The aims of correctional research are the improvement of the administration of criminal justice and the rational management of correctional administration and practice. To accomplish these objectives, an integrated research unit maintains an information system which takes advantage of electronic data processing, develops a system of measurement by which changes in the function of the apparatus can be gauged, and engages in experimental work aimed at the improvement of practice. This is the process of self-study which augments the application of research imported from outside the system.

A further analysis of correctional research operations would be beyond the scope of this study. It is apparent, however, that the nature of the tasks to be done requires certain professional specialties which are by no means abundant in today's labor market for intellectuals. Statisticians, social psychologists, and sociologists are difficult to engage at the salaries which prevail in public employment. Many of the most competent will prefer academic positions, thereby escaping the well-known dilemmas of the intellectual employed in a bureaucracy. It is thus that compromises are made, many to the considerable advantage of the system. Professionals find themselves lured into scientific work, often to the advantage of both the professional and the work. Much research is farmed out to organizations better fitted to conduct it, with the agency engaging to maintain a semblance of laboratory conditions. The worst compromise of all is that research is done and moulders on the shelf, a yellowing stack of mimeographed manuscripts.

For our purposes here, the lessons to be drawn are that research and practice must be mutually supportive, and that in this field the lines between the two can never be hard and fast. The professional worker in corrections may in good conscience abstain from some field of practice, but he is abdicating a part of his right to professional status if he does not maintain a minimum competence in the understanding of research method. At least he should be able to relate relevant scientific work to his own day-to-day practice. When called on to participate in a self-study project, he should be able to contribute intelligently. If the system in which he works is not content with stagnation, he will be called on, and frequently!

The implications for training are obvious. The professional worker planning to engage in corrections must have a reasonable grounding in statistics, at least to the extent that he understands the basic concepts even if he cannot operate the more sophisticated methods. The fundamentals of the scientific method as it applies to the inexact sciences should be familiar to him, and not merely by rote. Finally, a reasonable familiarity with the landmarks of social science literature, the major journals, and the bibliography of criminology and corrections should be imparted as a phase of graduate training just as essential to adequate performance as legal bibliography is to the law-school curriculum.

Some General Conclusions

Our survey has necessarily skimmed a surface, as surveys tend to do. What is needed next is a series of studies in depth of each of the correctional tasks which I have identified. Such studies will identify the minimum levels of required skill for correctional operation and propose a curriculum to qualify an aspirant to engage in it. It will probably be found that there are certain educational sequences appropriate to certain levels of activity. I suggest that my analysis supports the following distribution of educational effort:

Technical: General education, followed by agency in-service training. Preferably such training should include at least some residential experience in an agency-managed academy.

Professional (non-correctional): Complete professional education, followed by agency-managed in-service training designed for professional classes only.

Professional (control functions): Undergraduate education in criminology, followed by graduate courses in criminology and public administration as career requirements indicate.

Professional (resocialization functions): Graduate education in psychiatry, psychology, or *social work,* with specialized classroom instruction in criminology and correctional practice. At least a third of the supervised practice should be under correctional auspices.

Administration: Selection for higher administrative functions should be based on successful professional practice in either control or resocialization, followed by advanced graduate education in public administration.

To accomplish these goals, some major reorganization of both the correctional apparatus and of professional education will have to take place. It will not take place overnight, nor will it happen because everyone agrees as to its desirability. Steps will have to be taken, in the confidence that each step leads to another. Correctional progress cannot much longer be generated from in-service training. It needs specific and widely-used curricula preparing professional people for a difficult and changing task. We must now proceed to the analysis which will make such programs and such public servants possible.

Remarks

by DONALD R. CRESSEY

THE WORDS "profession," "professional," or "professionalization" are used about seventy times in Mr. Conrad's paper. If one did not go beyond such a count, he might conclude that the paper's principal objective is the furtherance of the "professionalization" of corrections. A more detailed analysis suggests that this conclusion is not quite correct. The paper's principal plea is for an upgrading of the educational level of correctional workers, so that a maximum number of workers will be "professional" but it also asks for a more effective division of labor among correctional personnel than now exists.

During the last ten years, increasingly more emphasis has been placed on higher and higher standards in American education. This emphasis has come on the heels of a trend toward making more and more years of formal education a prerequisite for more and more jobs. An upgrading of high school work has been followed by an upgrading of university work, and the years of formal education needed to be a "success" in our society have continued to grow. Accordingly, students must today work much harder than students of earlier generations worked—the high school student must work harder to get into a university, the university student must work harder to graduate, and a boy hoping to become a "professional" must be prepared for more years of difficult educational work than people going into the same profession in earlier years had to have.

In short, high school students have been getting better, and increasing "professionalization" has made an increasing number of high school graduates desire a university education. As a consequence, there is intense competition for admittance into universities. This has led to a university phenomenon—occurring especially among private universities—called "the raising of standards." Some private universities have already raised their standards so high that, with few exceptions, students with anything less than a straight "A" average find it useless to apply for admission.

In general terms, Mr. Conrad's paper asks for a similar "raising of standards" in correctional work. The paper says, implicitly, that correctional work has now become so desirable that we can "raise the standards" up to the levels of "professionalism," which means that we will require more and more years of increasingly difficult work in formal education for those who join us.

I do not agree that correctional work is as yet so desirable that we can afford to make it more and more difficult for persons to get into it. In view of the changes occurring in the educational world generally, all men must be in favor of "higher standards," just as they are in favor of "creativity" and the control of man-eating sharks. Only a fool would make a plea for *lowering* of standards, even if he calls it "resetting our sites," "modifying our guidelines," or "raising our standards." I am such a fool. Some years ago I made a plea for professional work in corrections, and it is true that corrections needs the services of many types of professional personnel.[1] But this does not

[1] Donald R. Cressey, "Professional Correctional Work and Professional Work in Corrections," *National Probation and Parole Association Journal,* Vol. 5 (January, 1959), pp. 1-15.

mean that the solution to the manpower problem in the correctional field requires more "professionalization" of the kind involving high levels of education. Correctional institutions and agencies must organize themselves in a way which will enable them to utilize effectively the correctional skills of men with a high school education at most. There are two lines of reasoning behind this proposal.

First, the evidence is clear that every move toward "professionalizing" an occupation has had as one of its consequences a decrease in the number of personnel in that occupation, in proportion to population.[2] Among other things, "subprofessional" or "sub-standard" training centers close down, leaving a few centers with the burden of training all the personnel needed, a burden they are not prepared to bear. Moreover, prospective practitioners turn away from the new, more rigorous, more technical, more "professional," and more lengthy training expected of them, and go into respectable but "non-professional" work.

Second, a "lowering of standards" in correctional work is needed to get us out of a trap in which we are caught, as far as the rehabilitation of offenders is concerned. Ironically, we set the trap ourselves, inadvertently, by subscribing to the psychiatric theory of rehabilitation promulgated by psychiatrists, social workers, and other psychiatrically-oriented personnel. As far as rehabilitation procedures are concerned, this kind of theory implies, by and large, that until one has had about ten years of university training, he is not qualified to try and rehabilitate a criminal. Moreover, we sometimes are even warned, on theoretical grounds, that a person who does not have about ten years of university training—a non-psychiatrist—may do irreparable harm to the psyches of delinquents and criminals if he tries to rehabilitate them. The theoretical position, then, has led us to the conclusion that rehabilitation by other than "professionals" is both ineffective and potentially dangerous.

Of course, there are some exceptions. A few years ago, it was conceded that in certain situations it was all right for "subprofessionals" with only about six years of university work—social workers—to talk to criminals, provided that they were closely supervised by a man who had gone to college for ten years; and now these former "subprofessionals" are saying that they, too, are "professionals," and it is they who are now conceding, rather reluctantly, it seems to me, that in certain situations it is all right for "uneducated subprofessionals" with only an A.B. degree to talk with delinquents and criminals provided that they do it under the watchful eye of the new "professional." As a mat-

[2] Theodore Caplow, *The Sociology of Work* (Minneapolis: University of Minnesota Press, 1954), pp. 137-140.

ter of fact, I have even witnessed the third step—the man with the A.B. degree in speech, philosophy, English, or French, who manages to get a job as a probation officer, takes an in-service training course, declares himself a "professional," and then points a long finger at the "subprofessionals" who only graduated from high school.

The trap is this: We subscribe to a theory of rehabilitation that can be implemented only by highly-educated, "professionally-trained" persons, and then scream that there are not enough of these persons to man our correctional agencies and institutions. According to the last count I have (for the spring of 1954), there were only twenty-nine psychiatrists working fulltime in all the state and federal prisons in the United States.[3] Twelve of these men were located in California, and seven in New York, leaving ten psychiatrists for the rest of the country's institutions. Eighteen states had no psychiatric services at all, and only nine had the services of a full-time psychiatrist. There are many more social workers than psychiatrists in correctional work, probably because members of this profession have moved in to partially fill the vacuum left by psychiatrists; but no matter what the number of social workers in corrections is, it is too small.

If we retain the psychiatric notions about rehabilitation, the "correctional industry" will be able to use every psychiatrist and social worker produced in the United States in the remainder of this century, leaving none of these professionals to work with mental patients, with thc middle-class ladies of Beverly Hills, or with other persons needing their services. Further, I am convinced that even if universities doubled or tripled their output of psychiatrists and social workers, corrections would not get its share of professional personnel of this kind in the future, for the same reason it is not getting its share now—their ideology and theory are such that they really don't want to try to rehabilitate criminals, at least not at the salaries that corrections can offer them.

To get through the mountain of inconsistencies we have so nicely constructed, I propose that we start tunnelling from the other side of the hill. Instead of continuing to try to bore through by means of louder and louder pleas for more and more training for greater and greater numbers of highly-trained psychiatrists, social workers, and similar professional personnel, let us start digging a tunnel that will enable us to make maximum use of the personnel actually available to act as resocialization agents. There is no shortage of mature, moral, average, fine, good, run-of-the-mill men and women of the kind making up the

---

[3] "What's New in Prison Psychiatry and Psychology?," *Correctional Research*, Bulletin No. 5 (June, 1954), pp. 6-7.

majority of the personnel now manning our factories, our businesses, our mental hospitals, and our prisons—men and women with a high school education at most. With increasing automation, in fact, more and more personnel of this kind will be leaving "production" occupations and will be available for "service" occupations, including that of rehabilitating criminals. Our first task, a simple one, is to recognize the tremendous force of manpower available to us. Our second task, and, in my opinion, the most difficult and important task that criminologists and correctional personnel will face during the remainder of this century, is the development of sound rehabilitation theory (and procedures for implementing that theory) which will enable us to utilize this vast reservoir of manpower.

The task is not impossible. Compared to the task of trying to shuffle an increasing proportion of our population through schools of medicine or social work, it is a simple one. We have already made some feeble theoretical beginnings which will enable us to use the personnel ready and willing to serve, but I cannot discuss them here.[4] If the citizens of the United States can put a man on the moon, they can develop sound rehabilitation theory and sound systems for using that theory to change criminals. Both the theory and the systems must be "practical," in the sense that the systems must be based on theory that recognizes that highly educated personnel are not available to change criminals into non-criminals, any more than highly educated personnel are available to change non-criminals into criminals. We are logically inconsistent when we say that a working-class boy can become a criminal even if (or partly because) his world of experience includes few highly educated people, but that this same boy can then become a non-criminal only if his world of experience includes personal interaction with the most highly educated men in the world.

It is quite probable that Americans will get to the moon. If they do, it will be because they have constructed a highly efficient organization for doing so. This organization includes a division of labor of the kind Mr. Conrad asks for in his paper. In terms which grossly oversimplify a very complex situation, the organization that is going to get us to the moon is made up of four principal types of personnel—policy makers, theoreticians, engineers, and technicians. Mr. Conrad's terms are different, but when he asks for scientists, for several varieties of professional personnel, for administrators, and for technicians, he seems to have the same kind of division of labor in mind. It is this kind of division of labor, plus a lot of money provided by policy makers, that has

---

[4] Donald R. Cressey, "Social Psychological Theory for Using Deviants to Control Deviation," *Experiment in Cultural Expansion* (Sacramento: California Department of Corrections, 1964), pp. 139-152.

increased the rate of technological change in the years since World War II. It is the ambiguity and softness about a division of labor of this kind that makes it necessary for those in correctional work to participate, over and over again, in conferences devoted to discussion of manpower and training in corrections. We have been insisting, by analogy, that the psychiatric theoretician also be both the engineer that puts theory to use and the technician that actually turns the loose screws, cracks the nuts, and straightens out the kinks.

We do not ask physicists and mathematicians to assemble moon rockets. Why, then, do we insist that the highly educated theoreticians in corrections be people-changers?

I do not imply that the correctional technician cannot make a contribution to the theory. Neither do I imply that correctional theoreticians, "engineers," or technicians have no voice in policy-making decisions. I do say that it must be the policy that correctional theoreticians continue to try to develop theories of rehabilitation which agency administrators ("engineers") can implement by creating an organization made up principally of men trained on the trade-school level to be skilled people-changers (technicians). Parenthetically, I have reason to believe that we will eventually discover that the most effective people-changers working in corrections will be ex-criminals, but I cannot develop that point here.[5]

My position differs from Mr. Conrad's only in degree. I want to put most of the money available into developing people-changers on the technician level while he wants to bet on the development of more professionals. His position is more widely accepted than mine. It is difficult to determine how we came to develop the notion that "efficiency" in correctional work depends upon utilizing more and more highly educated men. There seem to be three basic reasons:

First, American society has been characterized by increasing specialization and division of labor, and a trend toward professionalization of the many specialized occupations. In the early part of the century, educational institutions adopted a pragmatic emphasis that transformed a large proportion of high school and college curricula into vocational courses on subjects previously taught in an apprenticeship system. A reversal of this trend has begun, but occupational specialists continue to band together, to call themselves "professionals," and to demand that the qualifying educational level be raised. I expect, therefore, that

---

[5] *See* Donald R. Cressey, "Changing Criminals: The Application of the Theory of Differential Association," *American Journal of Sociology,* Vol. 61 (September, 1955) pp. 116-120; and Rita Volkman and Donald R. Cressey, "Differential Association and the Rehabilitation of Drug Addicts," *American Journal of Sociology,* Vol. 69 (September, 1963), pp. 129-142.

if we do develop skilled correctional technicians on the trade-school level, there will soon be agitation for college courses for these men so that they can be "professionals." Social work—outside corrections—developed in somewhat this way—and now social workers are so well trained that they would not dream of carrying food baskets to the poor.

Second, the traditional division of labor between correctional education and practice has been inconsistent, for most college and university courses dealing with crime and corrections have been taught by sociologists, while most people working in corrections, including the professionals, have only a vague knowledge of sociology. Moreover, high schools give courses on how to change machines (automobile mechanics), on how to change landscapes (agriculture), and even on how to change the weather (air conditioning), but they are not training any people-changers for the corrections industry.

Third, the agitation for "professionalization" would put psychiatrists, social workers, and other members of the "helping professions" in charge of correctional practice personnel who are not research-oriented. The "helping professions" are, by definition, professions whose members put into practice other people's ideas about how to give help, but in correctional work, members of the "helping professions" who might be viewed as analogous to engineers, have in effect been trying to be policy-makers and theoreticians as well as helpers and implementers. Men who have come into corrections as technicians, even if highly educated technicians, have successfully lobbied for the notion that they should be the engineers, theoreticians, and policy-makers. Yet, as Mr. Conrad points out, the conventional professional in the correctional field is essentially a colonist from another domain. This important point must be recognized to understand the operation of correctional institutions and agencies. Mr. Conrad is saying that few, if any, professions are as generic as their practitioners think they are. I would add only that movement toward colonization of the correctional field by the "helping professions" has necessarily meant that research and theory will be neglected. For example, until quite recently, it was common to assume that every student majoring in social work or psychiatry would be a practitioner, and that, negatively, no students majoring in these subjects would be researchers or theory-builders.

For these three reasons (and perhaps others), it has been difficult to visualize a division of labor in corrections comparable to the division of labor in physical science-technology or biological science-medicine. Accordingly, we have tended to ignore what I consider two important parts of the division of labor—theoreticians and trade-school-trained technicians. We have also ignored the fact that neither theoreticians nor members of the "helping professions" working in corrections need also be policy-makers, but here we share a fault with other scientists and practitioners who argue that they, and not politicians, should set policy.

In view of this background discussion, it is exciting to note that Mr. Conrad specifies research as one of the responsibilities of the correctional apparatus, along with control, resocialization, and the efficient utilization of manpower. Incidentally, two objectives of the correctional process which Mr. Conrad does not emphasize are punishment and the protection of criminals from society. We cannot ignore the fact that men are still sent to prison partly so that they will suffer. Neither can we ignore the vast amount of time and energy that correctional personnel devote to protecting criminals from those who would harm or exploit them in various ways. Participation in prison research made me sharply aware of the need to attain these two goals which society has assigned to correctional agencies, so I can only agree enthusiastically with Mr. Conrad that research into the causes and prevention of crime and the treatment of the criminal is now a responsibility of the correctional apparatus, and that "the scientist is essential to the correctional process." California leads here, as it does in so many correctional areas. However, I think that we will be in trouble if the theoretician is envisaged as an employee of a correctional organization in the way that we think of the technician as a correctional employee. I know no reputable researcher or theoretician who works regular hours, minds the boss, or routinely produces, on schedule, mimeographed manuscripts that "molder on the shelf." The theoretician must be free to arrive at his research findings, which may be used by policy-makers as a basis for introducing new programs. In no sense can he be "professional" who sees his occupation as one that applies an organized body of scientific knowledge. There is no "physics profession" or "biology profession" because physicists and biologists are devoted to changing the body of knowledge on which a profession could be based.

In summary, then, I believe that Mr. Conrad's most general conclusion is one that must be repeated again and again until it is finally implemented—"Some major reorganization of both the correctional apparatus and of professional education will have to take place." While, as I indicated, I do not necessarily like the terminology Mr. Conrad uses to lead to his conclusion, I cannot see how anyone can disagree with the general idea that correctional work must include several levels of specialists, or with the idea that each specialist should have the best training available. I disagree with the implicit assumption that a man must plan for at least six years of college training to make his mark in correctional work. If anything has been learned about mental hospitals and correctional institutions since World War II, it is that change in patients or prisoners depends more on the actions of attendants and guards—men hired officially to implement "the measures of control"—than it does on the actions of any other personnel. Our main job, then, is to make these persons into skilled correctional technicians—people-changers—who will do the real bread-and-butter work of resocialization and thus will be concerned with much more than the measures of control.

Remarks

by John M. Martin

There are a number of points made by Mr. Conrad with which I am in basic agreement. For example, I agree that a key responsibility of correctional agencies is to conduct research into the causation and prevention of crime and delinquency and the treatment of the offender. That this responsibility is not carried very far by most line correctional agencies makes Mr. Conrad's point all the more crucial.

I also agree with Mr. Conrad that few social workers come to correctional agencies prepared well enough to participate in such systems. Much adaptation and new knowledge and experience are needed if social work is to play a basic and important role in meeting the crime problem.

Moreover, I agree with Mr. Conrad that correctional agencies need to keep abreast of organizational theory. Long-standing studies of prison communities, as well as more recent work on total institutions, such as training schools and mental hospitals, make this abundantly clear. The subtle, but well-developed, conflict of interests between inmates and staff in such institutions, while disheartening perhaps to the administrator, points up, in realistic terms, the full measure of the task which he faces. The same is equally true regarding the concepts of formal and informal structure taken from the field of industrial sociology, which provide rich insights not only into the relationships in the inmate-staff world, but also into the relationships among different segments of agency staff.

Finally, I agree that knowledge which the social sciences have assembled on the nature of crime and the criminal must be communicated in a meaningful and applicable manner to the correctional practitioner.

But this last statement leads me to discuss the essential points of Mr. Conrad's presentation with which I am in basic and fundamental disagreement. Before discussing these issues, it might be profitable to make a general observation or two. The kinds of program which any society undertakes to deal with its problems of crime reflect, either implicitly or explicitly, the kinds of explanation that society accepts about the causation of crime. No better example of this proposition is found than in our own society's wide acceptance of psychoanalytic theory as *the* explanation of criminal behavior. True, not everybody "bought" this approach, but it is equally true that for over a generation—from about 1930 to 1960—this was the most prestigeful way of explaining crime, and hence programs based on it progressively were thought to be highly desirable inside and outside the correctional field.

Today, of course, the psychoanalytic view and psychoanalytically-oriented programs have lost some of their attraction although they remain powerful contenders. This is the situation, at least, in many sectors of our society, including the field of corrections. This decline in prestige of the psychoanalytic approach stems, in large part, from the impact of the teachings of social science and the awakened interest of social scientists in the practical application of their points of view on influencing public policy in handling crime and related social problems.

But it must be made clear that theories of crime causation alone do not determine programming. Some theories are so abstract and poorly articulated that they do not offer firm bases for program construction. Even more significant, however, are the roles played by values, interests, and community power—both in the acceptance of particular explanations of crime and in the endorsement of programs built on such explanations.

The history of criminology amply documents this last proposition. Whether we begin with the moral view of the Quakers reflected in their establishment of the Pennsylvania prison system, the biological view of Lombroso, or the more modern view of psychoanalytic theory, we see the more powerful, decision-making, elements in society typically finding their explanations of crime in the defects or deficiencies of individual criminals. Something is wrong, amiss, or out of tune with any man, woman, or child who breaks the law, and the task in dealing with such offenders is to remedy these defects by, as the case may be, religious ministration, corporal punishment, social casework, psychotherapy, or group therapy. It is this perspective into which Mr. Conrad's observations and recommendations seem to be placed—something is either wrong with the criminal or, in a very narrow, constricted sense, something is pathological about his environment, and it is the task of corrections to straighten him out, or to "resocialize" him. Such treatment, we are told, should consist of psychotherapy, group therapy, and therapeutic milieu management, by which is meant essentially the management of correctional institutions.

Don't misunderstand me. It is clear that Mr. Conrad is well aware that the correctional practitioner must be grounded in social science, and that the challenge facing the field of corrections is to incorporate the principles and insights of social science into its activities. Mr. Conrad's whole presentation argues to this end. He grasps quite clearly the need to move away from strict psychoanalytic theory and strictly psychoanalytically-oriented programs. What his paper fails to reflect, however, and this, I think, is its vital flaw, is that whole areas of analysis and schools of thought in social science argue against the proposition that the solution to the criminal problem lies in changing, rehabilitating, or resocializing individual criminals—the goal which is Mr. Conrad's primary interest and which he seems to insist must remain the primary, even sole, interest of the correctional enterprise.

Although Mr. Conrad's paper offers a good example of the transition from psychiatry to social science now taking place in the field of social work, Mr. Conrad and many of his colleagues seem to view social science through what might be called a "pathological lens"; that is, they are chiefly interested in seeing how social science can be used better to explain personality maladjustment or defect in the study of deviancy. Any use of social science in the correctional field is, of course, valuable and a vast improvement. It is a mistake, however, to assume that social science merely contributes to a better understanding of personality defect. Such principles and theories as culture conflict, differential association, differential social organization, and a host of others central to social-science explanations of crime, argue against such an oversimplification and distortion. Even the simple observation that there is an underworld as well as an upper world, and that in the upper world such things as white-collar crime exist, argues for viewing society as a differentially organized system and against corrupting social science into just another dimension for explaining personal maladjustment or defect more effectively.

Given the difference between the point of view I am trying to sketch and that developed by Mr. Conrad, which, I repeat, provides a good example of the transitional stage social work is in, I find unacceptable his insistence that corrections remain sharply, even exclusively, focused on the individual offender in terms of analysis, prescription, program execution, and evaluation.

Let us develop this objection simply in terms of the methods used in studying criminal behavior. Both social work and psychiatry are preoccupied with the case-study method as applied to individual clients or patients. This is also clearly the situation in corrections, as Mr. Conrad's paper implies. Even when the principles of social science are incorporated into such case studies—and they often receive only scant attention—a correctional process cannot be built on case methods of analysis alone, unless, of course, much of the methodological tradition of social science is simply ignored. Unfortunately, this is precisely what is being done in most correctional agencies today.

Among the methods social science has developed for studying both deviant and non-deviant human behavior, the case method parallels the epidemiological and situational methods of analysis. Epidemiological methods seek first to locate particular forms of behavior in social space and then to explain why they occur there. Situational methods seek to explain the configuration of events which bring about an event at the moment it occurs, and to explain why the event occurs at one time and not at another. In the study of the deviant behavior, Durkheim's *Suicide* and Cohen's *Delinquent Boys* are good illustrations of epidemiological studies. Cressey's study *Other People's Money* is an excellent illustration of the application of the situational line of analysis. It is my conviction that corrections must learn to utilize and adapt both of these methods, as well as the case-study method, in analyzing criminal behavior. To the extent that this occurs, two things should follow.

> *First,* a broad range of social-science principles will play an ever-increasing role in the analysis of criminal behavior undertaken by correctional agencies.
>
> *Second,* the center of focus in analysis, prescription, and program will gradually shift from viewing offenders in terms of their individual defects and their pathological milieux to viewing them and their behavior in the context of the social and cultural worlds in which they live, and in terms of the on-going situations to which they respond with adaptations which groups in society label "criminal."

One way of proceeding with incorporating the social-science perspective into correctional systems might simply be to supplement present case-study methods, which are highly psychogenic in perspective, with sociogenic case-study methods, as well as with epidemiological and situational methods of analysis. This would seem to offer one possible assurance against missing important emphases in the social-science approach to understanding criminal behavior.

My final criticism of Mr. Conrad's presentation is that it fails to specify that, despite all the rhetoric and mystique existing in corrections today, commitment to an institution or supervision in probation or parole essentially involves the application of penal sanctions. Most of the inmates, probationers, and parolees whom I have known understand this, as do their friends, neighbors, and the community-at-large. It is important, even vital, for correctional practitioners to understand this and also to understand the relevance of such related questions as Who makes the laws? Against whom are they enforced? And, why does the law work that way? Everything correctional workers do is influenced by the existence of penal sanctions and the circumstances governing their application. Much of the difficulty correctional workers have in doing their job arises from the fact that they are acting as agents of one element of society which is directing sanctions against another.

Let me end on a positive note, however. As Mr. Conrad states, vast changes ". . . have occurred in the structure and fabric of corrections during the last twenty years. . . . The new approaches require types and levels of service which were never contemplated by the designers of the nineteenth-century correctional models. They are still hard to incorporate into the well-worn and hard-pressed systems of today." I might add that the challenge facing corrections today is to incorporate types and levels of service which are not even contemplated into *present* correctional models. The application and use of valid insights and principles of social science, if they are really to exert an influence on the decision-making process, will require, I believe, vast innovations in the way correctional administrators presently perceive their job and carry out their function. The ultimate objective would seem to be the development of entirely new correctional programs that fall somewhere between the area-saturation efforts of a Mobilization for Youth and the narrowly-framed, individual-by-individual, approach typical of today's correctional agency. The task would require combining both social reform and individual adjustment within the objectives of the same correctional program. To accomplish such a goal, correctional workers would require quite different training than they now receive in schools of social work or outside them—that much is obvious. Precisely what the content of such training should be is much less clear at this point. But central emphasis would certainly have to be given to social science —perceived, understood, and used without the distortion of a "pathological lens."

An Assessment of Scholarship Aid in Corrections

by MILTON WITTMAN

IN EXAMINING scholarship aid in corrections in the United States today, it is necessary to be aware that no single resource reports all types of aid available and that the total dollar value of scholarship aid in corrections cannot be known because of the varied nature of such aid.

The federal programs which provide scholarship aid in corrections and delinquency vary as to their structure. To illustrate, the Department of Justice maintains court and prison facilities, some of which offer scholarship aid; the Department of Health, Education, and Welfare, through the Children's Bureau and the President's Committee on Juvenile Delinquency and Youth Crime, provides training through educational leave programs and through the support of short-term training and the National Institute of Mental Health of the U.S. Public Health Service offers demonstration grants and direct training grants and stipends for students in corrections and delinquency programs in graduate schools of social work, totaling $742,000 in 27 programs in 1963-1964. Each of these programs has developed along individual lines intended to meet certain program needs. The types of aid to students take the forms of stipends for short-term training programs and institutes, direct grants to students for full-time professional training, work-study arrangements permitting full or partial salaries while enrolled in school, and maintenance costs for students at institutions. There is no uniformity in these support programs, just as there is none in scholarship aid in other fields.

Some notion of the growth in the general volume of student aid may be perceived from comparisons of the number of grants awarded in social work, one of the several fields which supply personnel to the agencies commonly acknowledged as corrections resources. The data available from the Council on Social Work Education reveal an increase in the total number of grants in social work education from 2,178 in 1947-1948 to 6,200 in 1963-1964.[1] Unfortunately, these awards are not reported by field of practice, and consequently it is impossible to determine how these are distributed by field. Of 6,039 students enrolled in graduate schools of social work in 1962-1963, 5,135 received scholarship aid. Thus, the need for financial aid to help them complete their training is particularly urgent.

In a general survey of educational resources in corrections in the United States, Albert Morris compiled data on a variety of scholarship aid programs.[2] Morris reports, for example, that "approximately thirty-five correctional institutions in nineteen states provide internship opportunities for students."[3] He found three schools offering undergraduate majors, in addition to graduate work, in criminology.[4] The numbers of students in these programs are not reported.

Levels of Training

The levels and types of training have not changed materially since 1960, when Bernard Russell briefly described such training programs. Mr. Russell categorized four general areas of training:

"1. Training at the master's degree level in social work, which normally requires two years of work beyond the bachelor's degree;
2. Training at the master's degree level in sociology, criminology, or public administration, which ordinarily requires one year of work beyond the bachelor's degree;
3. Training at the bachelor's degree level in social work, normally a four-year program beyond high school;
4. Training at the bachelor's degree level in sociology, criminology, or related social science, generally a four-year program beyond high school."[5]

To these general areas should be added doctoral training in criminology, correctional administration, and public administration which is now available at several institutions.

There is some lack of general agreement about the most suitable training for the corrections field. The career patterns of personnel in corrections and juvenile delinquency reveal that they have entered the

---

[1] *Statistics on Social Work Education* (New York: Council on Social Work Education, 1947-1963).

[2] Albert Morris, "What's New in Education for Correctional Work?" *Correctional Research,* Bulletin No. 13 (United Prison Association of Massachusetts, November, 1963).

[3] Ibid., p. 25.

[4] Ibid., p. 7.

[5] Bernard Russell, *Current Training Needs in the Field of Juvenile Delinquency* (Washington, D. C.: U. S. Government Printing Office, 1960), p. 7.

field through a variety of ways. The constellation of personnel in delinquency and corrections is varied and diverse. Law-enforcement personnel include police and juvenile officers, judges, and probation and parole officers. The prisons and other correctional institutions have their own personnel networks. As in the mental health field, there is a growing use of half-way houses or other bridging devices. The work-release system means close coordination of correctional institutions with community resources. A number of protective services for children require staff attuned to the delinquency-prevention opportunities in those programs. Most states maintain some form of training function to help induct new workers and provide on-the-job or in-service and staff development education to raise the quality of service. Annual institutes help meet this need.

As revealed by the 1960 Bureau of Labor Statistics study, the percentage of those fully trained—with master's degrees—in social work is relatively low. Eight percent of 5,254 persons in services to adult offenders and nine percent of 4,923 in court services for children had acquired their master's degrees in social work.[6]

The assessment of the personnel situation in corrections reveals several problems: First, the need for more training in corrections is widespread and urgent; second, the field cannot rely on present methods alone for solution of the manpower problem; third, the field is relatively more deficient in fully-trained social work personnel than most other fields listed in the 1960 study. This emphasizes the need for an urgent effort to develop training resources for all correctional personnel, since it takes trained people to produce trained people.

Training Resources

The cursory survey by Morris in 1963 revealed a paucity of training resources in all the professions involved in corrections programs. While corrections field placements in graduate social work education increased from 225 in 1958 to 433 in 1963, the rate of growth has been small and not commensurate with the growth in other fields. The investment of the President's Committee program in training-center support has many implications for long-range expansion of educational opportunities. The National Institute of Mental Health programs permit immediate accretions to the field through support in twenty-seven schools of social work which received 156 stipends for corrections in 1963-1964. But since these are for both first- and second-year students, the numbers moving directly into practice are about half of those in training.

---

[6] *Salaries and Working Conditions of Social Welfare Manpower* (New York: National Social Welfare Assembly, 1961), p. 39.

The work of the Children's Bureau in improving standards of practice and supporting training through educational leaves and through direct grants has had and will continue to have a positive effect on program development in corrections. The private organizations also have created a climate for self study, assessment, and evaluation of program development for training, and have enhanced communication in the field, through annual meetings, regional meetings, institutes, and workshops; but the shortages of trained personnel continue to plague the field.

Implications for the Future

The Arden House Conference includes papers on the basic issues in producing unified action to develop corrections and delinquency programs in the United States. To look at a stipend program apart from these issues is unrealistic. In fact, there is some danger in viewing stipends as an entity when considering the corresponding and vitally important need for teaching grants as well.

The following are some impressions about what next steps the corrections field must take to advance its training capabilities:

1. The present training operations in state and federal programs represent an opening wedge to larger-scale developments. While the present investment in research and training is vastly insufficient to the need, it is a beginning which will provide a foundation for later expansion.
2. As there is a move toward substantial support of existing training programs, there should be a concerted move to promote experimental training programs which will provide answers to the criticisms of present training. If full professional training is not needed for adequate service in *all* cases, how can a division of labor be evolved? The question is how to train personnel to deal with all components of a difficult caseload. The values of full professional training are apparent; but the needs for fully-trained staff will exceed the supply in the foreseeable future.
3. Organizational structure has an important influence on policy development. There is a great variation in the state level organizational structures for administering corrections and delinquency programs. Moreover, the court system and the institutional system too frequently operate in disparate frameworks, and this is a barrier to close integration of services. This lack of horizontal unity within a state and the lack of coordination suggest problems which prevent collaboration in developing training resources and scholarship aid. Frequently, one category of personnel has adequate support; another may have none.
4. The extension of the population growth curves makes it urgent to anticipate growing demands on correctional services. The provision of qualified personnel will be an important part of the future expansion of these programs. The need for direct service cannot be seen apart from the personnel needs for administration, consultation, re-

search, and training functions in corrections. Thus, program planning for training support should be broadly oriented to the total spectrum of personnel needs, including preventive as well as diagnostic and rehabilitation services.

There is a good prospect for improved communications in the correctional field as the federal and state programs continue to expand and increase. The manpower needs in corrections will be met only as training resources are expanded. More investment of personnel and funds in education and research in corrections is essential.

*Manpower Strategy in the Correctional Field**

by Joseph W. Eaton and Menachem Amir

An Old-New Problem

For centuries, the field of corrections has suffered from a negative personnel recruitment policy: *Too much attraction for unqualified people and too little attraction for those capable of confronting the complex challenges of penal work with imagination and dedication.* We will make a case for the view that even the introduction of civil service reform is *not enough* to overcome existing negative recruitment trends. Civil service rules that place too much emphasis on seniority and too little on demonstrated merit actually strengthen the influence of conservatism on penal policies. Correctional work must be structured to become an accelerated career opportunity. It must offer upward mobility for young men in search of an exciting life task, while encouraging turnover among personnel for whom their work means no more than a pay check.

Penal programs are compulsory for the body politic. As long as there are laws, law violators, and law enforcement, programs will be needed to handle people who are convicted. The quality of correctional manpower and its use are important to correctional programming. This paper will focus on this variable, although there are others that would also be very pertinent. For instance, far too little is being done to contain correctional problems by preventive means. We enforce gambling laws that make criminals out of citizens whose deviancies could be contained by more appropriate social controls.

But there are those criminal acts for which correctional agencies are necessary. These agencies need to be staffed by men, skilled in human relations, whose numbers are not enough to meet the great demand for them. Prison, reformatory, probation, and parole services experience great difficulty in attracting staff personnel with the proper technical and

* Dr. Eaton's and Dr. Amir's paper was submitted as background for the Arden House Conference.

human relations skills and in keeping those most highly qualified. The prestige of working with adult or juvenile criminal offenders is low—in spite of its social significance.

This Arden House Conference has been convened to explore strategies for encouraging the recruitment and retention of correctional personnel who are technically trained and socially motivated. At the first American Congress of Corrections in Cincinnati, nearly a century ago, the Secretary of the State Prison Commission of California, Reverend James Woodworth, read a paper which can serve as a platform for our deliberations. His definition of the situation in 1870 still seems timely in 1964:

> The task of changing bad men and women into good ones is not one to be confined to the first comers. It is a serious charge, demanding thorough preparation, entire self-devotion, a calm and cautious judgment, great firmness of purpose and steadiness of action, large experience, a true sympathy and morality above suspicion. Prison officers, therefore, need a special education for them, and prison administration should be raised to the dignity of a profession.[1]

Corrections as a Diverse Field of Specialization

Manpower strategy is concerned with the recruitment, training, promotion, and retention of employees.

The correctional field requires a broad spectrum of personnel. Prisons, reformatories, and other total institutions are self-contained communities which must provide most of the essential services of a small town. In addition, there are the community-centered probation and parole services. Then there are programs of delinquency prevention and penal policy development, few in number but highly important. The correctional field not only needs guards, parole officers, cottage parents, and other personnel peculiar to the field, but also electricians, cooks, psychiatrists, and librarians.

The task of evolving a general manpower policy can be simplified somewhat by reviewing two fundamental categories of employees: *administrative generalists* and *technical specialists.*

Administrative generalists serve in jobs defined as non-technical such as guarding inmates, checking the whereabouts of parolees, working as a house-parent, supervising a shift of employees, and doing overall organizational administration. Such jobs, while carrying different levels of responsibility, are open to a great variety of persons. Job applicants

---

[1] James Woodworth in *Twenty-Sixth Annual Report* of the Executive Committee of the Prison Association of New York and Accompanying Documents for the year 1870, to which is appended the papers and Proceedings of the National Congress on Penitentiary and Reformatory Discipline held in Cincinnati, Ohio, October 12-18, 1870 (New York: The Angus Company, 1871).

only need to satisfy a few, very general, qualifications. Generally, they must have good character, be a citizen, have completed a grade of high school education, and have good health.[2]

This category of employee has had an occupationally narrow reference group—other people employed in correctional settings; but access to administrative generalist jobs is wide open. Persons previously engaged in the correctional field, as well as those with experience in the armed forces, business, or farming can qualify. In contrast, *their mobility from the correctional field to other means of employment is limited.* Administrative generalists find it hard to transfer their experience and seniority to other careers serving people, such as teaching or social welfare.

Technical specialists have skills used in many settings, inside and outside the correctional field. A prison plumber, for example, must be licensed and be a union member. He usually can leave his job to work for a builder. In medicine and social work, fully trained people are in great demand outside the correctional field. *Their mobility potential for other positions is therefore very high.*

Technical specialists in the correctional field must be recruited under highly competitive conditions.[3] Demands for *fully* qualified personnel are far greater than the available supply. In 1960, for instance, of 105,000 persons in social work jobs in the U.S., only about 20,000 had the minimum professional training required and a master's degree. The proportion of such skilled social work personnel is even lower in the correctional field. In 1960, only 14 percent of the social workers serving juvenile and adult offenders had at least a master's degree.[4]

The potential supply of applicants for technical jobs is restricted by time-consuming and intellectually-taxing training requirements. No one can become a physician, accountant, or electrician as easily as a farmer can become a prison guard or a retired major can take a job as correctional administrator.[5] Administrative generalists can come from every walk of life and can enter the field at almost any age.

---

[2] See, for instance, the job description of a correctional officer in the Federal Prison Service, Washington, D. C. (U. S. Civil Service Commission, Bureau of Programs and Standards, Standard Division, GS 007-0, February, 1963).

[3] Evan Clague, "U. S. Manpower in 1960," *Public Personnel Review,* Vol. 22 (July 1961) pp. 162-168.

[4] U. S. Department of Labor, Bureau of Labor Statistics, *Salaries and Working Conditions of Social Welfare Manpower 1960* (New York: National Social Welfare Assembly, 1961) Table 18, p. 39.

[5] Army officers have historically played a major part in developing and maintaining penal programs. They still have leading posts in many countries. Prison jobs and many parole services function as a second career for retired military men. But they rarely have the qualifications for staffing technical services.

RECRUITMENT HANDICAPS

Now, and even more so in the past, the correctional field has to compete for appropriate manpower with some disadvantages. If any strategy for improving the supply of correctional personnel is to succeed, these disadvantages must be systematically identified; and, to the extent possible, they must be counteracted. Following are some handicaps which recruitment for correctional work confronts:

1. Correctional work is viewed as being often *discouraging*. "A field without pride of ancestry and no hope of posterity,"[6] is how one observer caricatured this view. Correctional workers deal with people known to be "very difficult."[7] Recidivism is common.[8] Prospects for rapid reformation are dim except for a few offenders. Such difficulties represent a challenge to some people; but even for them, there are numerous occasions of psychological discouragement. Sol Rubin sums up this widely prevailing set of attitudes as follows:

> "Expert after expert, study after study, have shown the cost in lives and property of unreasonable caseloads and inadequate staff. But, in addition to these costs, there is the inevitable effect on correctional workers themselves.
>
> "Personal motivation and interest—even dedication—can carry workers to magnificent lengths to keep up with the overwhelming task.
>
> "But in time they reach their saturation point.
>
> "They become hard-shelled, indifferent, frustrated, demoralized, or cynical. Or they run from assignment to assignment to escape or they retire without leaving their desks. Or they quit."[9]

2. Correctional work has a reputation of great risk of *physical injury*. Actually, the frequency of injury to personnel is lower than that in many industries and in mental hospitals. Insurance rates for correctional workers are *not* higher than in most industrial jobs. But prison riots and instances of injury to parole officers are highly publicized. This reinforces the public image that correctional work is dangerous. Women are not allowed to work with male inmates, in contrast to the practice in mental hospitals, where nurses are usually in charge of wards.[10]

---

[6] Junius L. Allison, in remarks made at the Planning Conference for the Arden House Conference, New York, Statler Hilton Hotel, February 12, 1963.

[7] Frank Loveland, "Methods of Handling the Severely Recalcitrant Inmate," *American Correctional Association Proceedings* (1955), pp. 155-157.

[8] Sol Rubin, "Recidivism and Recidivism Statistics," *NPPA Journal,* Vol. 4, No. 3 (July 1958), pp. 233-241.

[9] *Viewpoint, Crisis in Corrections,* California Probation and Parole and Correctional Association, California, Vol. 2, No. 3 (November 1963) p. 4.

[10] This fact reduces the manpower reservoir. In Sweden and Israel, this restriction does not apply. Women work in prisons, especially as social workers.

3. Correctional work takes place in *total institutions* and in administrative units which are highly structured along military command lines. Work must be performed under conditions of heavy emphasis on security and discipline. Each employee is held strictly accountable for what he is doing at all times. Correctional workers are in the middle and must be on their toes against both their superiors and their subordinates.[11] Every major decision (and many minor ones) is a matter of public record. These decisions may be scrutinized closely by administrative superiors and the general public. Many institutional and parole agencies are large, impersonal, and resistive to experimentation and innovation.

4. Correctional institutions are plagued by the coexistence of *competing hierarchies* which come to serve different and conflicting goals. Organizations which have recruited for decades on the basis of spoils-system considerations tend to see technically qualified and socially motivated personnel as "threatening" and personnel who do not make good "organization" men. They have judgments of their own, and, at times, feel it necessary to express them. Intra-organizational rivalries are also likely, when technically qualified personnel are engaged to serve side by side, with or under the supervision of, old style personnel. Trained persons may be in the "out-group," rather than the "in-group," of the bureaucracy.

5. The correctional field is an area of major public policy ambivalence. Conflicting attitudes and intellectual uncertainties "with respect to punishment and treatment" coexist. Some public officials and opinion leaders assign a very low priority to correctional matters. Others accept correctional plans as being equal in importance to other welfare programs. Many believe in both maximum safe-keeping and experimentation. They may want prisons to be both tough and to give criminals "another chance." Correctional officials are expected to make day-to-day decisions involving these basically inconsistent expectations, often without clear-cut directions on what the "right" policy is. There is, therefore, little wonder why the administrative process is rule-ridden and hamstrung with compromise.

Recruitment Incentives

These special occupational complexities for the employee are only occasionally balanced by organizationally-planned incentives. Until re-

[11] Lloyd E. Ohlin, *et al.*, "Major Dilemmas of the Social Worker in Probation and Parole," *NPPA Journal,* Vol. 2 (1956), pp. 211-255; also G. M. Sykes, *The Society of Captives* (Princeton: Princeton University Press, 1958), Chapter 1, and "The Corruption of Authority and Rehabilitation," *Social Forces,* Vol. 34 (1956), pp. 257-262.

cently, salaries in the correctional field were almost always lower than other fields requiring the same type of personnel.[12] Tenure was unprotected by civil service standards. The prestige of working in a correctional setting was lower than that of other helping professions. A psychiatrist in a prison was and is less likely to be held in esteem than a psychiatrist in a public or a private mental hospital. Among psychologists, employment in a prison or parole agency ranks lower in status than most other forms of public or private employment.[13] The status hierarchy is somewhat more conducive to positive recruitment in the field of social work, but even in this field, correctional social work has not acquired the same status as psychiatric social work or child welfare work.

Since World War II, the field of corrections has begun to pay competitive salaries in a few jurisdictions.[14] These are exceptions, not the rule; but they could become precursors of a trend. These correctional officers are no longer in the same salary range as unskilled laborers. This is indicated in the following comparison of selected federal and New York State salary ranges in 1962.

Salary Comparison for 1962—Selected Correctional and Other Occupations, New York State and Federal Government[15]

Occupation	Federal Government Pay Line Derived from 1962 BLS Report	New York State Fourth-Year Rate Salary Grade
Corrections Officer	$6,585	$5,684
Psychiatric Social Worker	6,585	6,687
Staff Nurse	5,335	5,090
Telephone Operator	3,820	3,927

Social work salaries in corrections are also becoming competitive with other forms of social work practice. In fact, social workers can currently earn relatively high salaries in the federal correctional service, especially in work with youth. U.S. Civil Service Commission Announce-

[12] John Schapps, "Salaries are Strategic," *NPPA Journal,* Vol. 3, No. 2 (April 1957), pp. 149-157.

[13] H. Polson and R. Bendix, "Psychiatry in Prison," *Psychiatry,* Vol. 14 (1959), pp. 73-86.

[14] Howard Ferguson, "Nation-Wide Competition and Professional Pay," *Public Personnel Review,* Vol. 22 (July, 1961), pp. 168-177.

[15] From Civil Service Employees Association, *State Salary Study, January 1963* (Albany, Civil Service Employees Association, 1963). (In both jurisdictions, salaries for all personnel and correctional personnel in particular are high by comparison to those in most other parts of the United States.)

[16] United States Civil Service Commission Bulletin No. 251, Washington, D. C., December 13, 1960. The actual salaries paid can be surmised from a comparison of median salaries paid to members of the NASW, which is at the end of this report.

ment No. 251, issued December 13, 1960, listed the following range for different kinds of social workers.[16]

Medical and Psychiatric Social Work	$7,560-12,210
Rehabilitation Advisor	7,560-13,730
Correctional Social Worker	7,560-10,635
Child Welfare Worker	5,355- 8,955
Public Assistance Worker	4,345- 6,435

Civil Service: A Reform or Stagnation Device?

Before World War I, much of the staffing of government jobs was based on political patronage or the personal preferences of top policy-makers.[17] There were no publicly-defined standards. This type of politically-tinged employment had little to attract gifted personnel who had many vocational opportunities. Technical specialists were particularly unlikely to put up with the "spoils system." Why would a competent physician practice in a politically-ridden setting? On the other hand, people with an employment handicap were likely to seek correctional settings as a "career," or, shall we say, "asylum."

Correctional leaders, at the national level, have for a long time believed, along with other civil service advocates, that a shift from patronage to the civil service system would result in higher personnel standards.[18] As far back as 1905, C. V. Collins, the President of the American Correctional Association, urged the nation-wide adoption of such an appointment system.[19] Subsequent proceedings always included speeches advocating this objective. In 1916, for instance, the program of the Association included two sessions specifically devoted to civil service problems.[20] Since then, almost every year the problem was raised at annual meetings. But action to take recruitment out of politics has been slow. The federal prisons were not covered by civil service until the establishment of the Bureau of Prisons under President Hoover in 1929. California had exempted its prisons and parole services from civil service until 1944. While most state prison services are now under civil service, personnel recruitment with a patronage flavor is still the method of staffing many local jail, probation, and parole agencies.

---

[17] *See:* C. R. Fisher, *The Civil Service and the Patronage* (Cambridge, Mass.: Harvard University Press, 1940).

[18] It was the assassination of President Garfield in 1882 by a frustrated claimant for a patronage office which led to the enactment of the Federal Civil Service Act.

[19] C. V. Collins, Presidential Address, *American Correctional Association Proceedings* (1906).

[20] C. N. Lathrop, "Development of Prison Administration," *American Prison Association Proceedings* (1916), pp. 99-113.

Civil service limits the ability of persons elected to public office to surround themselves with subordinates of their own choosing. It reflects the belief that public services should be largely in the hand of non-partisan technicians. They should be able to serve under many types of top-level policy-makers. The theory of civil service assumes that democratic principles are adequately implemented when elections are restricted to a few top policy-makers, such as governors and legislators.[21]

Civil service regulations have removed much of the risk that used to be inherent in being a public servant. Government employees no longer need be apprehensive before every election because their position is dependent on the re-election of a particular political leader. Public employment can be a career service. This means that appointments, promotions, transfers, demotions, and separations are procedurally determined. There are rules intended to minimize personal influence. Working conditions are neither individually negotiated nor defined. There are provisions for measuring entrance qualifications and for setting salaries, tenure conditions, vacations, educational leaves, and other fringe benefits.[22]

This gain has to be weighed against the fact that it is difficult to use job security as an incentive for employees. Public policy is often conceived as being made at the top, but much of it is determined at the lower operational level.[23] Civil service offers job security to all with tenure, almost irrespective of their skill and devotedness to public service. At the 1936 meeting of the American Correctional Association, the famous civil service scholar Leonard White warned that when civil service rules are first adopted, both the "good" and the "bad" employee are blanketed in.[24] Those who fought for a civil service reform must then work with existing personnel, many of whom were selected on the basis of political considerations, rather than merit. An organizational power struggle may ensue in which the fundamental issues of correctional practice will take less than second place.

Unless blanketed-in employees are or will become identified with correctional reforms, the introduction of civil service will tend to freeze

---

[21] *See:* L. D. White, *Civil Service in the Modern State* (Chicago: University of Chicago Press, 1926); also A. C. Klein, *Civil Service in Public Welfare* (New York: Russell Sage Foundation, 1940).

[22] *See:* H. L. Henderson, "Civil Service as a Means to Better Prison Administration," *American Correctional Association Proceedings,* 1928; also L. D. White, "Prison Service and Civil Service," *American Correctional Association Proceedings,* 1936, p. 279.

[23] S. M. Lipset, "Bureaucracy and Social Reform," *Research Studies* (State College of Washington, 1949), p. 17.

[24] L. D. White, "Prison Service and Civil Service," *American Correctional Association Proceedings,* 1936, p. 279.

the status quo. New personnel, selected on the basis of higher standards, can be hired only slowly, either as replacements, or when correctional services are expanded.

The Danger of Negative Retention

A "Gresham's Law" becomes operative when civil service is introduced without a conscious policy to favor qualified personnel who had not been attracted previously. Old-line employees, who have no identification with the correctional movement, will, by their presence and influence, drive out those with many idealistic motives. Both the new and the old will be covered by the same civil service tenure. But unqualified employees will have few places to go, nor will they be highly motivated to look for new employment. More idealistic and qualified personnel have greater job mobility. They are therefore less likely to tolerate unsatisfactory working conditions.

Civil service may be a necessary prerequisite for a sound personnel policy, but it is not sufficient. It exists today in many correctional systems which are inferior and which have few qualified professional employees.[25] They are without an *enforced* policy of upgrading standards. This fact favors the retention of marginal workers. If allowed to go for a decade without a policy of reaching out for and retaining technically skilled employees, an entire correctional system will be characterized by the retention of poor performers. Organizations will have the personnel they deserve, since civil service will protect the poor performer. Thus, it will reduce his readiness to support reform for which the merit system has been originally introduced.[26]

Such conditions will further discourage positive recruitment. Those who apply to work in such a stagnant service might easily include a large segment of "little choice" personnel who may have done poorly in previous jobs. The possibility of such negatively weighted recruitment is greatest for the more closed occupational roles—the professions and the skilled trades. Technical specialists, such as physicians, accountants, and teachers, are in demand in many fields other than corrections. There must be special inducements and incentives for such public servants to be attracted to corrections. Merit systems are an improvement over po-

---

[25] Data on the nature and extent of civil service in the correctional field are not available for the state and local correctional jurisdictions. This lack is illustrative of a more generalized insufficiency of data on correctional manpower. Some pertinent data may be made available through a planned study of Professor David Rogers of the Department of Sociology at the University of Pittsburgh, "Comparative Study of Corrections System Structure."

[26] O. W. Wilson, "Toward a Better Merit System," *The Annals of the American Academy of Political and Social Science,* Vol. 291 (1954), pp. 87-97.

Occupational Roles	Qualification and Training Requirements	Ease of Entry	Mobility Outside or External Competition	Instrumental Importance in Prisons	Prestige in the System	Prestige Outside the System	Turnover
ADMINISTRATIVE GENERALISTS							
Policy implementers, such as superintendents, workers, deputy wardens and business managers.	Variable. Possibility of training on the job.	Wide open.	Little.	High.	High.	Low.	Low.
First-line officers, such as guards, probation and parole officers doing surveillance.	Generally low. Training on the job.	Wide open.	Little.	High.	Low.	Low.	Varied.
TECHNICAL SPECIALISTS							
Treatment professionals, such as psychiatrists, psychologists, social workers, and probation-parole officers giving treatment.	Generic. Higher education, plus internships.	Limited to persons with prior training.	High.	Low (When custody emphasized.) High if treatment is stressed.	High.	Low.	High.
Research analysts (statisticians, sociologists, anthropologists, and psychologists).	Generic. Higher education plus research experience.	Limited to persons with prior training.	High.	Low.	High.	Varied.	High.
Skilled occupations, such as maintenance workers, supervisors.	Specific. Apprenticeship plus trade school training.	Limited to persons with prior training.	High.	High.	Varied.	Varied.	High.

litical patronage, but they cannot alone solve the problems of attracting the right personnel, keeping them employed in corrections, and insuring high standards of performance.

The Job Analysis Approach

A manpower strategy, a strategy which will differ somewhat for each of the diverse talents needed in the field, is therefore necessary. To simplify outlining such a strategy, let us review selected aspects of the diverse jobs in the correctional field in terms of five major occupational roles:

Administrative Generalists:	1. Policy implementers.
	2. First-line officers.
Technical Specialists:	3. Treatment professionals.
	4. Research analysts.
	5. Skilled occupations.

Each of these roles is different from others in many characteristics, including:

a) Qualification and training requirements.
b) Ease of entry or access to work role.
c) Mobility and promotional potential within the system.
d) Mobility and promotional potential and competition outside the system.
e) Prestige within the organization.

A summary of these work role types is found in the chart opposite:

Policy Implementers: There are persons with planning roles. They must be capable of choosing between policy alternatives, based on technical requirements and political realities. Wardens, prison department heads, parole boards, parole chiefs, and other administrators are in this category. They tend to be administrative generalists who have major responsibilities for matters that are quite complex and of great significance for public policy. For instance, they must allocate their limited budget and manpower along alternate and related programs, such as custody, production, maintenance, education, therapy, and religious work.

Policy implementers are more often than not recruited without a generally enforced set of standards.[27] Justice Haim Cohn, of the Israel Supreme Court, suggests that in most countries, including his own, "a considerable portion of administrative policy making is entrusted to

---

[27] Many penal reformers decry this tendency and give high priority to recruiting technically qualified personnel for these higher echelon posts.

officials who have no special qualifications for their jobs; in the course of their years of office they acquire such know-how and experience as they have.[28]

Pay rates and fringe benefits are often higher than those of other positions outside the correctional field that would be available to these persons. These can be incentives in recruiting qualified persons, but they can also inhibit personnel turnover. Access to an administrative career can be through many channels, but experience in such a post does not confer much occupational mobility.

Correctional administrators are not generally credited with having administrative experience required in other types of organizations. This situation may make them conservative; they can't take many risks with their jobs because others of equal pay outside the field are not within their reach. Change and experimentation tend to be viewed as more of a threat than a challenge.

First-Line Officers: These are personnel required for direct work with inmates such as correction officers, guards, custody-oriented parole officers, cottage parents, and lower-echelon, middle-range administrators. Their work experience is primary to the successful execution of their assignments. Physical strength and "common sense" loom large among their role expectations. Through their direct service roles, rather than their technical skills, they have a strong impact on the way correctional institutions are run. No unusual technical skill, educational background, and experience are required to be accepted in their line of work. They perform many complicated tasks, however, such as "mothering" large groups of hard-to-handle boys, settling quarrels between inmates, spotting symptoms of psychic disturbance, and enforcing discipline. First-line officers apply organizational policies to individual inmates.

These lower-echelon administrative generalists are inadequately prepared, trained, and supervised for their many intricate assignments. In some jurisdictions, they receive in-service training, in awareness of the fact that their impact on the organization is direct and of paramount instrumental importance; but they have insufficient theoretical training in dealing with conflicting demands made upon them by administrators, custody chiefs, and treatment-oriented professionals. Chances for promotion and advancement for these administrative generalists are very limited, but in recent years their salaries have risen much above the compensation for other types of semi-skilled work.

In federal and in some state prison services, a correctional officer is hired at the federal grade of GS-6, with a starting salary of $5,035.00

---

[28] Haim Cohn, Preface to Joseph W. Eaton's *Prison in Israel* (Pittsburgh: University of Pittsburgh Press, 1964), p. x.

a year. High school graduation is a minimum educational qualification for this job. Social workers, who must be college graduates and have either two years of graduate work or certain equivalents, have a beginning salary that is only $500.00 higher. These salary conditions help to attract correctional officers, but they can also make some of them very cautious about any change which might threaten their relatively well-paid, semi-skilled jobs or undermine their power over the inmates. They could not shift easily to another job outside the correctional field.

Treatment Professionals: These are technical specialists with higher education, such as ministers, physicians, social workers, psychologists, dentists, and teachers. The correctional field is neither a primary nor a professionally esteemed setting for the practice of these professions. The occupational mobility potential of these professionals outside the penal system is very high, while it is more limited within the service. If this were not enough of an obstacle to recruitment, there is also the fact that professionals in the penal services are frequently subjected to pressure toward compromising their professional and ethical standards. They confront conflicting demands to satisfy both treatment and custody goals. Often they have such large caseloads that there is little opportunity to apply their professional skills.

Their professional training is generic and tends to focus on abstract principle. Their specific applications to work with social deviants in correctional settings have to be learned on the job. They have a high status because of their educational background, but they come to their job with little or no experience on the basis of which they can function with confidence in prisons and parole-probation agencies.[29] Some social work and criminology training programs try to bridge this gap by requiring correctional field placements.

In the past, professionals in correctional agencies have been employed largely in posts clearly identified with their fields. Access to these jobs was restricted to persons with recognized credentials. In change-oriented jurisdictions, professional requirements are also being specified for some jobs that in the past were open to administrative generalists. This is particularly true of probation officers, workers in juvenile institutions, and associate wardens.

Research Analysts: These are academically trained personnel assigned to analyze the effectiveness of preventive and correctional programs or to inquire into the causes of crime. They are concerned with "exploration, monitoring, and experimentation."[30] They are expected to differen-

---

[29] D. R. Cressey, *Limitations in Organization of Treatment in Theoretical Studies of Prison Organizations* (Social Science Research Council Pamphlet No. 15, 1954).

[30] Daniel Glaser, "The Prospect for Corrections," p. 25.

tiate between what administrators hope to accomplish and what actually occurs. These roles are threatening to the administrators since deficiences as well as achievements are highlighted at every level of operation. Researchers should know all facets of the correctional system intimately, but they rarely have sufficient personal experience with it to acquire such knowledge. They tend to define research problems in a theory-oriented fashion, in contrast to administrative and treatment specialists, who face these problems at the operational level.

Research analysts are identified with both academic and correctional reference groups, but cannot make their reports equally meaningful to both. Their vocational mobility is great outside the correctional system, since their research skill, if well developed, is in heavy demand in universities and other research settings. In the correctional agencies, their mobility is very limited, unless they are willing to move into administrative positions.

They have a high status reflected in better-than-average salaries, relatively unstructured working conditions, freedom to participate in research conferences, and direct access to high-level administrative personnel. They are often regarded as key personnel since their findings are likely to affect policy; but the organization can function without them. Their impact is not direct and of little instrumental importance. They often are identified with experimental programs and innovations, but they cannot assume responsibility for the implementation of these programs without risking loss of their own scientific objectivity.

Skilled Occupations: These include persons with manual skills, such as carpenters, farm superintendents, electricians. They are needed in prisons either for plant maintenance or as vocational training foremen. These people must undergo a lengthy training period. They often must be members of a labor union, and this may impose additional restrictive barriers. Technical specialists with the proper credentials can usually find good employment outside the correctional system. They have a high occupational mobility potential.

The correctional field generally does not pay people in these skilled occupations wages as high or higher than could be earned elsewhere; but it offers security, as far as tenure is concerned. It is therefore likely to attract persons who place a high value on security. Here, as in other occupational roles, the correctional field is inclined to emphasize stability rather than change.

Seniority and Organizational Efficiency

This schematic analysis of correctional job categories has been deliberately focussed on our key hypothesis: There are recruitment handicaps and negative retention trends in the correctional field. Civil service tenure and higher salaries alone are not likely to counteract them. Stability and organizational stagnation, rather than reform, are likely consequences of introducing civil service procedures without a well organized scheme for selection and promotion based on technical competency.

Such standards always include elements of vagueness and uncertainty. Someone has to take the responsibility for deciding which of the several candidates for a position, each with somewhat different qualifications, should be selected. No matter what the choice is, it is inevitable that someone will be dissatisfied.

Administrators are thus sometimes tempted to base their personnel decisions on a simple and automatic concept: Seniority. It is a seemingly "objective" standard. Length of service is rewarded. The person with the "most" experience is favored. The principle of seniority also makes it impossible for executives to use personal and political considerations in making decisions regarding personnel.

When seniority becomes an important element in an organization's personnel policy, however, young people with outstanding ability are discouraged from entering that organization's employ. Promotions come slowly, and this often results in intra-organizational jealousy, failure to maintain communications,[31] and other negative responses. Meritorious service is not given sufficient reward. It will not shorten the time needed by the unusually gifted public servants to acquire status.

An excessive emphasis on seniority also discourages bringing in personnel from the outside, except at the lowest level of an organization. When seniority is paramount, policy making by tired old men will be a highly likely outcome. Men who are bustling with initiative and innovative capability will have a difficult time in correctional service.

Elements of a Strategy

There are many ways of improving the personnel situation in an organization. Indirectly, there can be manpower savings by reducing inappropriate uses of existing personnel. More directly, there can be a policy to upgrade efficient employees already in the service, facilitate job changes by those who are uninterested in their calling, and encourage new talent to enter the correctional field.

Recognition of loyalty to an organization reflected in length of service must be balanced by the encouragement of employees to develop their skills and be innovative. Many top leaders in corrections entered the field during the pre-World War II Depression. It was an opportune

---

31 Bernard Levenson, "Bureaucratic Succession," in *Complex Organization: A Reader* (New York: Holt, Rinehart & Winston, Inc., 1961), pp. 362-376.

time to recruit men of unusual talent. Since there was heavy unemployment, occupational choices were limited for persons even with outstanding abilities.

But what about the present era? There is a shortage of persons with professional training. Individuals in skilled occupations are in somewhat less demand, but they can generally find ready employment if they are willing to move to areas of the country where there are pronounced labor shortages. Persons employed in both of these categories, therefore, make careers in corrections which sometimes leads people to ask: "What's wrong with them? Why are they making a career choice that affords them less status, recognition, and comfort than is theoretically available to them?"

Matching of Motivations

Work with prisoners will be especially attractive to persons who are appropriately motivated. Since the correctional field has always attracted some highly qualified persons, we need to examine the questions: What are the incentive factors? What conditions outweigh the "dis-incentive" variables? While no systematic study has been made, we suggest the following for further investigation:

The Mission Aspect: Certain officials have always been attracted to the correctional field because of a dedication to the challenge of reforming social deviants. Just as missionaries have done, they knowingly selected a complex field of endeavor without being concerned with the career disadvantages they would face. They were imbued with the ideals of the correctional movement.

The probability of attracting such men is maximized when recruitment is unhampered by politically inspired barriers, such as residence and state citizenship requirements. An exceptional challenge will not recognize any recruitment frontiers. One cannot expect that Pittsburgh, Pennsylvania or, for that matter, any other place, will always be fortunate enough to find among its inhabitants or among the citizens of the Commonwealth of Pennsylvania men who are needed to upgrade its correctional services.

Psychic Compensation: Some employees get great satisfaction from exercising authority and control, but they still function constructively. Correctional institutions often can make good use of such persons, but need to be on guard against those with tendencies toward sadism, homosexuality, or other psycho-social deviations. The correctional setting can provide opportunities for self-satisfaction for persons whose motivations are functional, without becoming an asylum for persons whose interest in their work is pathologically rooted.

ORGANIZATIONAL PLANNING

Wage Incentives: Salary is a major and concrete index of both income and social status. While man does not live on bread alone, he at least needs bread and some status. In more and more correctional jurisdictions, there are positions with pay incentives and fringe benefits which compare favorably with other career opportunities. Pay incentives help to counteract some of the problems of work in the correctional field, such as the low public esteem in which it is held and the difficult problems of the client system.

Wages are only part of an organization's opportunity structure, however. Monetary incentives alone rarely will suffice unless they are very large. Competing public services units cannot get approval for more than relatively minor wage level differentials between essentially similar jobs of different organizations.[32] There is usually more leeway in the provision of fringe benefits. An agency's competitive potential is strengthened when it can offer medical and life insurance programs, a pension plan, paid sabbatical leaves, free uniforms, meals at work, good housing near penal institutions, and similar fringe benefits.

Periodic raises in salaries also provide inducements for the retention of employees. It may be administratively convenient to calculate raises on a uniform, "across the board" basis. But such an undiscriminating policy must be weighed against the probable advantages of giving normal increments for good service, providing a stepped-up rate of increments for very unusual performance,[33] and skipping increments of clearly marginal employees. Routine salary raises or accumulated pension rights that terminate if a man leaves his job serve unintentionally to keep dissatisfied or ineffective staff personnel from voluntarily terminating their employment.

An attractive compensation plan, administered without recognition of merit, will often be insufficient to hold top employees. They can often do better in another organization. But it will clearly discourage marginal staff members from trying to find another job!

Special Opportunities: There always are employees with limited opportunities and handicaps in occupational mobility. This is true of minority group members, immigrants with health or language handicaps, and persons who could not complete their formal education. In

---

[32] *Federal Salary Reform Act of 1962—Principal Features* (United States Civil Service Commission Bulletin No. 530-1), p. 4.

[33] The United States Army provides proficiency payments to enlisted men at three levels—$20.00, $50.00, and $100.00 a month. These bonuses are earned on the basis of proficiency tests and ratings. The ratings are reviewed annually and aim to recognize current levels of proficiency. See Army Regulations Nos. 611-208, Headquarters, Department of the Army, Washington 25, D.C.

addition, there is in every correctional organization a dormant reservoir of capable people who never have a chance to show what they can really do. There are men who may not have graduated from school, but who can relate themselves therapeutically to disturbed inmates. Immigrant physicians with foreign degrees will be kept out of private practice, regardless of their actual skill, by regulations of many states. Not every psychologist who had to go to work before obtaining his Ph.D. degree is substandard.

Correctional employment has often appealed to persons living in areas where jobs are scarce. There also are many population pockets with large surplus of manpower, due to automation. In cities such as Pittsburgh, thousands of high school graduates have no prospect of employment. Some of them could be recruited to make a career in the correctional field if its potentialities were brought to their attention.

In progressive penal systems, employees already in the service are given opportunities to study. Classes are conducted within the system. Employees may be given time off to take courses at a university, and, on occasion, their organizations will pay part of the tuition. Persons without formal professional training can learn to function therapeutically as group counselors, in milieu therapy, and as welfare workers. Working to them, therefore, is not only a way of making a living, but also an opportunity for improvement and a chance to upgrade their capacity to be of service.

Structural Flexibility: An opportunity structure is created when job requirements can be met by alternate means, and when minimum educational standards can be waived for persons who have learned from experience or through in-service training. Rules which safeguard minimum standards of performance must be relaxed for persons who exceed such performance. For instance, in the group counseling program of the California correctional system, persons with no formal education are encouraged to engage in therapeutically-oriented activities with inmates and parolees.[34]

In the civil service structure, promotion is usually slow and often depends on the availability of a promotional "slot." Many people must wait until someone else retires or dies before they can advance to a position commensurate with their capacities. When the California Institution for Men was opened at Chino in 1940, the new director received permission to hire correctional officers at a higher classification than was true of the rest of the system. A large proportion of these officers were promoted rapidly. This was possible, in part, because the

---

[34] Joseph W. Eaton, *Stone Walls Not a Prison Make* (Springfield, Illinois: Charles C. Thomas Co., 1962), p. 93ff.

Department of Corrections was an expanding organization. In addition, its administrator was able to persuade the state to authorize new middle-range administrative and treatment posts to which people with recognized abilities could be appointed.

Such a procedure is possible in a young organization. Persons who enter it can, from the very start, think of themselves as future managers. Few are likely to be "brainwashed" by having an excessively lengthy apprenticeship during which they cannot express an opinion affecting organizational policy. But such infusion of new personnel must be within a framework of evaluative procedures to differentiate between various levels of performance. This can be done by such merit system techniques as pre-service training, probationary periods, a periodic review of efficiency, proficiency payments, and periodic shifts to new positions within the system to broaden the employee's horizon.

Emphasis on Experimentation: Most people like to be associated with a progressive organization that explores the frontiers of practice. Being a part of such an organization enables the employee to realize that he is doing more than earning a pay check and that he is part of a significant social effort. His personal status and his self-confidence are affected by the innovative reputation of his organization. By conducting research and experimental programs, and by publicizing them, a number of correctional jurisdictions have developed a public image that enables them to compete on very favorable terms with other organizations for scarce technical and custodial personnel.

Risk Sharing: When deciding to assign a sex criminal to a minimum custody institution or when placing him on probation, correctional officials assume calculated risks. If they place too much emphasis on security, the prisoner or probationer doesn't get the opportunity to demonstrate his capacity for self-control. If the public wants civil servants who will assume responsibility for matters in which there is no sure rule for decision-making, it must permit them freely and with administrative support to use their best judgment, even at the risk of their making a "wrong" judgment.

Physicians must often make decisions that involve issues of life and death. Not all operations are successful, and yet, the failure to operate could also be fatal. When an operation does not succeed, the doctor is not made the subject of a public investigation unless there is strong evidence of negligence. However, breakdowns in correctional security, such as a prison riot or the commission of a crime by a parolee, are very likely to subject otherwise responsible correctional officers to considerable personal harassment. Public officials and legislators must be prepared to support subordinates who use reasonable care and common sense in the making of necessary, though risky, decisions.

Recognition of Initiative: In many organizations, the individual employee is noticed only when he gets into trouble. In progressive organizations, management goes to great lengths to recognize unusual performance at every level. For instance, in the California correctional system, the director wrote a personal letter to every group counselor who participated in the experimental development of the program at Folsom Prison. Top-level personnel meet with employees on lower echelons in formal and informal settings and show that they recognize the contributions of these employees to the total service.

In the average bureaucracy, there are many barriers of communication between lower-echelon employees who deal directly with inmates and parolees and those who are responsible for policy decisions. A high level of morale can be maintained when recognition is given for suggestions made by any employee, regardless of rank.

Professional Planning

Specialized Education: The field of corrections has always been one identified with administration. Experience in correctional organizations has been recognized as a factor in employment, but the role of training has not been clear-cut. The core knowledge needed by the field has been vague. But it has gained in specificity. Courses such as criminology, crime prevention, treatment of criminals, and juvenile delinquency are now being taught in many settings. Such training is being increasingly expected of both middle-range and top executives. Correctional specialists are currently trained in many departments of sociology[35] and in schools of public administration. Treatment-oriented specialists are being trained more often at graduate schools of social work and departments of psychology.[36] The University of California at Berkeley and the University of Florida at Tallahassee now offer doctoral level training in criminology.

From the point of view of recruiting manpower, specialized criminological training has both advantages and disadvantages. It helps to identify students in this emerging field and sensitizes them to the need to find better answers to the field's many unresolved problems; but if such specialized training were to become prerequisite, it would limit the sources of personnel recruitment. Students are not likely to take these courses unless they are already committed to a career in the correc-

---

[35] William T. Adams, *A Study of Curriculum Content of Juvenile Delinquency Courses* (Boulder City, Colorado: Western Interstate Commission for Higher Education, April, 1962).

[36] *See:* Elliot Studt, *Education for Social Workers in the Correctional Field,* Volume V of the "Curriculum Study" (New York: Council on Social Work Education, 1959).

tional field. The field now also attracts more generically trained manpower than any of the academic disciplines and the helping professions.

The pros and cons of specialized training in corrections are giving rise to considerable controversy.[37] An important fundamental issue is whether corrections is becoming a specialized profession or whether it should be viewed as an administrative structure employing many types of professionals. Before the issues and alternatives can be intelligently considered and resolved, more information is needed on the education of middle-range and professional personnel and their functioning in the correctional field than is now available.

Domestic Service Utilization: Correctional service requires commitment but is not necessarily a life-time career. Persons who work with hardship problems, such as the mentally deficient, and chronic and terminal illnesses, may get discouraged, callous, or fatigued. But they often give a great deal of themselves at first. They may be relatively inexperienced, but they may show an enthusiasm that marks them off from many of the more "seasoned" workers who have reached a "career fatigue point." Many correctional jobs require that employees live in remote places, where the larger prisons and work camps are often located. Employees sometimes have to be available on a twenty-four hour basis, seven days a week. Dedicated personnel can meet these requirements, but they are likely to become increasingly burdensome if they last a lifetime.

Correctional services require, among other things, an adaptability to hardship conditions that warrant the designation of corrections as an underdeveloped domestic service field. It could attract people who wish to devote a few years to a significant social welfare task which challenges their imagination. Work with criminals and delinquents can be viewed as a *"moral equivalent of war,"* a concept coined by William James before World War I.[38] In times of peace, many young men feel that they have no opportunity to render service to their country. Some prefer an alternative to military service, without necessarily wishing to call themselves conscientious objectors. In any case, only a small minority of young people are required to give military service. Selective Service has become a lottery through which a few "unlucky" men or those "who do not know how to work the system" get caught.

The concept of national service may well be expanded to include difficult but significant non-military tasks. The correctional field could

---

[37] D. R. Cressey, "Professional Correctional Work and Professional Work in Corrections," *NPPA Journal,* Vol. 5, No. 1 (January, 1959), pp. 1-15.

[38] William James, "The Moral Equivalent of War," first published in *McClure's Magazine* (August, 1910), reprinted in William James, *Pragmatism and Other Essays* (New York: Washington Square Press, July, 1963), pp. 289-301.

place many thousands of such service corpsmen and women as correctional and parole officers. Appealing on the basis of a national service, the field could also recruit young doctors, psychologists, social workers, and other technical specialists. These people may have no practical experience, but if they have a service-oriented outlook, they can contribute much to the advancement of the nation's welfare by confronting challenges of the correctional services.

Correctional Reform: Correctional personnel are required by law to deal with drug addicts, gamblers, homosexuals, and prostitutes who cater to human weaknesses which are not morally acceptable. But the law and present enforcement procedures probably complicate, rather than ease, procedures for containing these vices.

Until the repeal of the Prohibition Amendment, federal prisons were filled with gangsters who lived on the proceeds of producing and selling alcoholic beverages. They were put out of business by the repeal of the Prohibition Amendment. Alcoholism is a serious social problem. But prohibition made its control *more,* not less, difficult.

The law now helps to support drug "pushers," gambling czars, and pimps who make parasitic gains from pandering to human passions. Law enforcement discourages few of these entrepreneurs. Often it helps to escalate the price of vice, thus adding a "get rich *even quicker*" incentive for those willing to still take a chance on not getting caught.

Public lotteries and legalized bingo will do more to eliminate the numbers racket than will doubling the police vice squad or raising the gambling penalties. There are no numbers racketeers in Nevada. Those in New Hampshire, where gambling was recently legalized, have probably already moved to states where gambling is illegal.

Nor can homosexuality, drug addiction, and prostitution be stamped out by repression. The experience of the Public Health Services with the control of venereal disease warrants careful study to see how medical, rather than police, controls might be employed to deal with homosexuality among mutually consenting adults, drug addiction, and prostitution.

Legal reform is a vastly under-explored region of crime control. It is highly doubtful that penalties for felonies and imprisonment are really effective in coping with deviant human passions which enjoy some social acceptance because "they don't harm anyone but the person who is addicted."

Local penal institutions could also be relieved from housing and taking care of many inmates by changing archaic bail practices. The imposition of bail results in a double standard of American justice. An accused person who is poor must stay in jail until his trial; well-to-do suspects are released on bail.

As public employees, correctional officials must be very circumspect in their advocacy of controversial penal reforms. Private citizens are under fewer restraints, and so are professional organizations. The Boston, New York, and Pennsylvania Prison Societies were prominent as innovators of reform practices during the nineteenth century. Similar community-oriented programs are sorely missed today. The correctional field has all but ignored the potentialities for bringing about major penal reforms through public discussion of fundamental issues and through organized advocacy of reform legislation.[39]

Matching Fund Subsidies: There will be greater agreement with the aforementioned strategy for upgrading correctional personnel and using them more efficiently than there will be funds available to accomplish this task. Corrections is only one of many public services which are being maintained much below the standards of those who are responsible for them. The taxes of local and state jurisdictions often bring in as much money as can be raised. Their expansion may be politically impractical.

In such fields as education, public welfare, mental health, and services to children, local services are being upgraded through matching fund subsidies from state or federal sources, which can yield larger tax revenues than smaller jurisdictions. While there is much objection to centralized control, there is much support for encouraging reforms, recruiting better personnel, doing research, or building modern structures through offers of money to correctional agencies ready to adopt improved levels of practice.

Conclusion

These generalizations regarding correctional manpower were distilled from an examination of a few jurisdictions where personnel are now generally screened and standards are being upgraded. There is no systematic body of data on which we can draw. But the analysis that was made and the strategy that has been proposed generally fit developments in the federal correctional system. As the setting changed from being patronage-ridden into one favoring the leadership of technically qualified people, the following results were perceived:

1. Top-level policy-makers identified the inadequacies of correctional personnel as a problem requiring special attention.

[39] This generalization is not without a few noteworthy exceptions. For instance, *see* Charles Ares and Herbert Sturz, "Bail and the Indigent Accused," *Crime and Delinquency,* Vol. 8, No. 1 (January 1962), pp. 12-20. It reports on action-oriented research study sponsored by the Vera Foundation. Important social action programs are also sponsored by such organizations as the National Council on Crime and Delinquency and the American Law Institute.

2. They gave considerable political and budgetary support to the task of correcting these shortcomings.

3. Reforms began at a time when qualified men had difficulties in finding employment that challenged their imagination and afforded them an opportunity for a significant career.

In 1929, when Herbert Hoover became President, his newly-appointed Attorney General, William Stewart Mitchell, held the view that "the prison situation presented one of the major problems that the Department of Justice would have to deal with" during his term of office. Part of this administrative reform was to provide for a professionalized work force. In 1939, untrained guards worked ten hours a day, seven days a week. They were replaced gradually by technically trained personnel. By 1964, all federal wardens, associate wardens, and the heads of various institutional services had no political obligations to anyone. An overall review of major policies was undertaken. A unified Federal Bureau of Prisons was set up. Congress approved a policy of facilitating more individualized treatment of different categories of inmates.

> It is hereby declared to be the policy of the Congress that institutions be so planned and limited in size as to facilitate the development of an integrated, federal and penal correctional system which will assure the proper classification and segregation of federal prisoners according to their character, the nature of the crime they have committed, their mental condition and such other factors that should be taken into consideration in providing an individualized system of discipline, care and treatment of persons committed to such institutions.[40]

The reformed federal prison system took shape during the depth of the Great Depression. Employment was scarce. Young men with vision had more limited vocational opportunities than they had before. The federal prison system offered such persons more than a job. It also espoused a cause that enjoyed top-level political support: penal reform.

The reorganization of the California system[41] provided a similar illustration. Here, too, top-level executive attention was given to penal reform by a politically influential governor—Earl Warren, the present Chief Justice of the Supreme Court. He called the attention of the legislature to the gravity of the problem and introduced fundamental reforms with strong legislative support. And he began his reforms during

[40] "Federal Penal and Reformatory Institutions," Hearings Before the United States House, the Special Committee on Penal and Reformatory Institutions, 70th Congress 2nd Session, pursuant to House Resolution 233, 70th Congress, 1st Session, January 7, 1929 to January 15, 1929 (Washington, D.C.: United States Government Printing Office, 1929).

[41] Joseph W. Eaton, *op. cit.*

a time when California was solvent. There were funds to hire new persons at attractive salaries and good working conditions, competitive with those paid in other helping professions, particularly in the Department of Mental Hygiene and the field of social work.

Any national effort to strengthen the manpower available to the correctional field must take account of the previously described occupational role problems. Correctional services now constitute a welfare service frontier where a young man with ability can make his way. There is an expanding demand for staff since the number of prisoners in juvenile institutions is constantly expanding. The recognition of the need for correctional service by the general public is also increasing. Opportunities for promotion are considerable.

Whenever a field of employment suffers from too many negative factors affecting personnel recruitment and retention, this can be remedied by the development of an accelerated opportunity structure. This involves the provision of substantially greater opportunities to personnel than would be available in competing work settings. An organizational milieu must be developed in which communication, innovation, experimentation, and research are encouraged.

Such conditions will not come about by pious hoping. Planned action by professional organizations and citizen groups will be needed to develop a favorable climate of public opinion within which correctional work can be transformed from a low-status job into a distinguished opportunity for rendering national service to public welfare. Such a transition will help to attract new people and will motivate qualified persons already in the service to make corrections their career.

APPENDIX

Order of Salaries Paid NASW Members According to Type of Program*

	Median Salary
Community services	$8,900
Teaching social work	7,900
Services to adult offenders	*7,800*
Services to aging	7,600
Group services	7,200
School and social work	7,100
Medical social work outside hospitals	7,000
Court services for children	*7,000*
Rehabilitation services	7,000
Public assistance	7,000
Psychiatric social work in hospitals	6,800
Child welfare institutions	6,700
Medical social work in hospitals	6,700
Psychiatric social work outside hospitals	6,700
Family services other than public assistance	6,600
Child welfare outside institutions	6,600

* Ruth Becker, "Study of Salaries of NASW Members," reprinted from *Personnel Information* (New York: National Association of Social Workers, November, 1961), p. 8.

*Expanding Educational Facilities for Social Work Manpower**

by Ernest F. Witte

Manpower with social work training is a vital part of the total manpower needed by the field of corrections to provide its essential services.[1] The information provided in this paper on social work manpower in relation to corrections is that which was most readily available. There was not sufficient time to gather original data nor to analyze fully the implication for corrections of what information is available. Some of the data and the discussion related to social work may have broader relevance to other disciplines which are employed in corrections.

Basic Assumptions

In preparing this paper, it seemed essential to formulate certain basic assumptions which appear implicit in the presentation. They may serve to stimulate discussion and to help in arriving at a consensus on certain issues. These basic assumptions are:

1. The use of the term "corrections" in this Conference includes treatment services for juvenile and adult offenders after their conviction (in some circumstances, after their apprehension) and sentence. (Thus, programs of law enforcement, the administration of criminal

* Dr. Witte's paper was submitted for the Preparatory Conference on Manpower for Corrections.

[1] For an interesting and careful examination of the training proposed for juvenile probation officers, see "Implications for Education and Training," p. 34ff., in *Training for Juvenile Probation Officers,* Publication No. 398, Children's Bureau, United States Department of Health, Education, and Welfare, (Washington, D.C.: U.S. Government Printing Office, 1962) and *The Practitioner in Corrections* (California Probation, Parole and Correctional Association [Revised] February, 1964).

For a review of curricular offerings in corrections at colleges and universities throughout the United States, see *Report of the Ad Hoc Committee on Professional Correctional Education* (Camp Hill, Pennsylvania: The American Correctional Association, 1962).

law, or judicial processes and procedures are excluded, however related and important these are to treatment programs.)

2. Corrections requires the services of many professionals, including lawyers, physicians, psychiatrists, psychologists, vocational counselors, educators, social workers, and administrators. The services provided in corrections are thus interdisciplinary and must be organized and administered to facilitate the appropriate maximum contribution of each to the treatment of those being served.

3. Despite its interdisciplinary personnel, corrections can properly be identified as one of the "social services." It follows, therefore, that manpower for the field of corrections is directly affected by the situation prevailing in the total social work manpower pool.

4. Graduate social work education provides the most relevant preparation currently available for many persons expecting to enter positions involving treatment services for juvenile and adult offenders. There is continuing need for the improvement of the education offered by schools of social work for personnel in corrections.

5. The generic nature of graduate social work education gives correctional agencies the responsibility for providing graduates of schools of social work with the specific knowledge required for practice in correctional settings.

6. Undergraduate education has a substantial contribution to make in preparing correctional staff for appropriate tasks in designated positions. This contribution has still to be clearly defined and agreed upon.

The Facts About Manpower

Background Information on the Demand for Social Workers

The number of actual social work positions there are or would be today if personnel with the required qualifications were available to fill them is not definitely known. It is known, however, that, on the basis of population increases and the compounding of social problems, the demand is continually expanding. The Council on Social Work Education estimates that in recent years there have been some 10,000 to 12,000 continuously vacant positions in social work (and corrections) for which funds have been budgeted but for which no suitably qualified—not necessarily fully professionally qualified—social workers could be found. Other estimates indicate that the field must attract between 12,000 and 15,000 new recruits each year to replace workers leaving the field and to staff expanding programs and new services. Schools of social work are currently (1963) supplying only 2,500 graduates.

Another factor which must be considered in estimating our manpower needs is the rate of attrition for staff in this field. There are no comprehensive studies of the attrition rate in social welfare, but figures established for teachers suggest the possibility that from 5 to 8 percent of those employed in social work positions leave the field each year. Thus, the number needed just to replace those leaving the field annually is substantial in itself, ranging, on the basis of current employment figures, from 5,250 to about 6,000. These are not comforting statistics, but until the scope of the problem is fully understood we are unlikely to cope with it realistically.

We do not need any projections of growth in the number of social workers likely to be required in the next ten years to know that we must do better than we are doing to meet even existing demands. The number of persons now holding social work positions is no true measure of existing needs for such personnel. One has only to note the tremendous range in the reported number of social workers per 100,000 of the 1960 population by different regions, e.g., forty in the Southeast region and eighty-one in the Pacific states, to know that the existing number and their distribution is no true measure of need. Moreover, there are thousands of unfilled positions, positions which have been abolished or no longer budgeted for because of the lack of personnel to fill them, positions projected but never established because there was no prospect for filling them, and many new services and expansion of existing services being held in abeyance, until the necessary staff can be obtained. Projections that have been made for such fields and areas of practice as public assistance and public child welfare services for the nation as a whole and by California[2] of its overall needs for social work personnel are so far beyond the current supply that one can easily despair of coping with the problem in any realistic way.

If you would like to make your own projections as to the social workers needed in your state, one base from which you can start is to take the ratio of social work positions reported for the Pacific states —eighty-one for each 100,000 persons in the 1960 census—and apply it. Unless you think the Pacific states have a greater proportionate need for social workers than your state has, the estimate you arrive at may be considered to be minimum.

These few data on the demand side of our manpower problem, though far from complete, are adequate for all present purposes. It is not lack of information which prevents us from taking positive action on many fronts in meeting existing shortages.[3]

---

[2] Report of the Advisory Committee on Social Welfare Education, *Social Workers for California* (September, 1960).

[3] Ernest F. Witte, "Realities of Staffing Social Welfare Programs," *The Social Welfare Forum,* 1963, Official Proceedings of the National Conference on Social Welfare (New York: Columbia University Press, 1963), p. 178ff. For further details, see this article.

Number of Social Workers Currently Employed in Correctional Services

The factual basis for any analysis of the manpower situation in social work, and, therefore, corrections, is provided by two surveys made by the Bureau of Labor Statistics in 1950[4] and 1960.[5] In 1960, about 105,000 persons held social work positions in the United States. Of this number, 5,254 were employed in services to adult offenders, 4,923 were in court services for children, and 5,685 were in institutional services for children, although a substantial number of these institutions were serving dependent and neglected, as well as delinquent, children.[6]

These were exclusive of detention home attendants, psychologists, doctors, psychiatrists, nurses, clerical staff, accountants, librarians, receptionists, maintenance personnel, house-parents, teachers, jailers, and sheriffs.[7]

Following is a further breakdown:

Services to Adult Offenders	
All agencies	5,254
State or local governments	4,488
Federal government	537
State or local voluntary agencies	225
National voluntary agencies	4

Court Services	
All agencies	4,923
State or local governments	4,692
Federal government	12
State or local voluntary agencies	219
National voluntary agencies	0

Institutional Child Welfare	
All agencies	5,685
State or local governments	2,657
Federal government	11
State or local voluntary agencies	3,007
National voluntary agencies	10

Unfortunately for present purposes, these figures do not provide a complete answer to how many of the 105,000 social workers were actually employed in correctional services since there were overlapping

[4] *Social Workers in 1950* (New York: American Association of Social Workers, 1952).

[5] *Salaries and Working Conditions in Social Welfare Manpower in 1960* (New York: National Social Welfare Assembly, 1961).

[6] *Ibid.* Table 11, p. 27.

[7] *Ibid.* Table 4, pp. 18, 19.

classifications, such as institutional services for children, psychiatric social workers in settings other than hospitals, and group work.

If we can assume, in the absence of more specific data, that about half the personnel listed under Institutional Child Welfare were working with delinquents, then the total social welfare personnel in corrections in 1960, with the exceptions noted above, approximates 13,022.

If the other categories are added, the total correctional personnel in the United States in 1960 is estimated at 93,000.[8] This is a substantial number of people, whose education and qualifications for effective service are the concern of this conference.

If this estimate is near to the correct figure, about 14 percent of all correctional personnel in 1960 were classified as social workers. Unfortunately, the percentage of such personnel to the total professional personnel in the field, which would also be a significant figure, is not available.[9]

A question of crucial importance for this conference would appear to be: How many professionally prepared social workers are required to staff correctional services? A corollary question is: How many of those currently employed have the requisite education?

Again, since these data are not available, and since they are constantly changing, estimates based on such knowledge as is available must serve for the present. Is it reasonable to assume that all 13,022 social work positions reported in the 1960 Bureau of Labor Statistics study should have professional education in social work? It would seem so to many who are knowledgeable about the responsibilities such persons are expected to carry.

For example, the *Report to the Congress on Juvenile Delinquency* (Children's Bureau and National Institute of Mental Health, 1960) states on page 28 that at present there are an estimated 3,572 proba-

---

[8] This estimate is by Dr. Charles Prigmore, who states, "I am postulating the same ratio of treatment personnel to custodial personnel as in Pennsylvania, and also postulating that half the 'medical, education and treatment' category fall into the B.L.S. definition of social welfare." Dr. Prigmore further bolsters his estimate by reference to the *National Prisoner Statistics,* published by the U.S. Bureau of Prisons, March, 1963 (Number 31), which cites the number of full-time staff in all state and federal institutions for adult offenders alone as being 45,324 on December 31, 1961. The Children's Bureau, in its Statistical Series No. 70, estimated in 1962 that there were 16,600 full-time employees in public institutions for delinquents. If about 15,000 probation and parole officers, 10,000 employees in private correctional institutions and agencies, and 5,000 administrators, consultants, community organizers and researchers are added, a total of 93,000 is not an unreasonable estimate.

[9] The "Memorandum on Pennsylvania Correctional Personnel by Categories" appended to this chapter has a detailed classification of correctional personnel in Pennsylvania, which may be of interest to participants.

tion officers in juvenile courts in the United States. An estimated 7,220 officers are needed to handle the present workload if the recognized standard is to be met.[10] If we apply this formula to the 13,022 social welfare personnel, then it can be estimated that about 26,293 social work positions in the correctional field—current and potential—require personnel with full professional education. (This would, of course, add to the total estimated personnel in corrections [93,000] by the same amount, so that the proportion would remain the same.)

Another check on these estimates may be found in "Social Workers for California."[11] Based on the projected need in this state, the total for the United States would be 23,436 social work positions in corrections for which professional training is required. These two projections seem to support each other.

The Bureau of Labor Statistics study[12] reports the percentage of personnel with full professional education. Twenty percent (569) of personnel in child welfare (institutional), 10 percent (493) of those in child welfare (court services), and 8 percent (420) of those in services to adult offenders had full professional education. Thus, 1,482 persons in these three categories were reported in 1960 as having an M.S.W. degree or its equivalent.

Of all professionally trained social workers who are in these special categories, 2.5 percent are in child welfare (court services), 3 percent are in child welfare (institutional), and 2 percent are in services to adult offenders. Roughly, then, 7.5 percent of all personnel with M.S.W. degrees were employed in corrections in 1960.

According to some estimates, there are approximately the same number of other professional positions in the field of corrections—including physicians, psychologists, psychiatrists, teachers, and nurses—as there are social work positions in corrections. If these estimates are correct and if we apply recognized standards, there were approximately 120,000 individuals in correctional positions requiring professional preparation in 1960.

The director of the National Council on Crime and Delinquency recently wrote: "If probation and parole agencies are currently understaffed, they will be even more so when the full impact of the 50 per-

---

[10] Report reproduced from hearings before the Subcommittee of the Committee on Appropriations, House of Representatives, Eighty-Sixth Congress, Second Session.

[11] *Report of the Advisory Committee on Social Welfare Education to the Liaison Committee of the Regents of the University of California and the State Board of Education* (September, 1960), Table 3, p. 15.

[12] *Op. cit.*, p. 39.

cent increase in our child and youth population is felt within the next 10 years."[13]

Sources of Supply and Factors Affecting Supply

Many factors directly affect the supply of social workers. These factors are of crucial concern to correctional agencies seeking to upgrade the quality of their services. Among the more important factors are:

STUDENT ENROLLMENT IN SCHOOLS OF SOCIAL WORK

The enrollment of full-time students has climbed from 3,811 students in fifty-two schools of social work in November, 1956, to 6,592 in fifty-eight schools of social work in November, 1963. The annual number of graduates of the two-year curriculum has increased from 1,612 to 2,505 over the same period.

Two new schools of social work were accredited in 1963, and at least four, and possibly five, additional schools of social work are being developed. The present school capacity is being expanded through the acquisition of additional faculty, new physical facilities, and new grant funds.

Since from 10,000 to 15,000 additional persons must be recruited annually into the field of social work, the number of graduates of schools of social work is woefully inadequate, despite the substantial progress which has been made.

UNDERGRADUATE EDUCATION AS A SOURCE OF SUPPLY

An increasing number of undergraduate majors or sequences with a welfare and/or correctional content are developing throughout the country. Unfortunately, it has not yet been possible to devise a system of uniform reporting which would provide reliable totals of students enrolled in these courses.[14]

There is evidence, however, which indicates that graduates of these undergraduate programs have become an important source for recruiting personnel into corrections. More attention should be given to the nature of the undergraduate education of such personnel, the tasks most

---

[13] Milton G. Rector, "Significant Developments and Trends Affecting Probation and Parole," *Federal Probation,* Vol. XXVII, No. 2 (June, 1963), p. 10.

[14] In the California State College System, about nine of the eighteen colleges reported a total of 1,122 students enrolled in undergraduate social welfare sequences in the fall of 1963. These figures do not include students of other colleges in the system who may be enrolled in similar sequences but which have not been designated "social welfare."

appropriate for them, and the opportunities afforded them for further education for a career in corrections.[15]

NATIONAL RECRUITMENT EFFORTS

The National Commission for Social Work Careers was established July 1, 1962, under the joint auspices of the National Association of Social Workers and the Council on Social Work Education, as the successor to the recruitment program developed by the Council on Social Work Education. The commission functions on a unified basis for the total profession. It maintains a field service and is attempting to organize, with citizen participation, community-wide recruitment programs under local direction in every major metropolitan area in the country. Participation of correctional leaders in this effort greatly improves its effectiveness and enhances the possibilities for increasing the supply of social work personnel for staffing correctional services.[16]

STUDENT AID

During the 1955-56 academic year, 2,552, or 70 percent, of the 3,644 full-time students enrolled in schools of social work in the United States received some form of financial aid. This increased to 6,082, or 83.7 percent, of the 6,592 full-time students in 1963-64.

Of an estimated 3,500 fellowships, scholarships, and other financial plans listed by the Council on Social Work Education for 1963-64, roughly 150 were specifically related to future work in the correctional field, a very sharp increase from the 20 available in 1956-57.[17]

Student aid has significant influence upon which practice areas students choose for their careers. This is most clearly demonstrated by the scholarship grants made by the National Institute of Mental Health over a long period of time.

There have been relatively few grants which would encourage students to consider corrections as a field of practice. The development of funds for scholarships to be awarded students who indicate an interest in this field would substantially help recruit more social workers into corrections.

---

[15] The California State College System, with the co-sponsorship of the Council on Social Work Education and the Western Interstate Commission for Higher Education, and the cooperation of agencies in the field, has called two conferences at which representatives of all institutions of higher education were asked to consider the subject.

[16] For significant information with respect to when students entering schools of social work make their career choice, *see* Arnulf M. Pins, *Who Chooses Social Work, When and Why?* (New York: Council on Social Work Education, 1963).

[17] *Statistics on Social Work Education, November 1, 1963, and Academic Year 1962-1963* (New York: Council on Social Work Education, 1964).

SALARIES

A large increase in salaries of social workers between 1950 and 1960 was reported in the manpower survey of 1960. The trend is being accelerated by the shortage of manpower[18] and the increase in the proportion of males in the field. Average annual salaries increased 76 percent during the decade. Considering the rise in the cost of living during this period, the net gain in real income was 43 percent. The median salary of all social workers, as revealed in the 1960 survey, was $5,229. The median salary of all members of the National Association of Social Workers, who must have an M.S.W. degree, is $7,000. There is a $7,020 median salary for men who have received a Master of Social Work degree, as compared with $5,000 for men who have only a bachelor's degree. The median for men in the National Association of Social Workers in 1961 was $7,700.

In 1960, the Bureau of Labor Statistics found that caseworkers in courts had a median salary of $5,930. Caseworkers with adult offenders, employed by the federal government, had a median salary of $6,600.

Salaries, of course, are one of the major elements which influence the career choice of young people. The field of corrections needs to give continuing attention to the improvement of its competitive position in the area of salaries.

IN-SERVICE TRAINING AND STAFF DEVELOPMENT

Correctional agencies should give more attention to the potential contributions which in-service training and staff development programs can make to the upgrading of personnel in corrections. Such programs, when properly organized and administered, not only add to the knowledge and skill of staff but also improve morale and reduce turnover. When coupled with a well-developed leave of absence for training, the benefits are further increased.

There is a growing conviction that correctional agencies would have much to gain by establishing well-staffed regional training centers to which new and currently employed personnel might be sent for periods of training. These centers have much to offer beyond what any agency may be able to develop for its own staff. Such opportunities for training foster interest in the field on the part of prospective personnel who are seeking more than economic rewards.

NATIONAL EFFORTS TO UPGRADE CORRECTIONAL MANPOWER

In 1960, the Ford Foundation awarded a grant of $149,000 to the Council on Social Work Education for the establishment of a five-year

[18] *Salaries and Working Conditions of Social Welfare Manpower in 1960, op. cit.*

corrections project. The broad aims of this project are to increase the number of social work personnel preparing for careers in corrections, and to work toward a curriculum in the schools of social work with more correctional content and socio-cultural material that will better prepare future social workers for the correctional field.

In part due to the efforts of this project, more than half of the 58 accredited schools in the United States now have faculty members with correctional experience. Other developments include an increase in the number of students in field placements in correctional agencies from eighteen in 1956 to 433 in 1963; the increase in the number of schools with NIMH grants in corrections to twenty-seven; the closer relationship between the Council on Social Work Education, on the one hand, and the National Council on Crime and Delinquency and the American Correctional Association, on the other.

The Council on Social Work Education has also received grants from the President's Committee on Juvenile Delinquency and Youth Crime for the development of correctional teaching materials for use in schools of social work. The Federal Bureau of Prisons has greatly expanded its field-instruction facilities, and field-instruction units are being established under NIMH grants in two different reformatories. Regional seminars have been planned to help correctional administrators and policy-makers develop strategies for increasing the number of correctional field placements; the first seminar was scheduled for March, 1964.[19]

Another recent development of great potential significance to the field of corrections is the Council on Social Work Education study of curriculums in community organization launched in 1963 at the urging of and with a grant from the President's Committee on Juvenile Delinquency and Youth Crime. The committee's experience in attempting to staff its various projects with social workers having the requisite education to ascertain causes of and provide services to alleviate youth crime and delinquency led the committee to request the Council on Social Work Education to examine curriculums in community organization with a view to making them serve present-day needs better.

Expansion of Educational Facilities

Three questions have been suggested as being crucial for consideration in this conference as they concern the expansion of educational facilities. In considering these questions, the focus must be on social

---

[19] For a more complete report of these developments, *see* Charles Prigmore, "Corrections and Social Work—The Impact of the 1962 Curriculum Policy Statement," *Crime and Delinquency,* Vol. 9, No. 2 (April 1963), pp. 185-188.

work education, although the discussion may have broader implications. Following are the questions, in the order in which they were suggested:

1. Can the various accredited professional schools be expanded without damage to standards and quality of instruction? If so, by the use of what devices and means?

There is little question that existing schools of social work can expand significantly without endangering the quality of instruction. This conclusion is based upon: (1) the rather dramatic increase in the enrollment in existing schools during the past ten years, during which their overall enrollment has been approximately 100%; this was accompanied by a marked increase in the quality of the education provided; and (2) an almost unanimous opinion by a committee of deans representing a cross-section of the schools of social work that, given the resources, schools of social work would face no serious obstacles which would prevent them from continuing their expansion in the future.

The answer to the question, therefore, is "yes," but it must be qualified by making clear that, if significant expansion is to take place, the schools, and those working with them, must be provided with the necessary funds and time to enable them to recruit additional well-qualified faculty—including field instructors—recruit qualified students, locate and develop good field placements, augment library collections, acquire necessary classroom and office space, and employ needed auxiliary personnel.

The administrative and teaching personnel of most schools have the knowledge and experience necessary to expand their programs while maintaining or improving their quality, if the needed financial resources are made available. It is obvious, of course, that the potentials for expansion are greater for some schools than for others. It should be remembered, however, that, by the use of such devices as "block field placements," schools need not be limited in their expansion because of their location.

2. Is it advisable and feasible for the various professions and disciplines to unite to effect such expansions in capacity, and, if so, how?

It would seem of great advantage to social work, particularly because of its relatively weaker public appeal, to cooperate with other professional groups, such as medicine, nursing, public health, teacher education, law, and psychology, in an effort to get the financial support needed for expansion and the community understanding needed to provide the laboratory resources for field instruction. In limited measure, such cooperation has been achieved in a variety of ways, and these efforts need to be intensified to (1) secure additional public funds from federal, state, and local sources to support education for social work, since it is increasingly clear that public funds will have to finance any substantial expansion of education for social work; and (2) improve the climate in which social work education is provided.

It cannot be emphasized too strongly, however, that there is no substitute for action by all aspects of social work, including corrections, in taking the leadership in the effort to secure the resources needed to expand social work education.

No other professional group should be depended upon to do more than lend its understanding support, since each group is heavily burdened with similar needs in its own field. But if understanding support is sought from related professional groups, including the faculties of other departments of the educational institutions which have the schools of social work, it will be significantly beneficial to further expansion.

3. Are new accredited professional schools required to meet the manpower shortage? If so, how are they to be established? What role should correctional leaders play in this establishment, if any?

There is urgent need not only to expand the enrollment in present schools of social work but also to establish new schools. One illustration may help to indicate why. California estimates[20] that it needs 2,700 additional social workers annually. The three accredited schools in the state are currently graduating approximately 150 annually.

Thus, although it is hoped that these three schools will triple their enrollment within the next few years, new schools must still be developed if the gap between supply and demand is to be narrowed or closed.[21]

There is a significant body of opinion that every state should have at least one school of social work, not only because of the need for social workers but also because of other benefits such as the provision of professional leadership, having an institution which would serve as a center for research on the social problems of the state, the provision of consultation to legislative bodies, having a center for encouraging continuing study by practitioners, and serving the profession in a variety of ways. Currently, there are some nineteen states which have no accredited school of social work.[22]

There is no established formula which can insure the establishment

---

[20] *See: Social Workers for California, op. cit.*

[21] California is now undertaking to establish simultaneously three new graduate schools of social work scheduled to open in the fall semester of 1964. A brief explanation of how plans for these three schools were developed, which may serve to illustrate one process for increasing educational facilities, is appended to this chapter.

[22] Alabama, Alaska, Arizona (school now developing), Delaware, Idaho, Maine, Mississippi, Montana, Nevada, New Hampshire, New Mexico, North Dakota, Oregon (school now developing), Rhode Island, South Carolina, South Dakota, Vermont, Wyoming, and Arkansas.

of a school of social work, but there are some fundamental factors which contribute substantially to such a development on a sound basis. The employing agencies and the entire profession, including correctional leaders—even though they have an interest broader than social work—should agree on the need for a school or schools. Help in undertaking this process is available from the Council on Social Work Education, both in assessing the need for a school and the potential resources available for its establishment.

Educational institutions should be explored to determine their suitability for and interest in the development of a school of social work. Many factors need to be considered in determining the priority to be assigned to those which would be suitable. These include the strength of the liberal arts program, especially in the social science area, the institution's location for ready access to good social laboratory resources, its willingness to consider the development of a school and to help secure the needed resources. Once a suitable institution for a school is found, that institution must assume the leadership in the development of the schools; however, the original sponsors are obliged to help in getting needed legislation and funds, and to help create a favorable climate for the development of the school.

The effort to establish a school of social work may be greatly delayed or completely frustrated if those most aware of the need can not agree on a location, and if they carry on a public feud about this or some other important aspects related to the establishment of a school. Some schools have failed to develop their real potential simply because, for a variety of reasons, they did not get the support of the total field after they were established.

There is every reason to expect that leaders in correctional agencies will assert more leadership and will join with leaders in other areas of social work practice not only to help the establishment of new schools where this would be sound but also to help established schools expand their services.

APPENDIX A

Recapitulation of a Memorandum on Pennsylvania Correctional Personnel By Categories

A memorandum originally prepared by the Planning Committee of the Pennsylvania Council on Correctional Staff Development on November 14, 1963 showing the number of correctional personnel in Pennsylvania by position classification is of interest because it provides much significant information not readily available on a national basis. Its statistical data are tabulated below:

I. Adult Correctional Institutions

A. *Bureau of Corrections*

There are approximately 2,250 persons presently employed in the Bureau of Corrections. They may be broken down as follows:

1. administrative	49
2. correctional-clerical	242
3. custodial	1,323
4. medical education & treatment	211
5. industry & maintenance	429

B. *Adult Prisons Department—Department of Public Welfare, City of Philadelphia*

There are more than 500 employees in this department, classified as follows:

1. administrative	16
2. clerical	33
3. custodial	299
4. medical education & treatment	57
5. industry & maintenance	101

C. *Adult Correctional Institution, County of Allegheny*

There are more than 200 persons employed in these correctional institutions classified as follows:

1. administrative	5
2. clerical	8
3. custodial	166
4. medical education & treatment	24
5. industry & maintenance	20

D. County jails in the remaining counties employ more than 750 persons. This figure is not clear-cut, since in some cases sheriffs are included as they are the principal jail officers, and in other cases, matrons who are included among the custodial personnel are wives of sheriffs and so forth. The total may be broken down as follows:

1. administrative	64
2. custodial	580
3. other	110

II. Probation

There are almost 600 probation officers reportedly employed in Pennsylvania. They may be broken down as follows:

A. *Allegheny County* 88

1. 66 of these operate in the juvenile field.
2. 22 are employed as adult probation officers.

B. *Philadelphia* 237

1. quarter sessions	55
2. Philadelphia county (adult)	59
3. Philadelphia county (juvenile)	123

4. 38 of the above are considered to be administrative or supervisory.

C. The remaining counties employ 268 probation personnel. They may be broken down as follows:

1. exclusively adult—7 chiefs and 33 officers
2. exclusively juvenile—12 chiefs and 76 officers
3. exclusively domestic relations—3 chiefs and 26 officers
4. no specific—32 chiefs and 79 officers

III. State Board of Parole

The State Board of Parole employs 254 persons, fifty of whom are considered administrative and 204 operate as parole officers.

IV. Juvenile Detention Facilities

The state's nineteen detention facilities employ almost 250 persons. These may be broken down as follows:

1. superintendents or directors	20
2. teachers	21
3. child care personnel	170
4. miscellaneous	33

V. State Department of Public Welfare

Information not pertinent

VI. Police

There are approximately 14,000 police officers currently employed in the Commonwealth, broken down as follows:

1. Permanent State Police	2,147
2. Philadelphia	6,271
3. Pittsburgh	1,543
4. Other cities over 25,000 population	1,911
5. Cities under 25,000 population	2,284

VII. Education of Correctional Employees

For this report, no effort was made to determine the educational status of persons working in the field of crime and delinquency. However, the 1957 National Council on Crime and Delinquency study on probation in Pennsylvania reported that 73 percent of all the chief probation officers and 54 percent of all the probation officers had not completed college education.

Eighteen percent had graduate school education, 12 percent had some high school education, 32 percent were high school graduates, 11 percent had some college, 15 percent were college graduates, and 12 percent had graduate degrees.

APPENDIX B

The Board of Trustees of the California State Colleges has approved the establishment of five schools of social work, but has authorized only three of these for the present, located at Fresno, Sacramento, and San Diego.

The action taken by the Board of Trustees is the culmination of long efforts to increase the facilities for the training of social workers in California. The Department of Corrections, the Youth Authority, the Department of Mental Hygiene and Social Welfare have for extended periods made clear their need for additional professionally-trained social workers, and have worked appropriately with the schools of social welfare at the University of California (Berkeley and Los Angeles) and the School of Social Work at the University of Southern California in urging their expansion. These schools have helped to insure that in every study of higher education in California, social work needs were not overlooked. Thus, the Strayer Committee Report on the needs of California in higher education in 1947-48 included a recommendation that the subject be given further study. (*See* Monroe E. Deutsch, Aubrey A. Douglass, and George D. Strayer, *A Report of a Survey of the Needs of California in Higher Education* [Berkeley: University of California Press, 1948], p. 106.)

The following study was completed in 1955. (*See* T. R. McConnell, T. C. Holy, and H. H. Semans, *A Restudy of the Needs of California in Higher Education* [Sacramento, California: California State Department of Education, 1955], pp. 180-181.)

As a part of this *Restudy* there was appointed a special committee on social work to consider the education of personnel (at both the undergraduate and graduate levels) for this field. (See "Social Workers for California," The Report of the Advisory Committee on Social Welfare Education to the Liaison Committee of the Regents of the University of California and The State Board of Education, September, 1960 [Mimeographed]).

This report of the special committee contained numerous findings and recommendations related to social work education.

In 1961, the legislature of California established the Welfare Study Commission, and the governor appointed seventeen members, including three county welfare directors, four county supervisors, three county administrative officers, a superior court judge (named chairman), a district attorney, a county probation officer, and four representatives of the general public. Other representatives included the director of the Department of Social Welfare, chairman of the State Welfare Board, two senators appointed by the Senate Rules Committee, two assemblymen appointed by the Speaker of the Assembly, and ex-officio, the Directors of Public Health, Employment, and Mental Hygiene.

The commission employed special consulting firms to study and report on various aspects of its assignments. It made sweeping recommendations, including specific ones on the need for additional educational facilities to increase the supply of professionally educated social workers. The recommendations made were:

"*Professional Training:* Vastly increased numbers of persons trained in social work are needed in California. The present social work courses at the undergraduate level are few in number, lack standardization, and are of varying quality. The graduate schools, while training qualified graduates, cannot produce the number required to meet the rapidly increasing demand in this field.

"This problem has been studied, reviewed, and subjected to recommendation repeatedly in the last several years, but thus far no effective action has been taken. Further delay can only magnify the severe problem which exists. It is the opinion of the commission that:

"1. The state colleges and universities have a special responsibility to assist in meeting the shortage of professionally trained persons in this field. The need for such staff is by no means limited to the field of public assistance but extends to mental health, public health, corrections, probation, school social work, and a variety of other specialized programs. We recommend the following:

"a. Undergraduate courses in social work should be established on all major campuses of the state college and university systems and at all independent colleges which can be interested.

"b. The course content of pre-social work programs in these schools should be standardized and coordinated with equivalent courses given in other departments on the same campus.

"c. Within the framework of the Master Plan for Higher Education, graduate schools of social work should be established at five of the state colleges and at each of the major campuses of the University of California where one has not yet been established. In planning the establishment of new schools, consideration should be given to the 12-month master's degree program which has been proposed to the Council on Social Work Education.

"d. Existing schools of social work in California should be encouraged to triple their capacity as rapidly as possible.

"2. To help achieve necessary expansion of facilities for professional training, the commission will designate a committee of its members to explore with the Regents of the University System, the Trustees of the State College System, and the Coordinating Council on Higher Education these problems and the most effective means of dealing with them.

"The commission, in its discussions with social work educators, was made aware of the problems posed by the suggested expansion of training facilities as they relate to cost, internal administration, and accreditation. We believe, however, that there are solutions to these problems and that they can be worked out.

"3. In the event that the Regents of the University and the trustees of the state colleges find it impossible to undertake the suggested expansion of professional training facilities for social work, the commission recommends as a much less desirable alternative the establishment of an academy for such training under the direction of the State Department of Social Welfare. This academy should provide courses which are equivalent in content and quality to those currently provided by the graduate schools of social work."

(For complete report see *Welfare Study Commission Final Report,* January 1963, Sacramento.)

It was on the basis of these recommendations that the Board of Trustees of the California State College System acted in establishing three new schools of social work, all of which are giving careful attention to the need for personnel for the field of corrections.

The above brief account is far from complete and makes no attempt to describe the negotiations, meetings, conferences, and personal efforts that were necessarily involved in getting action on the educational recommendations included in the report.

Finally, it should be noted that all of the above-mentioned state departments in California are cooperating enthusiastically in making resources available to the new schools as a means of insuring the best possible field placements in corrections (both adult and youth), in psychiatry and in public welfare. One state department, Social Welfare, has substantially helped the Board of Trustees finance the necessary year of planning so that the three schools can get underway a year earlier than would otherwise be possible.

In any exploration of resources needed to finance education for social workers, the potential availability of federal matching (and other federal funds) should not be overlooked.

In a related development, representatives of the Youth Authority initiated exploration with a representative of the Chancellor's Office of the State College System as to the adequacy and content of current undergraduate education. This has led to a beginning examination of undergraduate course content, organization, and relationship to graduate professional education in California.

Expansion of Field Work and Internship Facilities for Training of Correctional Personnel

by BEN S. MEEKER

INTRODUCTION

WAYS OF SUBSTANTIALLY INCREASING facilities for field instruction of and internships for persons seeking professional training in the rehabilitation of offenders will be the focus of this paper. Unfortunately, there are limited opportunities for field training in agencies and institutions throughout the country. Many of these programs are related to undergraduate social-science subjects. Others are integrated with programs of graduate education in criminology, sociology, psychology, and, increasingly, in social work. In relation to the demand for qualified personnel, these education programs meet a fraction of the need. Ways and means must be found to exploit all such resources as fully as possible. One of the main obstacles to achieving this—a dilemma particularly felt in the field of social work education—is the dearth of adequate field work placements for graduate students bent on a career in welfare or corrections. Yet, progress has been made toward resolving this dilemma in certain states and communities, and an effort will here be made to assess the present state of affairs and suggest some steps for the future. Attention will first be focused upon field work at the graduate level. Later, undergraduate internships and similar forms of field training will be examined.

Because of the long association between social welfare and corrections, certain basic assumptions about the relevancy of social work training, with its rich heritage of field instruction, will be made at the outset. While certain specialized attributes of correctional treatment services will be recognized, the commonality of knowledge and treatment methods underlying the broad field of social welfare and corrections will be emphasized. There is still much controversy in the correctional field about what is the best kind of training, whether it comes from law, social work, psychiatry, criminology, sociology, anthropology, or some other source. A comprehensive treatment of this whole subject, which all of you should read, is contained in the November, 1963, issue of *Correctional Research,* the publication of the United Prison Association of Massachusetts.[1]

There has been a proliferation of training and educational programs designed to prepare personnel for correctional work. One major problem confronting us is the need to distinguish between professional education as preparation for practice in probation and parole or institutional counseling in the correctional setting, and vocational training for specific job placements. There is also a lack of discernment between the educational programs related to specific disciplines in the social sciences and the broadly-based professional training in professional schools of social work, clinical psychology, law, and medicine. Professional education for the helping professions has its origins in the great traditions of apprenticeship teaching. However, it is now recognized that the finest professional education is university-centered, reflecting a joint undertaking of fields of practice and academic resources of universities. To preserve the vital flow of information from practice to academic setting and back to practice, the helping professions—medicine, psychiatry, clinical psychology, social work and others—have developed elaborate systems of clinical and internship training for personnel entering these fields. Inevitably, these clinic, intern, or field work programs focus on a wide spectrum of values derived from ethical and philosophical systems, knowledge from a great variety of disciplines, and tremendous investment in methods of practice. The capacity to relate ethical values to decision-making processes and to apply the proper skills and techniques to the individual being helped, whether he be a medical patient, parolee, or a student in a special school, is one of the chief attributes of professional education.

Comment has been made on the role ambiguity of the professional worker in corrections. There is no unified body of theory and practice which is as yet generally accepted as a guide in trying to professionalize correctional practice. Perhaps one of the difficulties has been the confusion in the objectives of education. Have we not too often assumed that training in a social-science discipline such as sociology, criminology, or anthropology will somehow equip a student for practice as a probation or parole officer or institutional counselor?

This does not mean that an undergraduate or graduate degree in sociology, criminology, or psychology is not the right background for

---

[1] *Correctional Research,* Bulletin No. 13 (November, 1963).

further training, but does a concentration of theoretical courses in such academic disciplines prepare one for actual treatment and control practice in corrections any more than a concentration of academic courses in physiology or chemistry prepares one for medical practice? Courses in physiology and chemistry are necessary background for professional medical education, but the medical profession is clear about the difference between the role and expectation of a graduate chemist or physiologist and the role of the fully-trained physician. The physician has to undergo a rigorous clinical internship, in which the knowledge and theory from a variety of scientific disciplines are integrated with a set of values and well-defined treatment methods that prepare him for the practice of medicine.

Without suggesting that this analogy can be applied in an exact sense to the field of corrections, I believe that we must look closely at the available educational resources which have widely recognized professional content and method. The capacity of educational resources are so heavily taxed that we cannot afford to reject or overlook any source of recruitment and training.

Among these resources are the schools of social work throughout the nation. There is controversy about the relevance of social work training for correctional practice, but controversy is healthy and does not change my conviction that schools of social work have much to offer in this area and their resources have not begun to be exploited.

I would like to focus attention on the most unique and perhaps most valuable attribute of social work training, namely, the rigid requirement of field training which is integrated with academic instruction.

This field training which gives the schools of social work their special professional status is comparable to internships in medical education, for this is where the student begins to learn how to apply his theoretical knowledge to the every-day solution of the problems of those he is expected to guide and help.

The remainder of this section of my paper is based upon an assumption that the purpose of probation, parole, and correctional treatment is the protection of the community through the rehabilitation and control of the offender. It is my further contention that rehabilitation affords the best long-range protection of society. Control over an offender's behavior must come largely from within, although the external controls of parole conditions, the walls of an institution, or other objective legal symbols of restraint are reality attributes to be accepted and recognized.

There are numerous approaches, of course, to the education of persons in the treatment and rehabilitation of offenders, and we must continue to experiment with and exploit all of them. However, I know of none more adequate than the one provided by the schools of social work, particularly when field placements of students are available in correctional agencies.

I suspect that one of the main sources of our disagreement over the role of social work training stems from the failure of correctional agencies and administration to provide field work opportunities and internships—under competent pedagogical and professional supervision—to compete with other segments of the broad fields of mental health and social welfare.

It is time that the correctional field take stock of resources available in schools of social work and offer to work intensely on ways and means of adapting these resources more adequately to its needs.

SPECIALIZED EDUCATION

Some people believe that a new and independent correctional specialty should be developed; however, I doubt that this is either practical or desirable. I know of no country in the world where there is any serious effort to develop an independent correctional profession—instead, probation-parole and correctional treatment personnel are generally recruited from a variety of disciplines. In West Germany, personnel trained and experienced in social welfare and education are recruited. In the Netherlands, schools of social work cooperate closely with the director of probation and provide many practitioners. In England, the probation officer is considered a court social worker, and the entire program of after-care is closely integrated with the field of social work. In conversations I once had with a probation officer and a child welfare worker from one of Great Britain's central industrial communities, Nottingham, both commented on the absence of controversy about the training and work of the probation officer and the child welfare practitioner. Both had been trained in similar techniques, and I was told that all probation officers in England are now expected to acquire training in marital counseling and other aspects of casework. As the child welfare worker commented, "It is assumed in Nottingham that if a probational officer works with a particular family, he will take care of the child welfare, marital, or other problems, whereas if the child welfare worker were assigned to the same family, he would be expected to handle the after-care work or probation counseling services, too."

One of the most persuasive and thoughtful commentaries on this matter will be found in a discussion by Tadeusz Grygier of the recommendations of the Canadian Corrections Association in a 1959 memorandum:

> ". . . if the number of fully qualified professional practitioners needs to be increased, the aim is not to create a new professional group. 'Rather,

we conceive of correctional workers as drawn from a variety of disciplines, such as psychology, law, education and social work, but given in addition specialized graduate training in the theory and practice of the correctional field.' The Association recommends that universities which have either a department of psychology or a school of social work should enrich their curriculum by introducing correctional material to existing courses, and by adding specific courses in corrections. They emphasize that schools of social work and departments of psychology are most relevant to professional preparation for correctional practice. They urge the establishment of a chair of corrections in those universities that have the necessary facilities. 'Ideally, chairs of corrections should be located in universities that have schools or departments of social work, psychology, psychiatry, sociology, theology, and law.' This should enable the proposed chairs to draw on the resources of all these departments and schools. They believe that a chair of corrections should be located in either a school of social work or a department of psychology. . . .

"Developments at the University of Toronto have followed this approach. After all, the practice of corrections involves personality, and social diagnosis, casework, group work, community organization and supervision; it is therefore much more closely related to social work and to clinical psychology than criminology. Criminology provides the basic theoretical framework, but it does not create practitioners of corrective treatment at the professional level. This view was expressed by Mr. Kirkpatrick in his 1957 memorandum: He does not suggest that criminologists should not function as practitioners, but he thinks that social workers and psychologists are more expertly trained in the skills required by a practitioner, with the psychologist in addition placing emphasis on the functions of testing and diagnosis. . . .

"The approach currently accepted at the University of Toronto is that corrections does not represent a single scientific discipline but rather a combination of several relevant disciplines. Consequently, instruction at the university level is not confined to a specific course of study, but aims at a gradual penetration of correctional knowledge into the training designed for lawyers, psychologists, psychiatrists, social workers, etc. Correctional content in the curriculum has been increasing in all relevant departments of the University of Toronto and is particularly prominent at the School of Social Work."[2]

Whether or not we agree with our Canadian brethren, we must, at this stage of our development, exploit to the maximum all possible sources of recruitment and training for corrections.

Certainly, schools of social work are among the most valuable resources for such exploitation. As our distinguished colleague, the wise English jurist, Eileen L. Younghusband, commented at the conclusion of her Ford Foundation research project on corrections and social work in this country, "The major bottleneck in the training of more correc-

---

[2] "What's New in Education for Correctional Work?" *Correctional Research,* Bulletin No. 13 (November, 1963), p. 48.

tional workers by the schools of social work is in the absence of field placements."

A recent study by the Western Interstate Commission for Higher Education has reaffirmed this limitation. The Commission conducted a special institute in March, 1964, to explore ways and means of further expanding field work and intern opportunities for the training of correctional personnel. Aside from philosophical or theoretical concerns which suggest the value of expanding social work field training, a number of practical considerations merit review:

1. *General Availability of Schools of Social Work*

   There are now fifty-nine accredited schools of social work throughout the United States, all but a dozen or so of which offer some courses related to corrections. The history of social work education has been a history of meeting the needs of social agencies which have made their demands most articulate. If, during the next decade, the correctional field presents a strong case to the schools of social work for the need for trained personnel and simultaneously cooperates with these professional schools to provide field work opportunities in correctional services, to propose or make available additional teaching staffs and to seek stipends and scholarship aid, the schools of social work will respond to this demand.

2. *High Curricular Standards*

   The curricula of accredited graduate schools of social work are developed by individual schools in line with the official curriculum policy of the Council on Social Work Education, the body which is responsible for the development and maintenance of high standards of social work education. As the official accrediting body for graduate social work education, the Council conducts periodic reviews of all accredited schools of social work to make sure that current educational practices meet the criteria established for sound preparation for the social work profession. The Council on Social Work Education works closely with the National Association of Social Workers and other national social welfare agencies in developing standards which promote a closer relationship between practice and education. I know of no other comparable educational resource which can give the same assurance of high standards of field and academic education, systematically organized around a set of professional educational principles, ethics, and methodology, and adaptable to practice in corrections.

3. *Common Traditions*

The long, distinguished association between social work and corrections is evidenced by the early history of the widely acclaimed National Conferences on Charities and Corrections. In more recent years, evidence of renewed rapprochement is reflected in the collaboration between such organizations as the National Council on Crime and Delinquency and the Council on Social Work Education in developing joint conferences, seminars, and other mutual educational ventures.

4. *The Great Potential of Correctional Field Training Resources*

There are many opportunities which correctional agencies and institutions can offer to the schools of social work for field work training. State and federal correctional services could make their wealth of resources for field training available to the schools of social work, something that they have been slow to do. This would be particularly helpful since it has been admitted that the expansion of resources in schools of social work to meet the personnel needs of corrections has been limited by too few field work placements.

5. *Scope and Flexibility of Field Work Tradition and Social Work Education*

No professional educational program has had a longer or more disciplined experience with field work education than that of social work. Training for the practice of social work has from its beginning been deeply involved in field education. A unique characteristic of social work education is its rich tradition of field work training. This is where the student, planning to go into corrections, mental health, public assistance, or child welfare, begins to translate concepts and principles into practice. As. Dr. Katherine A. Kendall, Executive Director, Council on Social Work Education, has pointed out, "Social work education has traditionally been agency-centered. Approximately 50 percent of the student's time is spent in actual field training. It is in this area that social work education becomes a partnership between the practicing community service agency and the educational institution."[3]

---

[3] Katherine A. Kendall, "The Agency as a Training Center," *Proceedings of Spring Institute with Agency Executives and Field Instructors 1960-1961* (Washington, D.C.: Howard University, 1961).

6. *The High Relevancy of the Content of Education Provided in the Schools of Social Work to Practice in Corrections*

   The stereotype of social work education, which a decade or two ago tended to separate corrections from the mainstream of social work, is gradually changing, and one has but to examine the modern curricula of the graduate schools of social work to realize how much in this training is relevant to correctional practice. The modern curriculum in a school of social work is divided into three broad areas of academic education: (a) social welfare policy and services, (b) human behavior and social environment, and (c) methods of social work practice.[4] Solving problems through the methods of casework, group work, community organization, administration, and research is the basic technique taught in schools of social work.

   Adaptations are constantly being made to meet the demands of the field. A recent survey conducted by the Council on Social Work Education indicates that of the fifty-nine schools, twenty-nine now have field work placements and course content specifically focused on preparation for corrections. All schools include some specialized course content related to the field of corrections. As demands from the correctional field for additional course content related to it are made, the schools will respond. For example, the current catalogue of a typical graduate school of social work in a Western state contains a section titled "Corrections," which includes the following statement: "The practice of social casework in a correctional setting includes probation and parole services for both children and adults, as well as social service programs for prisons, reformatories, and training schools for boys and girls. Corrections is a rapidly growing area of practice . . . it differs from the more traditional areas of social casework in that it requires the use of social and legal authority as a part of treatment. Field instruction is offered."[5]

A number of schools of social work for years have employed faculty members recruited from the field of corrections and offered courses focused directly on corrections. The University of Chicago for more than three decades has maintained a vital program of field training in corrections, and has always had among its faculty an outstanding pro-

---

[4] *Official Statement of Curriculum Policy* (New York: Council on Social Work Education, 1962), p. 2.

[5] *University of Denver Bulletin: the Graduate School of Social Work 1964-1965* (Denver, Colorado: Colorado Seminary, 1964), p. 9.

fessor recruited from the field of corrections.[6] In addition to having a professor who devotes full time to teaching and directing research in corrections, the University of Chicago also employs three full-time assistant professors, all of whom are engaged in field instruction or research in corrections.

Other evidence of growing interest in the schools of social work incorporating additional conceptual and technical materials from the correctional fields is to be found in the interdisciplinary faculty positions in many schools. In the Columbia University School of Social Work, for example, an illustrious criminologist has been serving on the faculty for some years. This past fall an eminent criminal law professor received a joint appointment at the Law School and School of Social Service Administration of the University of Chicago. Appointments of faculty members in criminology, sociology, and anthropology, with special interests in corrections, are also rising. The University of Toronto, Canada, recently established a chair in its school of social work titled, "Special Lecturer in Corrections." Filling this chair is Dr. Tadeusz Grygier, an eminent clinical psychologist, lawyer, and former student of Herman Mannheim. Other members of the faculty accompany students to a number of correctional institutions and organize discussion groups on the programs in these facilities. Field instruction in corrections has recently been expanding and is being organized in the areas of probation, after-care, forensic social work, treatment of alcoholics, and special institutions for disturbed and anti-social adolescents. The director of the school of social work states, "Nearly one-half of current M.S.W. theses are in the field of corrections or in highly relevant fields, such as treatment of multi-problem families, behavior deviations in children, etc."[7] In its recent report, the Council on Social Work Education shows that in the past years the number of professors added to school of social work staffs who were recruited or who have special knowledge in the field of corrections has increased from perhaps six or seven to approximately fifty.[8]

In addition to this growing sensitivity by schools of social work to the needs of the correctional field, there is an increasing recognition by corrections of social work as a basic source of recruitment. Specific evidence of this is found in the literature of leading professional organizations in the correctional field, such as the National Council on

---

[6] Noteworthy among these have been Professors Harrison Dobbs during the 30's, Frank Flynn during the '40's and early '50's, and Charles Shireman during the latter part of the '50's to the present.

[7] *Correctional Research, op. cit.,* p. 24.

[8] Charles S. Prigmore, "What's Happening in the Corrections Project?", *Social Work Education,* Vol. XI, No. 6 (December 1963-January 1964), pp. 10-11, 24.

Crime and Delinquency. Job descriptions of probation and parole officers and educational standards for professional training are couched largely in social work terminology. The Federal Bureau of Prisons titles the position of institutional parole officer "social worker-parole," and recently, the Federal Probation Service established a top administrative position of "Supervisor of Social Service." In a number of states, such as Wisconsin, Michigan, Minnesota, New York, and California, much of the literature containing descriptions of positions indicates that a background of knowledge and training in social work is desirable. Last year, the Professional Development Committee of the California Probation-Parole and Correctional Association issued a publication titled, *A Profile of the Practitioner in the Correctional Setting,* which, while recognizing the interdisciplinary nature of corrections and the need to recruit from a variety of disciplines, emphasizes the importance of social work methodology, particularly casework, group work, community organization, and administration, as fundamental to adequate performance.[9]

This lengthy and perhaps over-detailed account of the background and current groundswell of activity of correctional agency and social work school administrators has been presented to indicate that it is time for further efforts to expand this sphere of training. In the following section, a somewhat more concrete appraisal of current developments will be presented.

The Current Status of Field Training in Corrections

There is a dearth of opportunities for field training available to students who are interested in a career in corrections, and many of the opportunities that are available are diverse and not standardized. In general, such field training opportunities can be classified in three general categories:

The first major category covers graduate school programs systematically organized and generally leading to a degree at the master's level. These programs can be subdivided into: (a) those offered by graduate schools of social work in which the curricula have been standardized to a large degree and in which the field work is closely integrated with the academic courses as well as agency practice; and (b) other graduate school programs administered by graduate departments of clinical psychology, criminology, or correctional administration. These programs are frequently one-year programs, and, by and large, there is no national standard-setting body to evaluate the curricula in many

[9] *A Profile of the Practitioner in a Correctional Setting* (California Probation-Parole and Correctional Association, May, 1963), p. 10.

of these programs, which, although they are few in number, have met a real need and have turned out many successful practitioners.

The second major category of field training is of quite recent origin and stems largely from the program of the President's Committee on Juvenile Delinquency and Youth Crime operating under the joint auspices of the Department of Health, Education and Welfare and the Department of Labor. Although the funds of these training grants are for projects primarily geared to research and demonstration, a number of them include field training opportunities. Grants for the creation of "training centers" have been made to twelve major universities throughout the United States. Another twenty-five grants have been made for "workshops, institutes, and seminars" under the auspices of both universities and community agencies.[10]

The third major category of field training covers the undergraduate field observations, internships, and work-study programs.

Fortunately, information about graduate field opportunities throughout the United States and Canada is now available. There are the reports from the corrections project of the Council on Social Work Education, and the fine report of the United Prisons Association of Massachusetts in the November 1963 issue of *Correctional Research,* ably edited by Professor Albert Morris, contains one of the most comprehensive surveys of current educational programs extant.

Special attention should be given the program of the Western Interstate Commission for Higher Education, which has brought a fresh and lively approach to the whole matter of training and recruitment of personnel for those services involved in prevention and treatment of juvenile delinquency.

Under the leadership of the Western Governors' Section of the Council of State Governments, a National Institute of Mental Health grant for a two-year research study of personnel and training needs was instituted in 1960. A unique aspect of this study was its approach to problems on a regional basis. About thirteen states were surveyed, and the response to this survey reflects the tremendous need and widespread interest in training efforts.

In six of the thirteen states, graduate schools or departments of social service offer field training in adult and juvenile corrections. In another state, the university is undertaking plans to open a school of social work which anticipates developing correctional courses.

About half of the thirteen states also indicated that graduate field

---

[10] "Summaries of Training Projects" under P.L. 87-274, *President's Committee on Juvenile Delinquency and Youth Crime* (Department of Health, Education, and Welfare and Department of Labor, September 1963).

opportunities were provided by other university departments, including schools of public administration, sociology, anthropology, and psychology.

The schools of social work in California, Colorado, Hawaii, Oregon, Utah, and Washington all have a significant investment in correctional field training at the graduate level.

The cost of graduate education during the past two decades has risen to astronomical heights. Professional education, whether it be for law, medicine, social work, or teaching, has become extremely expensive and highly competitive in the search for scholarship and fellowship funds. The reports of the Western Interstate Commission for Higher Education and the survey of the Massachusetts Prison Association make clear the importance of fellowship money as a stimulus to field work training. The correctional field as a whole has lagged far behind other areas of social welfare and mental hygiene in the demand for adequate stipends and fellowship grants. I am convinced that one of the main reasons that the schools of social work have tended to place larger numbers of graduate students in psychiatric, mental health, and public assistance field placements is because there have been substantial funds available to subsidize both graduate students and graduate field training instructors. Fortunately, funds are now becoming available for subsidizing graduate field placements in the correctional services.

The report of the Western Interstate Commission for Higher Education indicates that the graduate school of social work at the University of Southern California now receives National Institute of Mental Health stipends in corrections and "has an expansive program." The report also indicates that the graduate school of social work at the University of California, Berkeley, receives NIMH stipends for students in corrections.

The graduate schools of social work at the University of Denver, in Utah and at the University of Washington in Seattle, receive stipends in corrections from the National Institute of Mental Health.

The implications of these developments are clear. The field of corrections can attract its share of competent graduate students provided that: (1) funds for stipends for fellowships are available; and (2) adequate field work placements can be developed.

For many years, the National Institute of Mental Health found it impossible to allocate stipends to students placed in correctional settings, as the definition of "mental health" for which the NIMH stipends were made available was apparently not sufficiently inclusive to incorporate agencies in correctional settings. Recently, the concept of mental health has been expanded, and correctional agencies which meet certain standards can now be certified as placements eligible for NIMH stipends for graduate students. The great state universities are keenly interested in developing research, enlarging training opportunities, and developing field work services for persons who show a desire to train for careers in corrections. The challenge to those of us in corrections is to use imagination and leadership to raise standards and develop opportunities which can meet the accreditation standards of the various university graduate programs for field placements. Although Oklahoma was not included in the survey of the Western Interstate Commission for Higher Education, funds have been made available through the joint efforts of the Federal Bureau of Prisons and the University of Oklahoma for a full-time field instructor to train graduate students from the university assigned to the El Reno Reformatory. An able former federal probation officer from Wisconsin has been appointed by the University of Oklahoma to direct this program.

As the corrections project of the Council on Social Work Education has demonstrated, one of the most effective means for expanding graduate field work opportunities comes about through the appointment of a professor from the correctional field to the staff of a school of social work. An interesting example of this development is the remarkable growth of field work opportunities which have taken place in connection with the program of the school of social work at the University of Washington in Seattle. Some eight or ten years ago, a professor who had been a former probation officer was appointed to the casework staff. Afterwards, graduate field work placements in the correctional field were developed in the Seattle juvenile court, state prison, reformatory, a boys' school, and at the federal prison on McNeil Island. When leadership is provided either by a school of social work or by correctional agency administrators, universities respond to the leadership.

Recent developments in California are also noteworthy. The associate superintendent of the Reception-Guidance Center, Vacaville, California, reports that prior to 1958, the Center trained only one graduate student from the School of Social Work at the University of California, Berkeley, but in 1958, "We were able to negotiate a grant from the National Institute of Mental Health which is handled through the University of California and provides for the salary of a full-time field work supervisor at this institution and stipends of $1,000 a semester for each of the six to seven second-year graduate students in psychiatric social work who are now regularly assigned."

The assistant superintendent goes on to indicate that other training programs have been developed in connection with departments of sociology or social sciences from a number of other California colleges. These include, for example, six students in clinical psychology. He goes on to make the following eloquent comment:

"While the primary objective of the extensive student training program that is carried on here is to contribute to the training of practitioners and scholars who will be entering the various fields noted above, there is a secondary gain for the institutions and the department in that many of the students become interested in corrections and in correctional psychiatry and obtain positions in the institutions of the department after they graduate. No exact figures are available of the number of staff in the department who originally started as students, but a very large number of the professional staff were introduced to the field of corrections in this way. Under normal circumstances we generally recruit one person for every five or six that we train. It is my feeling, however, that it is no less important, and perhaps even more important, that we provide training for people who are going into affiliated fields where they are in a position as practitioners, college professors and in other capacities, to influence young people to enter the field of corrections."[11]

Other field work placements are available at the California Correctional Institution, Chino, where a well-organized program for "Correctional Casework Trainees" is in operation. The prison at San Quentin also reports that it has a civil service classification of "Correctional Casework Trainee," which apparently is a combination work-training program.

Other states reporting field work opportunities are Missouri, Iowa, New Jersey, New York, Illinois, and Wisconsin, to mention but a few. The Director of Corrections in Iowa reports that field work training in connection with the Iowa School of Social Work is now available at the Men's Reformatory and at the Boys' Training School. He indicates that they hope to broaden the field soon, "As we now have qualified supervision at our prison at Fort Madison and in our juvenile parole services."[12]

In New Jersey, the Bordentown Reformatory operates two programs in connection with the Rutgers University School of Social Work. One is an eight-week summer work program, and the other is a paid ten-month internship for graduate students. Internships in clinical psychology are also available at Bordentown.[13]

Perhaps the most comprehensive program of field training is in Wisconsin, where under the early leadership of our late friend and colleague, John Tramburg, and Russell Oswald, and more recently under the outstanding leadership of Sanger Powers, the entire state correctional program has remarkably exploited the resources of the University of Wisconsin. The Wisconsin program is in some ways unique since

[11] *Correctional Research, op. cit.,* p. 32.
[12] *Ibid,* p. 32.
[13] *Ibid,* p. 34.

it is geared not only to the recruitment of personnel who have completed field training, usually in connection with the school of social work, but also is committed to a strong staff development and work-study program. This program is characteristic not only of the Division of Corrections, but of the entire Department of Public Welfare. Under Department of Public Welfare policy, personnel employed as social workers in any of the four major divisions of which the Division of Corrections is one must have undergraduate degrees with majors in social science and be prepared to enroll in one of the four training programs sponsored and jointly administered by the Department of Public Welfare, Division of Corrections, and the graduate schools of social work in Wisconsin. These programs are: (1) *In-service training,* wherein the student enrolls in the University of Wisconsin for extension division courses in social work, and has intensive field work supervision for a period of at least one year. At that point, such students are encouraged to enroll in one of the programs leading to a master's degree in social work; (2) *pre-graduate training,* in which an employee commits himself to enroll in a graduate school within two years from the day of employment; (3) *work-study training,* in which an employee attends school at his own expense, but continues working in a correctional institution or agency adjacent to Madison or Milwaukee, thus earning part of his salary; and (4) *stipend training.* Under this program an employee who has shown competence may be granted an outright stipend, permitting him to enroll in any recognized school of social work in the United States to complete his professional training. Stipends range up to $350 per month, and students who apply for these stipends are expected to invest a year's employment with the Division of Corrections for each academic year of education.[14]

In response to a questionnaire from the Massachusetts Prison Association, Sanger Powers, Director of the Division of Corrections, wrote:

> "One of the major benefits of this new plan is a salary increase from $413 to $453 per month for persons with an undergraduate degree and no social welfare experience. This has resulted in a more competitive employment opportunity in relation to other professional groups; and because of this financial and educational plan we have been able to interest more than a sufficient number of people from our state colleges and universities to fill the vacant positions within the Division of Corrections. I might comment that the civil service examination for the Social Worker I position is open on a nation-wide basis.
>
> "Currently, we have 33 persons attending the school of social work on a full-time basis of which 14 will receive their M.S.W. in June 1963, and

---

[14] *Social Work in Wisconsin* (Wisconsin Department of Public Welfare, February, 1963).

> will be permanently employed by us. In addition, we have 23 people employed previously under our old program as pre-work study trainees of which 18 are expected to enter the school of social work on a full-time basis in September 1963. You may be interested to know that since our training program began in 1955, 79 people have gone through our training program receiving their M.S.W. degree (including the 14 graduating in June 1963) and as of this date, 68 are still permanently employed by the Division.
>
> "The Division has operated a graduate recruitment and training program designed to provide professionally trained staff for our probation and parole services as well as our institutional social service department."[15]

In Illinois, correctional field training placements are being used by all schools of social work. The University of Chicago has a full-time training instructor assigned to the Social Service Department of the Municipal Court, which serves the specialized city courts such as the Boys' Court, Court of Domestic Relations, and the Women's Court. Loyola University also assigns graduate students to the Municipal Court. For many years, particularly during the thirties and early forties, the Family Court of Cook County provided a resource for field training. Renewed interest in using this court has been shown, and Loyola University School of Social Work has established a student field training unit there.[16] Field placements are also available at the Municipal Court Psychiatric Institute and the Institute for Juvenile Research of the Department of Mental Health.

For more than twenty-five years, the Federal Probation Office of the United States District Court, Northern District of Illinois, has been an approved field work agency for the training of graduate students from one or more, and often all three, of the schools of social work in Chicago. This has been a program mutually beneficial to the universities and the court. During the past fifteen years, approximately half the probation officers employed first became known to the court as a result of having completed field training at the court. The University of Chicago has assigned an assistant professor full time to direct field training for a group of seven graduate students from that university. Graduate students from other universities are supervised by members of the probation office staff. During the past three or four years, the number of graduate students assigned to the Federal Probation Office has ranged from eight to fifteen during the academic year.

---

[15] *Correctional Research, op. cit.*, p. 42.

[16] In 1963, under auspices of the Citizen's Committee on the Family Court, the National Council on Crime and Delinquency completed its survey and report on the Cook County Family Court and noted the potential value of this court as a field work training resource.

My experience with this program convinces me that there is no better way to train personnel for a career in corrections than through the joint undertaking of an academic program integrated with the practicum of field work. Not only does the field work provide the student an opportunity to test and put into practice methods and concepts he has learned or is learning at the university, but it also affords both the agency and the university an invaluable two-way line of communication. There are, of course, administrative matters which have to be carefully worked out between the agency and the university, but where there are good will and a strong conviction, by both the agency administrator and the school, of the validity of this kind of education, these problems can readily be solved. It has also been my experience that once a university discovers the wealth of resources and superb learning opportunities available in a correctional agency operated on a sound professional level, there is much more interest in expanding and further exploring the use of such resources. The field work program has grown in the last ten years from the time when only one or two students were assigned each year to the present, when as many as fifteen graduate students are assigned in an academic year in this department. There are some additional values inherent in this kind of relationship which, although not directly related to the issue of expanding field work resources, have some bearing on the topic.

In the first place, more and more case material is borrowed from the probation department and incorporated into generic casework courses. Many of us believe that corrections will continue to be an interdisciplinary operation recruiting from a variety of disciplines and do not advocate the development of a specialized, independent educational specialty. At the same time, we are convinced that if the academic program of graduate schools of social work is to equip persons for competence in the field of corrections, social work training must incorporate the specialized techniques of corrections and all of the concepts related to the use of authority and the legal aspects of correctional work. One of the best methods to adapt social work training to our needs is to incorporate case materials and conceptual systems of thought into social work education. During the past decade, social work with so-called "hard-to-reach clients," youth club work with street gangs or street corner groups, and the so-called "aggressive casework" techniques have begun to alter many traditional social work notions.

Field placements in group work agencies, particularly in some of the settlements working in high delinquency areas and in the delinquency prevention programs of the street club workers, have high potential. School social work programs are also often identified closely with court services and may afford sound field work opportunities.

Growing interest in corrections is further reflected in the fact that two years ago, twenty-five graduate students from the University of Chicago completed specialized research projects in the probation department related to an assessment of aspects of social diagnosis, treatment, and control techniques in probation. This year, about eighteen graduate students are undertaking a research project on factors in the selection of persons for probation and parole.

In 1962, largely as an outgrowth of the renewed interest of schools of social work in corrections, a professor at the School of Social Service Administration, University of Chicago, in cooperation with the probation office, applied for and received a $374,000 research grant from the National Institute of Mental Health to conduct an intensive research project on factors related to the motivation, capacity, and opportunities of probationers to utilize the services of the probation office. This is a combination research-demonstration project to be conducted over a five-year period by a sizeable staff of probation officers and research personnel. This is an illustration of how one probation office can provide many opportunities not only for field training, but also for research and exploration of the many problems correctional personnel confront.

Two other schools of social work have indicated that, if and when funds are available, they would like to establish field work units under full-time supervisors employed by the university or under joint appropriations of the university and the probation department to expand graduate field placements. Persons involved in research and training know that these programs take a tremendous expenditure of time and effort, but they are essential if our responsibilities in recruitment and education are to be fulfilled.

The history of medical education reveals that the professionalization of medicine and the giant advances in medical education have come largely through the development of superior teaching hospitals. We in corrections have the same obligation to make available the resources of our institutions and agencies for field training, internships, work-study programs, and research, particularly those agencies which are adjacent to great universities.

Other Field Training Programs

In addition to graduate schools of social work, there are a number of other excellent programs throughout the United States which provide field training for students interested in correctional careers. Among these are such programs as those at Florida State University, San José State College, the University of Notre Dame, and Southern Illinois University at Carbondale. Programs at these universities, usually affiliated with departments of criminology or sociology, have arranged for graduate students to receive field training at state and local institutions and services.

One of the most interesting developments is the Center for the Study of Crime, Delinquency, and Corrections at Southern Illinois University in Carbondale. Under the program of this Center, which offers an interesting interdepartmental undergraduate and graduate program, field training opportunities are being developed both at state and federal institutions. Indeed, one reason for locating the Center at Southern Illinois University was because the Federal Bureau of Prisons was planning, and has just now opened, a new major prison a few miles from Carbondale. The university faculty and administrators in the Bureau of Prisons hope that this new prison will become a real laboratory and, in a sense, a teaching institution for preparing personnel for correctional careers. This kind of joint planning between administrators and universities can assure an expansion of field training and eventually lead to correctional teaching centers comparable to the great teaching hospitals and clinics in the medical profession.

Among the most significant developments in this field are the many field training programs and internships sponsored by the Federal Bureau of Prisons. Under the direction of James V. Bennett, Director of the Federal Bureau of Prisons, a sound program of internship training for undergraduate and graduate students has existed for many years. Six of the federal institutions now provide approved field work training opportunities for schools of social work. Under the aggressive leadership of the Bureau of Prisons, this trend will in all likelihood continue, and as funds are available, additional academic personnel will be assigned to conduct similar field training units.

I believe that a new field training project jointly sponsored by the Kent School of Social Work, Louisville, Kentucky, and the Bureau of Prisons Correctional Institution at Ashland, Kentucky, has just been approved.

President's Committee on Juvenile Delinquency and Youth Crime

Specialized Training Projects

A second general area in which field training is being developed is related to the recently developed broad-gauged program of grants to various agencies and institutions for field training and research experiments. Generally, these grants have been allocated for three purposes: (1) training centers; (2) curriculum development; and (3) workshops, institutes, and seminars. Let us examine briefly the grants approved for training centers and for workshops and student seminars.

Training Centers

Many grants for training centers are given with the objectives of examining community conditions, collating information about academic and community resources, examining agency policies, identifying gaps in services, and the like. Almost all of them also contain a charge to design and conduct training programs. These grants have been made to such institutions as Southern Illinois University, the Institute of Government, University of North Carolina, University of Washington, Training Center for Youth Development in Corrections, Wayne State University, Delinquency Control Center, University of Utah, Western Reserve University, Law-Medicine Research Institute, Boston University.

Published information about these various programs is limited. However, a review of the grants makes crystal-clear the constant emphasis on the need to explore and to develop more field training opportunities. Whatever the outcome of these programs, the training center grants will unquestionably stimulate and develop greater interest in and awareness of training needs in corrections.

Workshops and Seminars

There are about twenty-five or more other grants of specific interest given to a variety of institutions, agencies, and services for special workshops, institutes, and seminars. These grants also emphasize the provision of field observation internships and field work assignments. They are made to a large number of agencies in education, welfare, and corrections. Their areas of focus include delinquency prevention, police crime prevention programs, school social work, settlement services, community organization, and many others.[17] Out of these research and demonstration programs will come additional guidelines toward ways and means of expanding opportunities in field training in the whole field of corrections.

Internships and Pre-Professional Field Training Opportunities

The demands for personnel in the hundreds of local, state, and federal courts, correctional agencies, and institutions are so great that we cannot expect to recruit most of the necessary personnel from the graduate school programs which offer comprehensive professional field work training. The graduate school programs must provide us with much of our leadership and administrative personnel. However, we will still be faced with the practical, everyday task of filling scores and scores of jobs with persons whom we hope have at least completed college. Ob-

---

[17] Training Grants, President's Committee on Juvenile Delinquency and Youth Crime, *op. cit.*

viously, these potential employees should be encouraged to seek field training as interns or on work-study and observation assignments whenever possible. In its survey, the Massachusetts Prison Association found that approximately thirty-five correctional institutions in nineteen states currently provide internship opportunities for students. Internships, or what are termed "student assistantships," are also available in twelve of the federal penal and correctional institutions. Internships in federal institutions are of two types—those available in the summer to students who have completed at least three years of undergraduate work, and internships up to twenty-six weeks for undergraduates who are available during the school year. These internships are available in the institutional departments of classification and parole, education, medical and psychological services, and recreation. Compensation for these internships averages $100 per month.

The Bureau of Prisons is currently working on plans to provide training programs, in cooperation with the United States Public Health Service, for clinical psychologists and psychiatrists. The United States Public Health Service Hospital for narcotic addicts at Lexington, and the Medical Center for Federal Prisoners at Springfield, Mo., offer internships for a limited number of college students and psychiatric residences and internships for clinical psychologists. In Connecticut, the District of Columbia, Florida, Illinois, Indiana, Iowa, Massachusetts, Michigan, Minnesota, Missouri, New Jersey, North Carolina, North Dakota, Ohio, Oregon, Pennsylvania, Texas, Utah, and Washington there are a variety of internships and work-study programs. These programs range all the way from observation trips, which encompass no more than a day in an institution, to the intensive kind of paid internships provided in institutions in such states as California, Illinois, Michigan, Iowa, and Wisconsin, and those of the Federal Bureau of Prisons.

The Western Interstate Commission for Higher Education received over 1,300 returns on a comprehensive questionnaire related to the broad scope of its survey of training and recruitment needs. One of the questions submitted to each of the agencies was, "In what way would you suggest enrichment of educational programs for better preparation of students for fields of work with juvenile offenders?" The report of the findings reveals that "The most frequent suggestion, strongly worded by many, is the need for the development of some means of actual internship or field placement for the students in the colleges and universities who plan to enter this work."[18]

Some institutions and services in the states studied had neither seen the need for an internship program nor had they been approached by

---

[18] Western Interstate Commission for Higher Education report, *op. cit.,* p. 9.

universities to develop such resources. There is a general indication, however, that most states are looking for guidance in developing internships and other field training opportunities, and that the time is propitious for a concerted effort to develop leadership at a national level in the standardization, evaluation, and further exploitation of all possible resources for field training.

There is a need not only to expand field training opportunities but also to promote the interest of college students in corrections as a possible career. Today, as never before, we must compete with business and industry and the more glamorous professions of medicine, law, nursing, and education for the bright college students. Among the techniques for acquainting college students with correctional opportunities are the various college-sponsored "career" conferences. Are we participating in these as we should?

In addition to these efforts, the National Association of Social Workers, together with the Council on Social Work Education, has sponsored a program on "Careers in Social Work." The purpose of this program is to give college students—usually those who have completed their junior year—an opportunity to spend eight weeks between their junior and senior years in a social agency, serving as participants and observers in a variety of community social agency settings. In Chicago, the Welfare Council has accepted responsibility for administering this program, which has grown from the placement of three students in 1957 to 123 in forty-nine agencies in 1963. Last year, more than five hundred promising students from colleges and universities of the Middle West applied to the Welfare Council of Metropolitan Chicago for placements under this "careers" program.[19]

Each year, for the past three or four years, we have four of these young people spend eight weeks in our agency under a very intensive program of observation, and they perform some of the rudimentary duties of a probation-parole officer. I have been much impressed with their caliber and enthusiasm.

We in corrections must participate to a much greater degree in such career programs, and, where there are none, organize our own efforts to capture the imagination and interest of many more young college men and women. There must also be, of course, renewed efforts to raise the level of career opportunities, in salaries and tenure, to attract and retain personnel. The section of the report of the Western Interstate Commission for Higher Education dealing with the turnover in positions of

---

[19] Wm. H. Darrow, "Community Responsibility for Recruitment to Social Work Careers," p. 5. Unpublished paper read at Midwest Workshop on Social Work Careers Program, St. Louis, Mo., October, 1963.

persons employed in juvenile services reveals that more than twenty percent left in less than two years and more than fifty percent left in three years. In its section on "special problem areas," the report comments, "When a very close look is taken at the political involvement in this field, the findings reflect some matters of concern. Correctional institutions are political footballs in some states and with the changing state administration the institutional administration also changes. Many courts handling juvenile matters have elected judiciary who in turn select their court staff, detention staff, and probation staff. When these changes occur so do the professional positions. A large number of these positions do not have tenure and stimulate little desire on the part of personnel to seek further training."[20]

Conclusions and Recommendations

The issue confronting corrections is the need to expand field work training opportunities. Progress has been made on a variety of fronts. We have reached a point where we must consolidate these gains and reach some general agreement on the direction we are to go during the next decade. The optimum professional education of persons embarking upon careers of individual or group treatment, guidance, and counseling of offenders is the joint responsibility of correctional agencies and academic institutions. Field training of the highest order is a basic requisite for adequate professional performance. The problem becomes one of determining where we shall look for professional education, and how we can bring about the cooperative relationship which must exist between agency and university if the training is to meet mutual standards demanded of practice and required of education.

Although treatment and counseling methods applied to corrections will continue to reflect an interdisciplinary approach, realities dictate that we exploit to the fullest those educational resources which have developed the most comprehensive and standardized programs in field training. Thus, from the standpoint of their availability and long tradition of field instruction, is it not evident that we must continue to join forces with schools of social work in order to expand the availability of field resources, particularly through the utilization of our own correctional services?

In addition to doing this, we must develop guidelines and sound standards for the development of other field work opportunities in recognized universities. Finally, we must urge schools of social work, graduate departments of criminology, law schools, and other university fa-

---

[20] Western Interstate Commission for Higher Education report, *op. cit.,* p. 53.

cilities to work with us in further evaluating, standardizing, and expanding undergraduate programs to attract students toward service in the field of corrections. Following are some specific recommendations:

1. Through the joint auspices of the National Council on Crime and Delinquency, the Council on Social Work Education, the American Correctional Association, and other leadership organizations, an objective statement should be formulated outlining:
   a. the standards required of schools of social work and other graduate programs for the development of field work placements;
   b. the expectations of correctional agencies concerning the content of training and skills to be imparted to personnel referred for such placements.
2. Establish a commission or other form of joint interdisciplinary body to collaborate with schools of social work and various correctional standard-setting bodies in the field on long-range plans for field training.
3. Survey the entire field of corrections in an effort to determine the number of agencies whose standards are sufficiently acceptable to meet the requirements for field placements.
4. Develop an aggressive and comprehensive fund-raising program to provide instructional stipends for field work instructors, scholarships, and fellowships for college graduates who wish to take advanced professional training. In this regard, further exploration of the availability of substantial funds from the National Institute of Mental Health, foundations, and from state, federal, or county public funds is urgently recommended. An intensive study of the well developed Wisconsin program, which has now been in operation for ten years, might be in order.
5. Substantially raise the salary level of field instructors. Top administrative and supervisory salaries in the correctional field should be reviewed as possible guides to such salary adjustments.
   Although field instruction is primarily an educational technique, it does not differ markedly from the role of an agency supervisor. Such positions should receive equal or better compensation.
6. Develop and implement a strong commitment to the support of professional education in field training. Commitment in this sense means far more than lip service or permissiveness to the establishment and operation of field work opportunities. The administrators must demonstrate their conviction about the value of such training by:
   a. developing strong communication lines between the agency and the university;
   b. offering to provide adequate space, equipment, supplies, and agency support to field work units;
   c. seeking budgetary funds for the employment of full-time field work instructors. We can no longer rely on universities to provide field instructors for the majority of these placements. Practice demands competent practitioners, and we must go to the

universities and demonstrate that we are willing to invest money in terms of our own staff talents in this kind of training.

7. Sponsor joint agency administrator faculty conferences on field work training. If we are to acquaint universities with our needs, we must take the initiative and sponsor joint conferences not only with university faculties but with agency administrators of related health and welfare services in the community as well.
   At this time in our development, welfare departments, family agencies, medical services, psychiatric clinics, vocational programs, group work agencies, and many others are placing their demands squarely before the schools of social work. We in corrections have lagged far behind in presenting our needs.
8. Provide for research and evaluation of various approaches to field work training.
9. Endow the position of field instructor with the prestige and acceptance which it merits. Improving the salaries of field work instructors is, of course, one approach to this matter. However, it is even more important that the host agency of the field work unit integrate the field work program into the operation of the agency.
   All too often, field work units are set apart and considered sort of an appendage to the regular program. This tends to build a gulf between the line staff and the field work student and may result in defining the role of the field work instructor as less important than that of the agency supervisor or administrator. Actually, we should be moving toward giving special recognition to field work instructors, selecting only the best of our supervisors and regarding this position in the same light as the medical clinician is considered in medical education.
10. Examine and evaluate the whole field of group work, particularly noting the rapidly expanding delinquency prevention efforts of street club workers in high delinquency neighborhoods as potential areas for field training.
11. Seek imaginative ways and means to evaluate and greatly expand undergraduate internships and pre-professional field observation programs. Practical necessity dictates the recruiting of a majority of correctional personnel charged with counseling and casework responsibilities from among the ranks of those with only an A.B. degree. Perhaps an interdisciplinary commission on undergraduate educational programs should be established.
12. Support and expand the work of such groups as the Western Interstate Commission for Higher Education, the National Council on Crime and Delinquency, the Council on Social Work Education, and the President's Committee on additional specific research focused on the relative values of field training in relation to future practice. It is evident from the comments of the Commission's report, the collation of the Massachusetts Prison Association, and the observations of Mr. Sidney Berengarten that practitioners, in looking back on their training periods, generally rate field training as the most valuable of all.

In a very interesting paper on field training in professional education, Sidney Berengarten eloquently presented the value students place upon the practicum of clinic or field training. He wrote, "My colleagues in the medical school tell me that the mentor who exercises the most profound influence on the medical student's emerging professional identity is the clinical professor or preceptor, and I have no question whatsoever that in social work education it is the field work instructor, of all mentors, who is closest to the student in action, in feeling, in thinking, and in behavior. . . . " Mr. Berengarten continued, "A major finding of our Curriculum Study is the fact that both the students and alumni were in complete agreement about the greater importance to them of the field training experience than any other aspect of their professional education. Questionnaires administered to students in Social Work Seminar sections, and the discussion held with them during the fourth semester, confirmed the impression that field instruction was regarded as the highlight of their school experience. The response to the questionnaire showed that, first, in the technical content areas of social study, diagnosis, and treatment formulation, the students perceived field work primarily, or a combination of class and field, as the sources of learning; second, professional self-awareness was viewed overwhelmingly as the primary contribution of field work; third, the field was said to contribute most to understanding of agency structure and organization."[21]

Mr. Berengarten pointed out the importance of a two-way traffic along the bridge field instruction provides between practice and classroom theory. How can field work instructors be kept abreast of the new knowledge constantly being incorporated in the academic social work curriculum? How can academicians be kept abreast of new developments in the field of practice? Obviously, the most effective method is to keep communication lines open between agency administrator and university faculties. In Chicago, a joint conference of administrators of all agencies involved in field work training and the deans, directors, and research personnel of the three schools of social work was held to discuss the very problem of expanding and strengthening the field work services. This was a landmark meeting, and many issues concerning the current relationships of agencies to universities were raised and clarified. Out of this meeting came a much greater appreciation by the agency executives of the problems which universities face in recruiting

---

[21] Sidney Berengarten, "The Concept of the Training Center in Social Work Education." Unpublished paper presented at workshop on the concept of a training center, Columbia University School of Social Work, New York, May 5, 1961.

and assigning academic staff, arranging schedules to meet students' programs, establishing policy-making and administrative conferences between university faculty personnel and agency administrators on mutual problems growing out of field work instruction, and in the many practical problems related to stipends, scholarships, and the availability of funds to finance graduate education.

It may be said that this paper has approached the issue of field work education in much too conventional a manner. This is perhaps true, but novel solutions are not easily found and frequently prove to be novel in name only. However, whatever we do we must approach this matter with a determination to experiment, demonstrate, and apply our most creative imagination to the development of new ways in correctional education.

Remarks

by H. G. Moeller

From a humble beginning in 1958, with one student from the University of Washington School of Social Work at the United States Penitentiary at McNeil Island, Washington, the field work program for social work students in Bureau of Prisons institutions has continued to grow until today, when we have field work placements in six of the thirty-two institutions and are planning such programs in four more. The six placements include a unit of students at the El Reno Reformatory for which the University of Oklahoma school received a grant from the National Institute of Mental Health. One might logically ask why we were so late in developing field work placements when other federal agencies, such as the Veterans Administration, have long had a major role in training social workers. For many years, we have had numerous student interns from universities offering specialties in corrections or criminology in their sociology departments, and student interns from schools offering degrees in corrections or correctional administration on both undergraduate and graduate levels.

I suspect that if we were to identify the reasons for this apparent delay, they would include many of the factors which Eileen Younghusband identified as responsible for the small number of field placements in corrections in this country as a whole. In this connection, it is significant that our 1958 venture at McNeil Island resulted primarily from the interest and efforts of Professor David Gronewold of the University of Washington School of Social Work, who was for several years a member of Mr. Meeker's staff in Chicago and who has not only a deep and abiding interest in corrections but also some familiarity with corrections on the federal level because of his experience in federal probation. His interest, understanding, and influence unquestionably helped to bridge the gap between the institution and the school. Currently, Dr. Prigmore seems to be fulfilling this role quite admirably on the national level.

In response to the question of why we have been concerned with developing field work placements in our institutions, one of the primary reasons is that the development of ties with schools of social work is one of the best avenues for recruitment of trained social workers. Another benefit is the upgrading of present personnel through the utilization of faculty members of the schools in in-service training, a service often provided field work agencies. It also gives us an opportunity to become better acquainted in the professional community, improve relationships with other agencies, both correctional and non-correctional, gain knowledge of their programs and the resources their programs offer, and perhaps collaborate with them in staff training as well as other programs. In short, it has helped to reduce the isolation of our institutions from other agencies and community services with whom they should be working very closely. This self-isolation has historically been a major problem in corrections.

Collective Responsibilities

Along with these and other benefits which accrue from relationships with schools of social work go some responsibilities. Ordinarily, the institution must provide a staff member as a faculty field work instructor. To qualify for such an assignment, he must have a master's degree from an accredited school of social work and generally must have at least two years of post-master's experience and be approved by the school's field work committee as a field work instructor. Most schools require that he devote approximately four hours per week to each student. This includes time spent in reviewing case records, in supervisory conferences with the student, in selecting new cases, in attending meetings at the school, and the like. Students usually spend two or two and one-half days each week at the institution unless the placement is a block plan arrangement, in which case he or she spends twelve to twenty consecutive weeks at the institution. This is a greater investment of staff time than statistics indicate because usually only one or two members of the staff of any one institution qualify as field work instructors, and those who qualify are almost without exception the better trained individuals who are key people and to whom we look for above-average, if not outstanding, performance on operational assignments. The additional responsibility of supervising students reduces their responsibilities in other areas, and this makes it even more difficult for the administrator, particularly since he is already faced with the problem of an overburdened staff. Some schools provide one of their faculty members as field work instructor. This is the case with the grant-financed unit at El Reno, and at McNeil Island, where we had one group student assigned last year.

Both the school and the student also have responsibilities. The school should be expected to assign students with sufficient capacity and maturity and the motivation to work with offenders in a correctional institution. Schools of social work, of course, screen applicants carefully prior to admission. We cannot expect, however, that the students assigned to field work placements in a correctional institution will necessarily have correctional work as a goal, because the majority of schools have a generic curriculum, and the primary considerations in assigning a student to a particular setting are his educational needs and "readiness" for the demands of a particular field work experience. Some might consider this a disadvantage to a particular agency, but the trained recruit with broad experience in several settings is as valuable as, if not more valuable than, a person with experience primarily in one setting. In the long run, it is also helpful to the entire correctional field and to the whole area of social welfare to have persons who have some experience in and understanding of the field of corrections working in other agencies. While we do not require a work commitment from field work students, we ask that the students to whom we give financial aid come to us free of other commitments and with at least an open mind to the possibility of developing a career interest in corrections.

Field work students should not be looked upon as "extra help." They are at the institution as part of their education, in which they are investing considerable time and money. In assuming responsibility for field work training, we must bear in mind that our primary responsibility is to work with the school to provide the student with a social work education and not to train "correctional technicians." Although it is often tempting, especially in view of our already overburdened staff, to utilize their services on a production basis, doing this can only have unfortunate and distasteful results for all concerned—the student is neither staff member nor student, and our agreement with both the school and the student may be abrogated. It is important that an institution or agency does not assume responsibilities for field work unless it is fully prepared to meet these responsibilities.

In accepting a field work placement, the student accepts responsibility for following and supporting established policies and procedures, although he should still feel free to discuss his questions about them with his supervisor. He is responsible for meeting deadlines and conducting himself in such a manner which reflects credit on him, the school, and the institution. He must, of course, maintain a good academic standing.

In considering an agency for field work training, schools are guided by standards developed by the Council on Social Work Education which include: (1) evidence of good practice in casework by qualified staff members; (2) evidence of sound interdisciplinary relationships (other disciplines with which the student should have the opportunity to work include psychiatry, psychology, sociology, medicine, nursing, and other social or behavioral sciences); (3) involvement in research activities; (4) the attitude of the agency leadership toward training and the commitment of the agency to its responsibilities in this area.

While practically all of the student placements in our institutions are made for the training of caseworkers, we hope that it will soon be possible to offer field work training in social group work. We have done this when the school provides a faculty member as field work instructor.

Financial Aid to Students

Corrections has lagged far behind other fields in offering financial assistance to students and this, of course, is one of the major reasons for this meeting. There has been, however, some improvement in this area, both directly and indirectly, in recent years. While this improvement has been very slight in relation to the total needs, we can be encouraged by recognizing that there is at least a growing awareness of the need. It is ironic that this lag has existed, because the students to whom corrections admittedly looks to meet its major manpower needs in the future are primarily male students with family responsibilities who have the greatest need for assistance. Financial aid frees them from work obligations that might interfere with their educational program and frequently is the factor which keeps them in school. While schools of social work now have considerably more funds available from public and private sources which may be utilized to assist students who are interested in a career in corrections, the need for funds earmarked specifically for training people for corrections is obvious.

The financial aid which we provide students is parallel to that in the Veterans Administration program. It is limited to second-year students, who are paid $2.79 per hour spent on their field work assignment at the institution. If the student is interested and if the school permits, he may do work at the institution beyond the hours required by the school and be compensated for this extra time at the same hourly rate. Institutions able to offer financial aid are in a more competitive position for better qualified students, since professional promise is usually a primary consideration of schools in nominating recipients of financial assistance. Our program by no means offers the largest amount of assistance available and is limited by being tied to a specific agency; however, it is quite competitive with other correctional agency-sponsored programs. Field work assignments to our institutions are generally considered quite desirable by students. Students are usually enthusiastic about the assignments and regard them as a very satisfactory educational experience. The assignments are an excellent means of acquainting a large group of potential correctional workers with the rewards and satisfactions of correctional work. We have not as yet been able to recruit as many people as we had hoped to as the result of these programs, but one of the major reasons for this is a procedural one within our own organization which we must work out.

In addition to the training program for social work, criminology, and correctional administration students, we have in recent years initiated training programs for law students, psychologists, and psychiatrists, the latter two in cooperation with the United States Public Health Service and supervised by their personnel assigned to our institutions. A number of second- and third-year law students are now coming to us for a fourteen-week summer intern program. The majority of these students have been assigned to the central office; however, more recently, we have assigned a few to selected institutions and have also worked out a cooperative agreement with a few United States attorneys permitting the student to spend part of his time at one of our institutions and part with the United States attorney's office. The enthusiasm by law students and law schools for this program is reflected in the fact that there are about ten applications for each available summer internship position.

The impact of students from these disciplines has been a healthy and helpful one because of their questioning minds, their reluctance to take anything for granted, and their efforts to synthesize their experience with their classroom work. We avoided trying to develop the social work students into "correctional technicians," and the same can be said for students from other disciplines. With law students, for example, we not only provide them with some experience in criminal law but also help them develop a greater awareness of both legal and social issues in corrections and related fields.

Staffs of the various institutions have come to accept student programs as a part of the mission of their institutions. Administrators now more appreciate the fact that an individual with a professional degree is not a journeyman but an apprentice, and that it is not only advantageous to but a responsibility of their institutions to provide the climate and resources which will enable the professional to continue to consolidate and sharpen his skills.

The experience with social work students has provided additional impetus to our efforts to make a more realistic and selective division of labor for social workers—particularly in the use of diagnostic services and services which are not only non-social work tasks but which do not necessarily require professional training. There are at present two programs concentrating on these problems. One is intake screening of adult offenders, which has as it primary purpose the early identification of specific diagnostic services required for an individual upon his arrival at the institution instead of running all individuals through the same "diagnostic mill." The second is the assignment of correctional officers as "case aides," to perform tasks which do not require professional training but which heretofore were assigned to social workers. This permits the time and skills of the professional to be more appropriately applied. One of the very important by-products of this arrangement has been the training this provides correctional officers. This has proven so valuable that as funds become available to expand this program to all institutions, such an assignment may well become a prerequisite for promotion of correctional officers to supervisory positions. The latter point reflects the enthusiasm our custodial people have for this program.

The Role of National Professional Organizations in Resolving Manpower and Training Problems in Corrections

by JOSEPH P. ANDERSON

IT IS EXPECTED that one of the results of the Arden House Conference will be the creation of ongoing vehicles for the resolution of manpower and training problems in corrections. There is already an impressive number of organizations interested in some aspects of corrections. The need for new or additional machinery will be seen more clearly if each existing organization would recognize the changes having an impact on society and the major trends influencing the development of community services. The need for new approaches to the problem of manpower and training will be more apparent if each organization (1) would appraise its present efforts in this area, (2) see how these activities can be improved, and (3) see how its contribution can be enhanced through coordinated and cooperative action with other organizations.

One outstanding development of present-day American society is the growing sense of interdependence among individuals and groups. As new advances in transportation and communication continue to shrink the distances between various parts of the country, the realization that every individual is increasingly affected by forces beyond his personal control grows greater. This has led to development of new methods for adapting ourselves to the situation. Increasing attention is being given to common efforts which will facilitate the adjustment of people to each other, to other groups, and to the changing larger society. There is also a thoughtful concern about people, not only as units in a particular ethnic group or an industrial organization or as members of a particular community, but also simply as human beings.

This feeling of interdependence has led to a greater acceptance of certain concepts of significance to all persons providing community services. The first concept is related to the role of government in helping to meet the health, education, and welfare needs of people. The second concept is that society as a whole cannot be healthy if any significant proportion of the population is not healthy, and that a democratic society cannot maintain itself and preserve the freedom of its people if any large proportion of the population is economically, socially, or politically deprived. The third concept is related to the maintenance of a minimum standard of living for everyone. The fourth concept is based on the conviction that health, education, and social services should be made available to whoever needs them.

The most important changes having an impact on society can be grouped under the following headings: population growth, mobility, technological advance, civil rights, and community services.

Population Growth

The rate of population growth of the United States is one of the fastest in the world. It is estimated that there will be an increase of about 30,000,000 by the end of 1970, bringing the total population up to more than 210,000,000. The tremendous population growth has been accompanied by a dramatic increase in the high risk-vulnerable groups. These include the very young, the very old, the handicapped, the emotionally and physically ill, and the unemployed.

Mobility

Another development which has important social, economic, and political implications is the gradual but irresistible mobility of people. There is movement from the farm to the city, from the city to the suburb, and from one section of the country to another. A move into a new and strange community can have an effect on every member of the family. Young children of uprooted families have their education interrupted, their personal security undermined, their family relationships upset, and their future careers jeopardized. Individuals and families face problems of social and emotional adjustment which challenge and frequently overwhelm their strengths, resulting in families breaking up, children developing serious emotional problems, and some youth becoming seriously delinquent.

Technological Advance

Another important characteristic of our growing economy is the rapid pace of technological change. The impact of automation, with its new ideas of substituting mechanical means for human hands and the human brain, is felt in every field of endeavor. We are in a second industrial revolution, the results of which will be a shorter workday, a shorter workweek, and more leisure time for all workers and their families.

More married women, even mothers of young children, will be employed. The social implications of these developments are self-evident.

Civil Rights

Civil rights—the effort to eliminate discrimination and segregation—picked up considerable momentum during the last decade. There still exists, however, deep-rooted prejudice and fear by many individuals who do not wish to give minority group members their constitutionally guaranteed right of equality. Much permanent and meaningful progress has been made by court decisions, Presidential orders, state and municipal laws, and by the simple recognition by an increasing number of citizens that discrimination and segregation are morally wrong. But the social conflict which the struggle for equality engenders will leave scars on many communities.

Community Services

There have been significant developments which have had an impact on community services. One outstanding development which has had an impact on social services has been the growing emphasis on prevention of crime and a positive approach to rehabilitation. There have been several experiments and demonstrations which have shown the validity of the principle of prevention and rehabilitation. Another important development has been the increased understanding and recognition of the value of social services and a greater acceptance of them as an integral part of community life. There is acceptance of the fact that as our society increases in complexity, much of that complexity can be expressed in terms of changing human relations. Social services have demonstrated that they can adapt to these changes, to provide the help necessary to establish and maintain socially healthy individuals in socially healthy communities.

There have been significant trends which reflect these developments. The first is the tremendous expansion of the public social services. Responsibility for planning, organizing, administering, and financing many social welfare programs has been assumed by national, state, and local governmental agencies.

A second trend is that social services are now being offered in a large variety of new settings and under auspices other than those usually associated with social welfare.

The development of a constructive and mutually productive relationship with other disciplines is another significant trend. The "team approach" in clinics, correctional institutions, hospitals, schools, and the traditional social agencies is increasingly emphasized. This team approach makes possible a planned and coordinated program of service to an individual, a group, or a community.

A fourth trend is the growing spirit of self-evaluation and a willingness to assume responsibility for validating social work's body of knowledge and for testing the effectiveness of its methods through planned programs of disciplined research.

Another trend is the increasing interest in contributions of the social sciences to social work practice. Concepts developed by the social sciences are tested and utilized in an increasing number of social work programs.

The past decade has seen a steady movement away from an emphasis on agency auspices and functional groupings in planned community social welfare programs. Institutional loyalties are being tested against the goal of establishing and maintaining a flexible network of services to meet a community's changing needs.

The growing interest of the average citizen in community service programs is a trend of special significance. More attention is now being directed toward providing programs of interpretation designed to give the lay public an accurate and practical understanding of the objectives and programs of social welfare organizations and to enlist the participation of volunteers in program planning and operation.

Finally, the trend toward an acute shortage of qualified personnel to man the expanding community service program continues. It is because of this trend that this Conference on the Manpower and Training Problems in Corrections has been called. The magnitude and complexity of the manpower and training problem in corrections will require different kinds of action on a variety of fronts. This paper will focus on the role and contribution of national professional organizations.

An effective program of corrections requires the services of individuals in a number of professions. Currently, and for the foreseeable future, education, law, medicine, psychiatry, psychology, and social work will be represented in correctional agencies at various levels of authority and responsibility. The national organizations of professional practitioners have a special obligation and an opportunity to contribute to the resolution of the manpower and training problems in corrections.

The professional association is an organization of practitioners who judge one another as being professionally competent and who have banded together to perform certain functions which they cannot perform as individuals. Professional associations may vary in structure and organization, but they have common objectives and perform certain common functions.

The objectives of the National Association of Social Workers are:

To promote the quality and effectiveness of social work practice through services to the individual, the group, and the community;

To further the broad objective of improving conditions of life in our democratic society through utilization of the professional knowledge and skills of social work, and

To expand, through research, the knowledge necessary to define and attain these goals.

The functions of professional organizations can be grouped under two general headings:

1) The extension of services and improvement of the quality of practice.
2) The contribution of expert knowledge to the formulation of broad public policy.

A high standard of service depends on a number of factors, the most important of which are manpower and training. The national professional organization performs a variety of functions which can contribute to the solution of the manpower and training problems in corrections.

Manpower and training problems in corrections have their own distinctive flavor; however, in many ways they are comparable to the problems in mental health, public welfare, and other programs of community service. There have been studies in these areas and a testing of a variety of approaches. As a result, a number of elements have been identified which need to be in programs dealing with problems of manpower and training regardless of the field of practice.

These elements include:

1) A clear statement of agency purpose and function, and a description of the different kinds of services which are needed to carry out this function and those services which require fully professionally qualified personnel and those which can be provided by persons not having full professional training.
2) Sound organizational policies and procedures designed to achieve the purpose and function of the agency effectively and efficiently.
3) A consciously developed plan for dealing with manpower and training problems; responsibility for the implementation of the plan would be assigned to appropriate groups.
4) Enough funds to underwrite costs of manpower and training programs.
5) Employment conditions conducive to maintenance of high quality and quantity of production. Reasonable workloads and assignments which provide opportunity for growth will increase the efficiency and effectiveness of staff personnel.
6) An adequate salary schedule to provide necessary financial incentive for all personnel.
7) Analysis and classification of service demands. This will highlight manpower and training needs.
8) Deployment of staff to use available skills most effectively.

9) Planned, ongoing, comprehensive staff development programs. This should include: (a) preparation and use of training materials; (b) orientation programs for new employees; and (c) programs for current staff through institutes, workshops, and seminars.
10) Opportunities for all staff personnel to participate in local, state, and national conferences, institutes, and workshops as part of staff development programs.
11) Educational leave policies to enable staff members to complete their professional or technical training. Policies should make it financially feasible for employees to take educational leave.
12) Provision for promotion and upgrading within the agency on the basis of additional training and improved performance.
13) Research and experimentation to discover new and improved methods for utilization of personnel and for development of training programs.
14) Cooperation between fields of practice and educational institutions so that new knowledge gained from studies of practice can be incorporated in educational programs to improve professional preparation of each succeeding generation of practitioners.
15) Development of a constructive and mutually productive relationship with other disciplines. The need and responsibility for interprofessional cooperation springs from the fact that life is too complex to permit any one profession alone to meet the wide variety of demands requiring special competence.
16) Testing and utilization of concepts developed by the social sciences.
17) Planning and coordination of community services, with the goal of establishing and maintaining a flexible network of services to meet a community's changing needs.
18) A continuing program of recruitment, to acquaint high school and college students about career opportunities in a particular field of practice.
19) Interpretation and community education programs, emphasizing importance of qualified personnel to assure high standard of service.
20) Evaluation at regular intervals of efforts to deal with problems of manpower and training.

A conference of this kind provides an opportunity for an appraisal of these elements as they apply to a particular field of practice—corrections. It can identify those which have special meaning for corrections, identify additional elements, and suggest action priorities. It can also provide better understanding of programs of professional organizations designed to deal with manpower and training problems. In so doing, it can highlight areas which need special attention and suggest ways we can work more productively to achieve our common goals.

The National Association of Social Workers is a professional membership association established in 1955 by members of seven social work organizations. Its establishment was a significant step toward a unified profession.

NASW is an organization of individuals who have met certain criteria qualifying them for membership and for carrying out the purposes of the association. Its program consists of those services and activities which grow out of the experiences and needs of individual members in professional practice. Both the purpose and program are related to the nature of the fundamental responsibilities which are accepted by a professional organization.

The NASW has adopted the following purposes which it seeks to implement through its structure and program: 1) to improve administration of social work services, 2) to advance research and study in social work, 3) to improve social work practice, 4) to improve social work education, 5) to improve social conditions, 6) to improve salaries and working conditions, 7) to gain public understanding of social work, 8) to recruit for the profession, 9) to certify competence of social workers, and 10) to develop, promulgate, and enforce the Code of Ethics.

The NASW has a membership of 39,500 organized in 167 chapters in all 50 states. In states having two or more chapters, state councils or committees exist to coordinate chapter activities on state-wide issues.

Since it is an organization of individual members, ultimate responsibility for association affairs rests with the members, who act directly in two ways—by mail referendum and a biennial Delegate Assembly. Responsibility for the conduct of NASW affairs is vested in elected officers and a Board of Directors, who are assisted by an employed staff.

The program of the association is carried on by standing committees with specific assignments and three major divisions: The Division of Knowledge and Practice, Division of Professional Standards, and Division of Social Policy and Action. Within the Division of Knowledge and Practice, nine councils provide opportunities for individual members to participate in division activities. Seven councils are organized on fields of practice—corrections, community planning and development, family and children's services, group services, health and medical services, mental health and psychiatric services, and social work in the schools. The two remaining councils are on social work administration and social work research.

Corrections and family and children's services received scant attention during the early years of NASW operations. The existence and activities of other national voluntary organizations in these fields, the creative and sustained attention they gave to these practice areas, and the nature of the fields themselves may account for the fact that there was no demand to establish program units in the NASW.

These units were included in the revised NASW structure because of the conviction of the members that no matter how competent the work of other organizations is, the professional membership association has a unique responsibility to its members practicing in any field.

There are three program areas of special significance for the profession and the various fields of practice:

1) The NASW program of publications—which includes *Social Work,* a quarterly journal, *NASW News,* a news bulletin reporting on developments in the association and in the field, *Personnel Information,* a periodical containing position openings for which agencies are seeking applicants, brief articles and reports on personnel issues, the *NASW Washington Memorandum,* issued by the Washington office, which reports on legislative and administrative developments, and a pamphlet and book publications program.
2) The Washington office of NASW, staffed by a full-time person, represents or arranges for representation of the NASW in congressional hearings, maintains liaison with federal agencies, Congress, and other professional organizations, keeps the membership informed on current issues, and mobilizes support for particular measures in keeping with the association's *Goals of Public Social Policy.*
3) The Academy of Certified Social Workers, established in 1961, which identifies, for other professions, clients, and the general public, the NASW members who meet basic requirements of education and social work experience.

The NASW can contribute to the solution of manpower and training problems in corrections by its activities in five areas:

1) Study of developments in practice.
2) Development of professional literature.
3) Establishing and maintaining standards.
4) Recruitment and community education.
5) Social policy and action.

Study of Developments in Practice

Every profession has a continuing obligation to be alert to developments in practice which influence its scope and function. The professional membership association provides the best auspices for an ongoing, orderly review of the changes in clientele being served, new service demands, and available community resources. From such a study, new insights are developed, new techniques and skills are tested, and new knowledge is gained. Areas in which there is need for joint study with other professions can also be ascertained.

Of particular importance are the studies being conducted on the utilization of personnel in community service programs. The acknowledged crucial shortage of fully trained professional workers has prompted a series of studies of how best to utilize available manpower. Projects are now under way to determine which tasks should be assigned to a fully trained worker and which can be assigned to workers with less than full professional education. As a single, unified professional association, the NASW has an important advantage in conducting such studies.

Results of studies in one field of practice can be tested in other settings, and all fields of practice can benefit from them.

Studies of practice, particularly as they relate to utilization of staff, should be supplemented by research experimentation and demonstration projects. Such projects should include measurement of results, testing of factors which increase efficiency of agency operations, and cooperation with other professions.

Development of Professional Literature

There is need for a wide variety of material—descriptive writing on developments in practice, reports on new service demands and how they are being met, reports on research experimentation and demonstration, original and creative thinking, administrative reporting, and operational statistics, and contributions by members of related professions.

This professional literature will serve two purposes: 1) It will help the practitioner to discharge his professional function more effectively, and 2) it will serve as the basis for changes and modification of educational programs in training institutions. The national professional organization provides an excellent means for publication and wide dissemination of professional literature and an organized channel through which knowledge distilled from practice, and views on educational needs as demonstrated by practice, are transmitted to educational institutions.

Establishing and Maintaining Standards

The foremost obligation of a professional organization is to set standards and to see that they are understood, accepted, and applied. The NASW has formulated personnel standards—objective criteria for determining competence, standards for personnel practices, conditions of employment conducive to a high standard of service, and a Code of Ethics in professional practice.

Nationally, and through its chapters, the association has brought its standards to the attention of public and private agencies employing social workers, civil service agencies and merit systems, other professions, and the general public.

In recent years, the association inaugurated a program to improve salaries by recommending a minimum salary for beginning workers and appropriate ranges for experienced workers.

As part of the NASW program for improving personnel policies, the association provides a structure for considering complaints filed by social workers against employers who allegedly have violated personnel practices.

Recruitment and Community Education

An important step designed to extend and strengthen a recruitment program for social work, nationally and locally, was taken with the establishment of the National Commission for Social Work Careers. Sponsored by the NASW and the Council on Social Work Education, the commission has as its aims: 1) The recruitment of new persons to the social work field, 2) the encouragement of persons in social work jobs to take further professional training, and 3) the retention of trained personnel in the social work field.

The association also recognizes its responsibility for carrying on a program of interpretation and education which emphasizes the relationship between competent staff and a high standard of service.

Social Policy and Action

Social work is the profession which concerns itself with facilitating and strengthening basic social relationships among individuals, groups, and social institutions. For this reason, it has a social action responsibility which grows out of its social function and professional knowledge.

This social action responsibility is discharged in three ways. The first is by identifying new and emerging needs among individuals and groups. Most social workers, whatever their specialty or setting, act as agents of society in meeting needs or facilitating social adjustments of individuals. It is their job to make a complex social machinery meet the needs of persons: a) by providing the benefits of existing programs, policies, and knowledge, and b) by calling attention to the areas where society's machinery is not functioning effectively. This is especially important in a dynamic society, where shifting economic conditions, a high degree of population mobility, and rapid social change constantly create new needs for particular groups. The social worker, whatever his function or setting, is in a key position to spot these needs as they begin to emerge and to interpret their development to the society which he serves.

The second way in which social workers discharge their social action responsibility is to contribute their knowledge of social conditions, social constitutions, social needs, and social feasibility to the advancement of the standard of mutual obligation between individuals and their social organizations. They are necessarily concerned with all social conditions which affect the welfare of individuals, groups, and communities, and they accept an obligation to support the broad social programs which will eliminate the needs and ameliorate the problems with which they deal.

Thirdly, the social action function of social work in areas of social policy and program involves the application of specific knowledge, experience, and inventiveness to those problems which can be solved through social welfare programs. In the growing complexity of modern social organizations, both governmental and private, few policy makers can be expected to have the technical knowledge in all the fields of social responsibility with which they deal. The professional organization provides an excellent channel through which the technical knowledge and experience of its membership is made available to those who make social welfare policies in legislative, administrative, or community leadership capacities.

The National Association of Social Workers recognizes that many professional organizations and other groups share its concern about social progress and that social advances can be accelerated through cooperative efforts.

Such collaboration should be directed toward:

1) Providing opportunities for discussion of common problems and exchange of information about major changes in existing services or the development of new services.
2) The establishment of effective working relationships among all community service agencies to make possible a coordinated approach to community problems.
3) Sponsorship of activities designed to improve the quality of service.
4) Carrying forward a continuous process of sound community planning.
5) Creating greater public awareness of social problems, and developing public understanding of and support for services necessary to deal with these problems.

A great challenge confronting American democracy is the need to develop broad, enlightened, and productive participation in public affairs by all its citizens. The National Association of Social Workers helps its members to meet this challenge by providing opportunities for their participation in a social action program and by encouraging their own involvement as individual citizens in the affairs of their local community, state, and nation.

The Legal Profession's Responsibility in the Field of Corrections

by JUNIUS L. ALLISON

THE ADMINISTRATION of criminal justice, like ancient Gaul, is divided into three parts: The area of arrest and formal charge of the commission of a crime, the trial and possible appeals, and that broad field of what happens to the defendant after he is convicted. The first function has been romanticized in literature and song, from the classics to the "Ballad of Tom Dooley," and publicized by Sherlock Holmes, the FBI, and the Texas Rangers, to say nothing of the impossible feats of the modern "private eye." The trial has been dramatized even more widely, especially by radio and television. Unfortunately, the equally important third phase, that of corrections, has not been glamorized. Its significant role is unrecognized, its scope of service unevenly defined, and its great potentialities for rehabilitation unappreciated.

Among the potent forces which could be the most effective in giving luster and prominence to this noble service, the legal profession has probably been the least vocal and the most withdrawn from active participation in areas where its responsibilities are identifiable and extensive.[1]

Before I am accused of committing the legal profession to obligations far beyond the reasonable and pertinent functions of those trained in the law, or of creating a knight-errant, roving at will in pursuit of some system of unbounded benevolence, perhaps I should define some roles and limit some issues that I see are involved in the problem of manpower and training in corrections. For this purpose, I distinguish between the duties of law schools in regard to the scope of instruction

[1] The Report of the Joint Conference on Professional Responsibilities (established 1959 by the American Bar Association and the Association of American Law Schools) contains little that could be interpreted as relating to Corrections, even though it covers many specific as well as general areas. *American Bar Association Journal,* Vol. 44, No. 12 (December, 1958), p. 1159ff.

and the fields of practice for the lawyer, on the one hand, and the broad responsibilities of the organized bar, on the other. Certainly, the law school curriculum should not be limited to ancient common-law rights and wrongs, and should include more than such technical subjects as taxation and patents. And the practitioner must be concerned with more than the art of cross-examination and the "nice sharp quillets of the law." However, it is primarily the legal profession—the organization of those whose training, experience, and lifetime commitments grow out of the whole body of the law—that has broad, inescapable, responsibilities in the field of corrections.

Relation to the Legal Profession

The whole gamut of activities in the correctional field is carried out within the legal framework. Indeed, these *ex post facto* efforts to eliminate waste of human resources are an integral part of our legal system for regulating man's conduct toward his fellow man in a complex society. In a broad sense, the whole machinery for maintaining law and order must be evaluated by the success or failure of the third phase of the administration of criminal justice—that of preparing the convicted offender for his return to society. Members of the legal profession can with no more reason abandon the defendant in this post-conviction process than can the doctor forget his patient after he is wheeled from surgery to the recovery room or the patient recuperating in a sanitarium.

Legal limitations are both the floor and ceiling of a crowded world in which the probation officer and parole agent work to rehabilitate the man conditionally released or the one serving out an indeterminate sentence in a penal institution. These public servants do not operate in a vacuum (for instance, consider the mandatory minimum sentences, as in federal narcotics cases); they all work within a legal context created by legislators. What must be done by the correctional agent is inextricably enmeshed with rules and regulations that have their basis in the law of the land. Since law is so pervasive in correctional practices, the legal profession has a continuing responsibility to advise, guide, and actively support this vital part of criminal justice.

This responsibility, in a general, yet significant, way, also rests upon the lawyer as an individual. Because of his training and experience, he is a community leader, especially in matters related to the courts and extra-judicial activities. He serves on youth and adult commissions; he is on parole boards; he is an advisor for prison organizations; he is a legislator. In all of these roles, his work is interwoven with almost every activity at the correctional stage. These obligations must be faced if the legal profession is to fulfill its broad responsibility to society.

In addition to these wide areas of interest, there are more direct ones for some lawyers. James V. Bennett, who has promoted an enthusiasm for these problems more effectively than any other man, has called attention to numerous career opportunities in corrections for practicing lawyers.[2] He points out that almost all of the approximately 350,000 prisoners have legal problems which call for services of lawyers. Mr. Bennett also lists many positions in the Federal Bureau of Prisons which call for lawyers. He adds this significant comment:

> "But the role of the lawyer specializing in criminal law is really much broader. . . . The administration of justice does not stop at the gates of a prison. I emphasize this particularly because in my experience many people, including all too many lawyers, feel that once sentence has been imposed, the appeals, if any, concluded, and the man in fact committed to custody, his case can be checked off as completed. . . . Nothing . . . is further from the truth. In a real sense the *administration* of justice . . . has only begun."

Recently, in a carefully prepared paper which discussed the role of a parole board member—as well as his selection, compensation, career prospects, and preparatory education—Lloyd E. Ohlin of the Department of Health, Education and Welfare emphasized the value of legal training. He outlined several vital areas where there is a need for improvement. "The situation could be changed," he said, "by defining more clearly a unique, but hitherto neglected, contribution which lawyers might make to parole board operations. I would like to encourage discussion of this role of the lawyer and the way in which law school education might be supplemented to enhance its visibility, significance, and effectiveness."[3]

These are some of the reasons why I firmly believe the legal profession has an unmistakable responsibility for taking a more active part in solving existing problems in corrections. This also applies, to a degree, to the education of the individual lawyer, for, as Justice Oliver Wendell Holmes told a group of law students in 1886, "To be a master of any branch of knowledge, you must master those which lie next to it."

What Is Being Done

Granting that the typical bibliography of material in this field contains few references to legal publications, that most law schools are re-

[2] Session paper No. 8b—"Career Opportunities for Lawyers in Corrections." Conference on Improving Career Opportunities for Lawyers in the Field of Criminal Justice (Harvard Law School, July, 1961).

[3] Session paper No. 8c, "The Lawyer's Role on Parole Boards and Adult Authorities," Conference on Improving Career Opportunities for Lawyers in the Field of Criminal Justice (Harvard Law School, July 1961).

luctant to broaden and enrich their courses in criminal law, that lists of research projects touching upon corrections include few sponsored by legal organizations, that institutes on manpower and training of personnel, such as this Conference, are usually inspired and carried out by disciplines other than law—admitting all this—we must still recognize several significant steps taken by legal groups to help solve the problem of manpower shortage in corrections and to give prestige to the concept of corrections in general.

The National Legal Aid and Defender Association

There are two programs of the National Council on Legal Clinics (a project of the National Legal Aid and Defender Association, which is financed by a Ford Foundation grant) which should be mentioned as an experiment in legal education. One is a "training program in justice and corrections," supported by a $42,000 grant from the National Legal Aid and Defender Association to the School of Law at the University of California. The purpose of this project is to provide both academic and practical training for students in the socio-legal phases of the administration of justice and corrections. Professor Paul W. Tappan, who directs this project, says that this experience should lead some of the more highly motivated students into careers in the correctional field. "Others," he says, "will be prepared to assume responsibilities more effectively as lay advisors, sponsors, board members, and other roles where lawyers should exert a greater influence than they do now." The experiment, which began in June 1963, will continue to November 1966.

The second project involves law student internships in correctional settings at the University of Wisconsin Law School, where the National Legal Aid and Defender Association made a grant of more than $41,000 (matched locally by a similar amount), to cover the June 1963—January 1967 period. In describing the plan, Frank J. Remington, director of this project, said that the object is to "increase the capacity of the legal profession to make a meaningful, professional, contribution to the administration of criminal justice, both adult and juvenile." He said further:

> The legal profession does not at present make an adequate professional contribution to the administration of criminal justice. Major areas of default include a failure to provide adequate representation . . . at all stages of the criminal process, including the police and correctional stages. . . . This field experience is designed to give the student a 'feel' for correctional programs in the view that this will (a) make possible more meaningful legal representation in regard to *what* will be done to a defendant rather than to the issue of whether he is guilty or innocent, (b) to pro-

vide opportunity for first-hand evaluation of correctional programs in relationship to sentencing . . . and (c) increase the student's capability of taking a leadership position in his local bar and of making a contribution to issues about criminal law administration which come to public attention.

In evaluating these two projects, Professor Howard R. Sacks, executive director of the National Council on Legal Clinics, commented, "Without being too visionary, it is possible to envisage a time when a large number of law students, as a matter of course, will spend the summer before their third year doing field work with an agency engaged in an important kind of public service."

In addition to these pioneering projects at California and Wisconsin, at least two other National Legal Aid and Defender Association clinic programs involve corrections indirectly—those at the Universities of Denver and Tennessee.

An important by-product of the National Council on Legal Clinics was the publication of needed teaching materials for the use of law schools in courses in criminal law.[4] In an excellent essay on the legal profession, in Mr. Schwartz's volume, the lawyer's obligations which touch upon "questions of procedure and institutional arrangements" are squarely faced. The author observes:

> The general public in today's society is probably more interested in convicting the 'criminal element' than in reforming the system in such a way as to lead to fewer convictions or shorter terms of imprisonment. . . . If there is to be a balanced popular comprehension and consideration of our administration of criminal justice, lawyers must bear the burden of explication.

Law Schools

By and large, however, the general curriculum of law schools remains traditional. Of several legal scholars who have been somewhat critical of the narrow approach to teaching criminal law, Andrew S. Watson has spoken out about the "scarcity or utter lack of teaching materials relating to the dynamics . . . of criminal motivation."[5]

Nevertheless, noteworthy developments have taken place in several law schools. One of the most ambitious on the specific subject of careers in corrections was the five-day institute at Harvard in 1961.

---

[4] Murray L. Schwartz, *Cases and Materials on Professional Responsibility and the Administration of Criminal Justice* (Chicago: National Council on Legal Clinics, American Bar Center, 1961), p. 196ff.

[5] "Critique of the Legal Approach to Crime and Correction," *Law and Contemporary Problems,* Vol. 23, No. 4 (Autumn 1958), p. 629.

The announcement of this conference, where more than 30 expert conferees met, included the following statement:

> We find ourselves facing a problem . . . since the career opportunities in criminal law and administration seem less inviting to young men of ability than those afforded in other areas of legal work. If the law schools were to give the training for work in this field believed to be needed, and could not place the men so trained in work that held the promise of utilizing their capacities, the school's efforts would be frustrated.

At this institute on "Improving Career Opportunities for Lawyers in the Field of Criminal Justice," nine nationally known authorities presented papers at the various workshops.

Another encouraging trend is the increasing number of schools or departments of criminology in universities which have added courses in criminal law to the courses of study required for degrees in criminology and corrections. Some of these have been established in cooperation with law schools. Majors and graduate degrees in these fields are offered at several universities, such as those of Florida State, Maryland, Michigan State, Southern Illinois, and California. The University of California has four legally trained men as instructors, as well as several judges and lawyers in the advisory council.

Further, about fifty law schools conduct legal clinic projects—most of them connected in some way with legal aid and defender societies. Indirectly, this experience gives law students background training and a philosophy favorable to future interest in corrections.

American Law Institute

Substantial advances have been made by the American Law Institute in promoting youth corrections programs established in several states and in the federal system. However, one of the most notable contributions of the institute was the drafting of a Model Code of Criminal Law (which, after years of work, is now in the final official draft stage). Part IV of the Code is devoted to "Organization of Corrections." Professor Herbert Wechsler says that the institute "proposes to consider not alone the law defining criminal behavior . . . but also the law governing the treatment of criminals. The hope is to emerge with formulations that will be of long-run aid to legislatures interested . . . in the revision and improvement of the codes of their respective states."[6] He reminds us that the Model Youth Corrections Act (1940)—another pioneer project of the American Law Institute—stimulated special measures dealing with the young offender (California in 1941;

---

[6] "Correctional Practices and the Law . . ." Proceedings of the 82nd Annual Congress of Corrections. (The American Prison Association, 1952.) p. 125.

Minnesota and Wisconsin in 1947; Massachusetts, 1948, and others). These are developments of a highly significant nature, even though, as Richard Chappell points out, "Members of the bar can claim very little credit for the development of probation and the juvenile courts in the early years of the life of these movements."[7]

Both the youth act and the criminal code have a direct bearing upon the question of personnel in the after-conviction stage of the administration of criminal justice.

The Judges

Judges have probably been more conscious of the problems in corrections than have lawyers. The agenda at many annual judicial conferences periodically include some closely related topics. For instance, the National Council on Juvenile Court Judges discussed probation staff qualifications and salaries in 1962, and a week-long workshop on "What Is Involved in Good Juvenile Court Probation?" was held in June, 1963. (Twelve state and regional conferences were held during the past year.)

As a by-product of the Juvenile Officers' Institute at the Center for Continuing Study at the University of Minnesota, a 170-page mimeographed edition of a revised study syllabus, *Legal Aspects of Delinquency Control,* was issued in 1960. Much of the credit for this institute and the teaching material goes to the Hon. Theodore Knudson, Judge of the Fourth Judicial District of Minnesota.

The Judicial Conference of the United States, held in March of 1963, authorized the creation of a permanent committee to "make a broad study of the Federal Probation System and to assume the additional responsibility for organizing and conducting institutes and joint councils of judges and others on sentencing in criminal cases."[8] Commenting on this resolution, Chief Justice Earl Warren said:

> The action of the Judicial Conference . . . is a recognition by the federal judiciary of the needs for concentrated re-study and re-examination of the qualification, training, organization, and supervision of federal officers so as to provide for more adequate enforcement of the probation laws and so as to develop a probation service capable of meeting the present and the future needs of the administration of justice in the federal courts.

In the past two years, the subject, "Sentencing and Probation," has

---

[7] Session paper No. 8a. "The Lawyer's Role in the Administration of Probation and Parole," Conference on Improving Career Opportunities for Lawyers in the Criminal Law Field. (Harvard Law School, 1961.)

[8] Warren Olney III, Address before the Advisory Council of Judges at the 1963 Annual Meeting of the National Council on Crime and Delinquency.

been discussed at more than twenty seminars for state trial judges. These conferences are sponsored by the Joint Committee for Effective Administration of Justice, a highly active agency of the American Bar Association with representatives of approximately fifteen national legal organizations.

Proposals for a Joint Study Committee

Whatever may be the contributions made in some areas by a few legal associations, individual lawyers, and judges to solve the personnel problems in probation, parole, and institutional corrections, they are not enough. The organized bar must use its great capacities to inspire, inform, and guide those who may have talents and interests in socio-legal careers in corrections if the legal profession is to maintain its traditional position of leadership.

The need for wider attention to this area has been documented by a pilot study of the American Bar Foundation in 1957, in which Sanford Bates concluded, ". . . problems were encountered in the whole area of corrections which clearly demonstrate the importance of an impartial, exhaustive study of matters that in many instances and in many places have been taken for granted or very superficially examined."[9]

Without further repeating high-sounding principles about the professional responsibility in this phase of the administration of criminal justice, I propose the following specific remedial measures:

1. That a Joint Study Committee on Corrections be created, with representatives coming from the American Bar Association (Section on Criminal Law), the American Correctional Association, and the National Council on Crime and Delinquency.

2. That the Chairman of the Committee on Sentences, Probation, and Parole of the ABA Section on Criminal Law take the initiative in suggesting this organization. (Fortunately, this chairman, James V. Bennett, is one of the truly outstanding authorities in the field.)

3. That experts knowledgeable in the field of corrections and representatives of other behavioral sciences be appointed to this special study committee with a nationally known man, but not a professional in the correctional field, named as chairman. The Hon. William J. Brennan, Associate Justice of the United States Supreme Court, could give this committee and its assignments the recognition and stature that Justice Tom C. Clark is giving the Joint Committee on Effective Administration of Justice.

---

[9] The Administration of Criminal Justice in the United States. Pilot Project Report (Confidential), Vol. VII, p. 19. Mimeographed (Permission to quote given by the American Bar Foundation).

4. That the ABA Section on Criminal Law and the American Correctional Association make a short-term, "emergency" grant to this committee to enable it to get organized.

5. That a more substantial grant be sought from a foundation to finance a two-year study by this committee.

6. That an executive secretary be employed to coordinate and administer the study program.

7. That the committee seek assistance from the American Bar Foundation or help from research resources within the American Correctional Association and other appropriate national organizations in carrying out its objectives.

8. That the following items be among the assignment of this committee:

a. Documentation of the specific personnel needs in relation to numbers, salaries, tenure, and education in the federal jurisdiction and in each state system.
b. Analysis and evaluation of existing classification of jobs and responsibilities of positions now existing in the states and federal system and recommendations concerning a more ideal arrangement, making use of expert assistance of an objective agency having job analysts on its staff.
c. Suggested job descriptions for each classification.
d. Minimum educational requirements for those who will have "professional" responsibilities.
e. Study of the feasibility of establishing a National School of Criminology, with centers of study in universities selected on a regional basis (such as California, Colorado, Wisconsin, North Carolina, and, perhaps, Texas) where there could be close cooperation between law and the behavioral sciences.
f. Curriculum recommendations, based upon the committee's study and the experience of several successful schools of criminology, leading to a degree, a certificate or registration in criminology—one that would mean for professionals in corrections what the C.P.A. means to accountants or the R.N. to nurses.
g. An outline of a promotional program to persuade the selected universities to inaugurate such schools, or departments, in partnership with law and the social sciences.
h. A plan for encouraging the federal government and the states to provide scholarships for trainees who would be pledged to return to their jurisdictions and to accept employment in the field of corrections.

9. That, after the two-year study, a detailed report and recommendations of the committee be made to the sponsoring associations.

10. That a National Board of Corrections, to include representatives of the related disciplines, be organized and incorporated, and financed through contractual arrangements with federal and state governments in order for the educational program to have continuity, security, and longevity.

For all the national associations represented at this conference, this is a challenge. For my own profession, in particular, it is an urgent call for the understanding of relationships, the recognition of obligations, the necessity of involvement, and immediate action in an area that is such an integral part of the administration of criminal justice.

APPENDIX

Since I realized, when I began this paper, that I am not an expert in the field of corrections, I asked for the assistance of several knowledgeable persons who have worked more closely in this area. Their responses were so helpful that I believe others would benefit from selected comments sent to me. Following are these pinpointed observations, which have not been published elsewhere and are not otherwise available:

Donald McIntyre, Director of Research, American Bar Foundation. Special staff conferences were held on this topic in December 1963. Summaries of the discussion, prepared by Mr. McIntyre, reflect the general viewpoint of this expert group:

> Once it has been established that the person is guilty of the charge, then there has been a tendency (of members of the legal profession) not to be concerned with what happens . . . thereafter. (The practicing bar) is concerned primarily with an effort to establish innocence and to enforce procedural and substantive rights . . .
>
> The judge (on the other hand) . . . must study data about the convict's past behavior and try to predict the effect different kinds of dispositions will have on both the individual and society. To this extent, courts have addressed themselves to the problem of corrections, but once the decision on the disposition is made, execution of this decision is left largely to the penologist or social scientist . . .
>
> (As to the academician:) Within the past decade there is evidence that a few members of this branch of the profession are becoming increasingly concerned with the way the law and the state handle persons convicted of crime . . .
>
> *Justification for the legal profession getting into the field of corrections:*
>
> 1. The spectrum of interest by the legal profession in the administration of criminal justice ought not to be limited to the area encompassing detection of crime (and) the adjudication of guilt or innocence.
> 2. The legal profession is the primary group dedicated to and equipped for the enforcement and establishment of human rights. . . . It is important that the legal profession address itself to the question of whether persons convicted of crime are given the benefit of modern knowledge about human behavior . . .
> 3. It is important that the legal profession associate itself with behavioral scientists. (The lawyer) is probably in the best position to define and to balance the twin objectives of criminal law: protection of society and the protection of individual rights.

Daniel Glaser, Visiting Professor of Sociology, Arizona State University:

> . . . The development in corrections, which I think is most significant for (this) . . . topic is that of increased recognition of the legal rights of prisoners and parolees. While heretofore the prisoner has been conceived as stripped of almost all rights by his conviction, hence transferable and

punishable by prison and parole officials almost at will, a series of recent decisions suggest the need for training correctional administrators in the legal rights of offenders . . .

Gerhard O. W. Mueller, Professor of Law, New York University:

. . . Inasmuch as execution of sentence is a direct consequence of the judgment of a court and, indeed, is the most significant single stimulus in the criminal law's game of producing certain response among the citizenry, it is of utmost significance that the legal profession play an active role in solving the personnel problem of corrections. Brutish custodial officers are as incapable of carrying out judgments of the courts as are the heartbreaking social workers ignorant of the major and the minor premises of the law. In sum, it is the obligation of our profession to see to it that we have a sufficient number of appropriately trained officers capable of carrying out the judgments of criminal courts within the spirit and policy of the criminal law.
. . . Ultimately, the law schools can exercise their best influence by teaching the teachers of correctional people. It would be a Sisyphus task for us to attempt to teach the correctional workers directly.

A. LaMonte Smith, School of Criminology, University of California:

We have both graduate and undergraduate students, many of whom are girls, preparing for careers in the correctional field. Our increasing enrollment indicates a growing interest for professional training in this area, and we believe that this will result in a higher caliber and better trained personnel for employing agencies. . . . The demand for such graduates certainly now widely exceeds the supply.

Hon. Florence M. Kelley, Administrative Judge, Family Court of the State of New York:

I strongly believe that the legal profession and the judiciary have a responsibility for helping to solve these (manpower and training of personnel) problems in corrections. Corrections is an integral part of law enforcement. Law enforcement necessarily plays a role in our concept of justice. Any lawyer or judge who is interested in justice through law must be interested in corrections and it follows from this, of course, that if there are problems to be solved in the area of corrections, the lawyers and judges must be interested in seeing that those problems are solved . . . I have felt now for some ten or fifteen years that lawyers, law teachers, and judges should do everything within their power to encourage young people to train for positions in fields dealing with human problems. The emphasis on science has assumed almost monstrous proportions. Something must be done to make a career dealing with human problems seem interesting and glamorous to our young.

Charles L. Decker, Director, Defender Project, National Legal Aid and Defender Association (Former Chairman, Section on Criminal Law, American Bar Association), Chicago:

I think that the basics of corrections are:

1. Teaching a man to make a living honestly and putting across the idea that it is easier than making a living by crime.

2. During the correctional period, requiring a high standard of performance and *recognition of anything* that the individual does well.

3. Making sure that the follow-up takes the individual into his own community or into a new one in such a way that he is accepted and feels that he is.

A. W. Peterson, M.V.S., Chairman, The Prison Commission, London:

(There is a) growing emphasis on the need for closer liaison between those whose responsibility it is to sentence convicted offenders and those who have the duty of carrying out these sentences . . .
. . . Sentencers, in particular, newly appointed sentencers, should be reminded of the importance of visits to penal institutions.
"There should be recognized machinery whereby a sentencer can obtain periodic reports about the progress and further convictions of an offender.

(These comments related to recommendations of a special committee appointed in 1958, under the chairmanship of Justice Streatfeild, to provide the courts with information necessary to enable them to select the most appropriate treatment for offenders.)

James V. Bennett, Director, Bureau of Prisons, U. S. Department of Justice:

Most assuredly the legal profession and the judiciary, being charged primarily with the effective administration of criminal justice, must look upon their responsibility as broader than merely participating in formal trials and passing judgment . . . Moreover, if the judiciary has no resources to carry out its decisions in a constructive and humane manner, it is all but an exercise in futility. There will be no resources unless the legal profession puts its shoulder to the wheel and helps solve the administrative, manpower, and training problems of its services, including corrections.

Hon. Henry A. Riederer, Judge of the Circuit Court, Kansas City, Missouri:

As to the training required, many judges feel that the social work field has stolen the show because of its persistence. However, there are other disciplines which have legitimate claims . . . I would create a whole new field which would uniquely qualify graduates to work in the increasingly needed field of domestic relations, juvenile, family, and criminal courts. Such students would receive especially developed courses in certain phases of the law and behavioral sciences.

Prof. Paul W. Tappan, Meyer Visiting Research Professor, Law School of Harvard University:

Developments in juvenile and family courts, sentencing, parole and probation revocation procedures have highlighted the needs . . . for more legal sophistication in correctional fields and . . . among lawyers. The extended persistence of undesirable procedures, especially in the decision-making processes, may be attributed to a very great extent to the non-involvement of the legal profession in the problems and practices in corrections . . . Only through drawing good legal minds into policy positions . . . will it be possible to develop a due process of correctional justice that extends beyond the finding of guilty in the criminal court. In my opinion, law teachers and judges can be most effective in appealing to the idealism of some youths to develop new roles in the administration of justice and corrections.

G. N. Elder, Chairman, Board of Probation and Parole, Jefferson City, Missouri:

Inasmuch as the legal profession and the judiciary play such a vital role in the prosecution, defense, and sentencing of the offender, they should, in turn, accept a portion of the responsibility as to the proper disposition and treatment of that offender, institutionally, as well as the area of probation and parole . . . the lack of training of correctional personnel is the greatest weakness of our present systems. While great strides have been made in late years, there is still a long way to go. Requirements and standards should and must be set as goals, but too often it is a matter of realistic practicality in selecting personnel from the group that is available.

Richard A. McGee, Administrator, California Youth and Adult Corrections Agency, Sacramento:

The matter of salary, availability of manpower, pre-training and in-service training are all inextricably enmeshed and must be considered and dealt with simultaneously. For example, in our efforts to recruit personnel with capacities for growth and development, we compete with the higher salaries of industry . . .

Hon. Paul W. Alexander, Judge, Court of Common Pleas, Division of Domestic Relations, Toledo, Ohio:

. . . The legal profession should do its part in encouraging good material to prepare itself for the correctional field. However, by and large, we don't know enough about the qualifications and requirements to give any advice to anybody, except to go to school and study the courses prescribed therefor . . . I personally take a dim view of the technical knowledge of the bar in the field of corrections. They understand criminal law and procedure, but they have only vague ideas about penology . . .

Livingston Hall, Professor of Law, Harvard University:

I do think that the law schools ought to take the lead in organizing courses for corrections people . . .

ABA Foundation Research Attorneys

I am deeply indebted to three research lawyers on the staff of the American Bar Foundation for reading the first draft of this paper and making many valuable observations. Donald McIntyre, Jr., William Eldridge, and Richard Janopaul spent considerable time reading the paper and discussing the various issues raised. In addition to their contributions, which are reflected in certain uncredited changes in the draft, I am paraphrasing other comments which I feel will be of interest. The three lawyers have had considerable experience in working with other disciplines on a number of research projects. Following are their paraphrased comments:

1. Problems of manpower and training of personnel cannot be intelligently discussed without considering broader issues in corrections.
2. The legal profession has responsibilities in this field, but it is difficult to identify specific areas where the lawyers can make the best contribution. The lawyers themselves are at fault in not learning more of the general field and for not insisting that the profession be heard in the formation of broad policies in corrections.
3. Research is needed as to what are the greatest influences in re-shaping the lives of prisoners. Much is known of what *is being done,* but little study has been made on what is the best way to re-condition. The prison atmosphere repels professional (and other) staff and makes it almost impossible to attract the best talent.
4. (One example: A warden told one of the research attorneys that he was unable to fill a vacancy with a reputable psychiatrist as the good ones were not content to conform to established routines of the prisons, and that the authorities did not want one who might be a disrupting influence.)
5. "Good" prisoners do not make good citizens—or good workers—when they leave the prison. After they are conditioned to doing their assigned tasks without question, they become depersonalized and lose the creativity which is necessary for successful employment after their release.
6. Correctional people don't really want to look objectively at what they are doing. They are blinded by their vested interests. They defend too much by saying that their first job is to keep the prisoners secure, as the court ordered.
7. Admitting that security measures are essential, something could be worked out between the minimum requirement of what the custodian *must do,* and what a good professional person, such as a psychiatrist or a lawyer, would admit as being necessary, yet not destroying his professional relationship.
8. There are specific areas that should be recommended to lawyers:

   a. Participate more actively in pre-sentence investigating, i.e., attempt to line up a job or place to live in the event of—and as encouragement for—probation. Supplement pre-sentence report.

   b. Upon release from prison, encourage the client to visit, and help in getting him a job and place to live. Become more interested in the person—not just the facts of the case.

c. Visit prisons to learn problems confronting both the penologist and the prisoner. Bar committees would be good for these visits, which would be a morale builder for prisoners and would give them a chance to associate with the pillars of the community.

Frank J. Remington, Professor of Law, University of Wisconsin:

. . . I consider the most fundamental question (to be that of) the extent to which the court ought to have an interest in and a responsibility for the total criminal justice process, including the correctional stage. It has sometimes been assumed that the best correctional system is one which is most removed from judicial control. This certainly has been the assumption in the juvenile justice field in the past. Yet, it appears to me that the attitude is changing and one sees more and more concern on the part of trial courts with police problems on the one hand and correctional problems on the other. My own view is that this is a desirable trend, although in saying this, I do not assume that lawyers are more able or intelligent than are police or correctional personnel . . .

John Ritchie, Dean, Northwestern University School of Law, Chicago:

It seems to me that judges, lawyers, and law teachers can encourage young people whom they know and who have manifested an interest in correctional work to train for positions in the correctional field. Members of the legal profession who are concerned with the administration of criminal law are in a particularly favorable position to offer encouragement and to underscore the need of society for trained personnel in correctional work.

Harry W. Jones, Cardozo Professor of Jurisprudence, Columbia University, (former Research Program Consultant, American Bar Foundation):

If there were an established professional or quasi-professional tradition in the correctional field, lawyers, judges, and, particularly, law teachers could undoubtedly be of assistance in steering qualified young people into corrections careers. Obviously this is a big *if.* The career must be there—a career offering reasonable compensation, vocational status, and genuine opportunity for service—before young people can be encouraged to train for positions in the correctional field. At the present moment, knowing as little as I do about the career possibilities of corrections work, I would not advise a young man to enter this area of public service. My guess is that most law teachers, lawyers, and judges would feel about as I do.

Groups such as the group who will meet with you at Arden House have, therefore, a twofold problem: *first,* the establishment of a career pattern, including educational programs and secure professional opportunities for persons interested in corrections work as an aspect of public service, and *second,* the announcement and explanation of that career pattern to young people who might be interested in the work and to other persons who might be consulted by young people. The situation is perhaps analogous to the development, within recent years, of a career in hospital administration. In that area, the medical profession saw a personnel need and assisted the universities in the development, at a few institutions, of a special training program. Once a career in hospital administration became available, able young people were attracted to it, either on their own initiative or through the encouragement of persons to whom they had gone for vocational advice.

Manpower and Training in Corrections: Suggestions from the Field of Mental Health[1]

by Daniel Blain

The author, with minimal experience with courts, prisons, or individual offenders, has a strong interest in corrections from active acquaintance with James V. Bennett, Richard McGee, Herman Stark, and certain members of the legal profession and judiciary; particularly with the Department of Corrections and the Department of the Youth Authority in California which he believes exhibit, in many ways, the best modern concepts in the field. As Director of the Department of Mental Hygiene in California, he had opportunities to discuss many common problems of both fields, and in working with the American Psychiatric Association, he had some experience related to the Committee on Legal Aspects of Psychiatry. "Forensic psychiatry" (legal aspects of psychiatry) is a subspecialty in the field of psychiatry.

The two fields of mental health and corrections, though radically different, have many similarities, many common problems, much to learn from each other, and they should be mutually helpful in many ways.

This paper is intended to present in a hurried and superficial fashion:

1. Certain apparent similarities in the two fields of corrections and mental illness-retardation.

[1] "Mental health" includes mental illness and retardation and encompasses efforts in the diagnosis, treatment, rehabilitation, and resocialization of persons suffering from these conditions; the prevention of the occurrence of these conditions; and the production of mentally healthy individuals and the maintenance of their mental health. Medicine and the specialty, psychiatry, is only one of the disciplines concerned, others being, career-wise, clinical psychology, social work, and professional nursing. Participation of other professions (and this may apply to corrections) include the ministry, teachers, lawyers, judges, law enforcement officers, social scientists, executives and foremen in industry, recreational specialists, civic leaders, and others. The mental health of people is strongly affected positively or negatively by all personal contacts and social conditions. (Vulnerability to antisocial behavior would appear to be related to these also.)

2. Some apparent differences.
3. The psychiatrist in correctional work—his availability, function, and usefulness.
4. The American Psychiatric Association Manpower Commission as a model, some parts of which may be of value in the field of corrections.

Similarities in the Two Fields

Both fields are large and important to an appreciable segment of the population—in a broad sense to all persons, and, in a narrow sense, to many. Both of these fields have to do with individual and a group problem with "mass" and "epidemic" properties and are potentially related to all people.

Both are costly to individuals and to society as a whole in money—far beyond available appropriations and loss of income earnings; in family disorganization; in human suffering and deterioration of individuals; and both are demoralizing to society when there is neglect and relatively poor facilities which are made available. These are examples of man's inhumanity to man. Some progress has been made and some institutions have improved, but obviously there is a long way to go, and there is some doubt that there is enough tax money.

The institutions related to services in both of these fields are chiefly tax-supported, but with the possibilities of greater involvement by private and non-governmental sectors of society, it is possible that the whole situation may be improved. Both are subject to decentralization of state services in the direction of local operation and local administration. This movement will assist both in the finding of manpower and in the utilization of many financial resources.

Vulnerability in both fields is related to genetics, growth, and development, and social, economic, intellectual, spiritual, and physical resources of the individual and society. Because of these, the situation is strongly dependent on public information or ignorance, attitude, traditional and historical perspectives, and proof of the ability to intervene successfully for "rehabilitation" or treatment. In both fields, there is conflict between the rights and needs of the individual and the rights and needs of society. This complicated situation in both fields, therefore, is unfortunately related to somewhat less advanced areas of scientific knowledge in which there must be more specificity and more basic clinical and operational research before much progress can be made. In the field of mental health, however, it can be said that there is more known than today can be acted upon because of the shortage of personnel. This is probably true of corrections also.

In both fields, preventive techniques are few and largely unproved. There is reason to believe that proper growth and development of healthy personality and the ability to handle stress situations are important as aids to primary prevention. The terms "secondary" and "tertiary intervention" are applied in medicine to the prevention of acute conditions becoming chronic or more of a handicap and the later phase of physical, mental, and social rehabilitation. There is a parallel to both of these areas in the field of corrections.

Both fields are in serious difficulties because of the shortage in trained personnel; they are both strongly dependent on professional personnel, in many categories, and are now able to develop usefulness of many nonprofessional groups and individual volunteers.

Both fields have a large professional body working in law and medicine, both are assisted by special groups, such as social scientists, and both must rely on the factors inherent in satisfactory growth and development, for both mental illness and retardation and for corrections, individual attitudes and activities of those who have contacted persons before and after breaking the law or becoming mentally ill are of great significance.

Both the legal and medical professions (psychiatrists) need a clear delimitation of their function to avoid what Virginias Ellison calls "creating a knight-errant roving at will in pursuit of some unbounded system of beneficence."

Both professions could go much further than they do at present in assuming interest in modification of conditions, which in either a positive or negative way strongly effect a production of strong, healthy, and law-abiding citizens and assist or hinder in their rehabilitation.

In both fields, the individual is the target unit, but these individuals are strongly affected by environmental influences and conditions.

Differences in the Two Fields

The author is presenting material based on assumptions that not all criminals and delinquents are mentally ill, and not all mentally ill are criminals. Nor are all people who are in trouble deviate in their behavior or showing signs of stress diagnosable as having a psychiatric disorder. Even though these two fields overlap each other, they should not be put under the same jurisdiction except where both diagnoses are present, at which time the major problem—"mental illness" or "antisocial behavior" should determine the jurisdiction. There is a difference between psychopaths with individual psychopathology, and sociopaths, where pathology is related to society as a whole more than, or in addition to, individual pathology. There is a difference between mental illness and antisocial behavior, and both groups suffer when they are lumped together in program, physical propinquity, and public attitudes.

Medicine and psychiatry have been traditionally more interested in and more effective in working with individuals, with the internal needs, conflicts, and origin of behavior of individuals, with the goals of individual health, reduction of individual pain, and prolongation of the individual life, although the public aspects of the profession are engaged in extending these individual benefits to large numbers of people.

It appears to me that, on the other hand, in the correctional field, the emphasis is on antisocial behavior as an object of primary interest, and that the field, by definition, is more primarily concerned with how society is affected than the individual. Again, it would appear that neither can be treated separately from the other.

The medical profession is avowedly interested in eliminating the occurrence of disease and insisting on the maintenance of health. I have not personally been aware that the field of law has had any such interest, although I am sure that the field of corrections has. I suspect that in both medical and legal professions, whatever interest they do have in primary prevention must be carried on much further.

Treatment and management of mentally ill and retarded are almost always in the hands of the persons trained in medicine, psychiatry, and some other specialties in psychology, social work, and nursing, with leadership and authority chiefly in the hands of medical persons trained in psychiatry. This is not true of the field of corrections. Although the law may be the primary professional group involved, it does not extend itself to administration of programs for adult or youthful delinquents, prisons, and alike, or the rehabilitation of convicted offenders, nor is any single profession interested in a major way in primary prevention of delinquency. It would seem to me that the field of corrections suffers seriously from this situation, assuming that I am right in my premise. It would, therefore, appear to be of great value to develop a professional group and a professional organization which has the inherent authority which the professions of medicine and law have.

The Psychiatrist in Court Work and Corrections

Assuming that the function which the psychiatrist can perform is important to those people who are in trouble with the law because of behavior, that is, delinquents or criminals, it is worthwhile to see how many psychiatrists are actually practicing this form of a subspecialty of the field.

In preparation for a conference on psychiatric education, a task force on recruitment and the distribution of psychiatrists gathered an appreciable amount of information related to the numbers, distribution, and utilization of psychiatrists.

For various reasons, thirteen states were selected for special study and contained exactly 50 percent of all of the psychiatrists in the United States. The following states were included: Alabama, California, Idaho, Indiana, Louisiana, Massachusetts, Minnesota, New Mexico, New York, North Carolina, South Carolina, Texas, and Wyoming, in an attempt to get the two largest and others from the deep South, the Southwest, the Middle West, the mountain states, and the Northeast.

Among other subjects taken up were the numbers of those employed in correctional institutions—federal, city, county, and private, including court work. The following results were obtained: 201 had something on their IBM cards which indicated that they belonged in this group. Seventeen of these indicated that they were in only one type of employment, that is, full time in this particular work. These were eight in California, one in Indiana, one in Minnesota, six in New York, and one in North Carolina; 184 had other additional employment. Of the full-time persons, fifteen were employed by states, and two by the federal government. Of the fifteen in the states, eight were in California, one in Minnesota, five in New York, and one in North Carolina. Of the 184, California and New York had the greatest number, and Massachusetts had equal numbers employed on a part-time basis in correctional institutions. California had twenty-one employed by the state, Massachusetts, twenty-three, New York, thirty-four, and Idaho, Indiana, Louisiana, Minnesota, New Mexico, South Carolina, and Wyoming either one, two, or three each in state service; Texas had four in state service in correctional institutions; all of these were on a part-time basis. County or city correctional programs had forty-five on a part-time basis, none full time. These were divided as follows: twenty-four in California, fourteen in New York, and the rest in Indiana, Louisiana, and Texas. Private correctional institutions had twenty-four people working part-time, and other institutions in which the type of control was not specified had ten others working part-time. Private institutions had, on a part-time basis, nine in California, thirteen in New York, and two in Massachusetts.

Another table indicates "employment with social agencies, courts, state and federal government." Those indicating work in correctional institutions, therefore, apparently, did not count their work with courts.

It must be remembered that psychiatrists working in state hospitals include those who are in the institutions or divisions for criminal insane in the state hospitals. The number employed here is not known, nor apparently has been singled out.

Out of approximately 5,500 included in the study, 200 represent slightly under 4 percent. In contrast, 847, or about 15 percent, obtained employment with social agencies, courts, states and the federal government, fifty-eight, or 1 percent, were employed in industry, 1,923, or approximately 35 percent, were employed in universities or other educational settings, 1,711, or 31 percent, were employed to some extent in general hospitals, 865, or about 16 percent, were employed in mental hygiene clinics, ninety-six, or approximately 2 percent, were employed in institutions for the retarded, 1,793 employed in mental hospitals (that is about the same in general hospitals), and 5,500 in private practice, or 100 percent doing some private work.

Of 11,000 members of the American Psychiatric Association, in listing their top three major interests, 975 included "forensic psychiatry," which presumably includes court as well as institutional work. Twenty-seven of these are women. The age distribution follows:—34, *74;* 35-39, *170;* 40-44, *167;* 45-49, *128;* 50-54, *144;* 55-59, *131;* 60-64, *85;* 65 and over, *76.*

The number of psychiatrists in any given state tends to parallel the number of physicians and other economic and educational levels of the state population. One third to one half of the psychiatrists remain near where they were trained. This points to the necessity for the development of local training programs.

The need for psychiatrists in the field of corrections parallels the need for others for the so-called mental health team, that is, clinical psychology, psychiatric nursing, and medical (psychiatric) social work. In addition, those who do counseling in group therapy must be considered as part of this group since they must have a certain amount of psychiatric skill.

Another important addition is the use of general physicians. There is a big movement on foot to train physicians for practice in psychiatry, to handle a certain part of the load; these will be increasing their usefulness to correctional facilities.

Let us review the interest of physicians as a whole in the legal aspects of medicine. All medical students are given a short course in applicable parts of the law, including contracts, malpractice, expert testimony, and compensation, among others. Certain specialties in medical practice have more contact with law than others, such as orthopedic surgery, pathology, neurology, and psychiatry. Psychiatry has the most because of the commitment to mental hospitals, the presence of mentally-ill offenders in psychiatric programs, insanity as a defense plea, the presence of mental illness in prisoners, the use of jails to house mentally-ill persons, and perhaps the anticipated acts of violence which the public associates with mental illness. In addition, I believe that legislative action and laws relating to the field of mental health are more related to psychiatry than to any other specialty of medicine.

The psychiatrist, in training to be a specialist, has a second course in "legal aspects." Some become active in "forensic psychiatry" on a part-time basis or, occasionally, as their full-time practice (see figure above). The old term "alienist" illustrates the major occupation of some physicians as expert witnesses for mental conditions. This term now has derogatory implications and has been largely abandoned. The difficulty in obtaining expert witnesses qualified in psychiatry is a serious factor in many rural jurisdictions. This is because three-fourths of all counties in the United States have no psychiatrist in residence. These counties, are, of course, small and have small populations, so the total percentage of people uncovered in this way is not as large as it might be; but the distances are there. Many psychiatrists loathe exposing themselves to cross examination in courts of law, and this cuts down the availability. Low fees for court examinations and time in court are also a deterrent. The legal framework surrounding expert testimony is also important; that is the presence or absence of something such as the Briggs Law of Massachusetts, or the competitive element when the person is employed by either the prosecution or the defense. The philosophy of some psychiatrists lead them to pronounce all criminals mentally ill; on the other hand, certain others rarely see mental illness in any criminal action. Both of these extremes are deplorable and bring no credit to the profession. An example of what might be done occurred in the psychiatric association of a large city in the Midwest, where all psychiatrists agreed that they would not accept employment by either the prosecution or the defense, but would restrict themselves entirely to the service of the court. Disagreement between expert witnesses when the reasons for these differences are not clearly understood has placed the profession in a poor light. Often to the psychiatrist these differences are just as reasonable as those which divide the Supreme Court in a 5-to-4 split opinion.

In a profession which regards treatment, release from pain, and saving of lives as of the greatest importance, legal work has a hard time attracting the interest and efforts of its members. In institutions for offenders, with few exceptions, the conditions of work are usually less attractive than other available opportunities, and the discouragement encountered in attempting treatment under the conditions that exist in most correctional institutions is devastating, according to a psychiatrist who is one of the leaders in forensic psychiatry in this country. He is more pessimistic than I in terms of improving recruitment. Even state hospitals of the mentally ill and retarded usually have better opportunities for professional satisfaction. If private practice of psychiatry is currently in such high favor and the opportunities for favorable locations are so plentiful—there is such a seller's market for psychiatric skills—correctional programs are likely to meet with small success in the near future.

This need not be so. Psychiatrists are putting more and more time in public service, especially on a part-time basis. Work with offenders can be most interesting and most rewarding; but these opportunities should be subject to careful scrutiny and efforts made to create attractive and professionally rewarding opportunities. The present favorable trend toward mental hospitals and clinics could be tipped to the advantage of correctional programs.

The following suggestions are made in terms of the current situation concerning psychiatrists in correctional work.

1. A study should be made in detail and depth to bring to light the current shortages among psychiatrists and others.
2. An organized effort with the professional organization representing the psychiatrists, psychologists, etc., such as the committee on legal aspects of psychiatry of the American Psychiatric Association and the Commission on Manpower of the APA, the National Association of State Mental Health Program Directors, the psychiatric association in each state, state personnel boards for proper working conditions, and other groups. An organized, nationwide, and locally distributed effort would yield considerable advances, in my opinion.
3. The possibility of shared treatment and training responsibility with other psychiatric programs such as a Department of Mental Hygiene should be considered in every state and local situation.
4. Personnel needs by wards of the correctional program should be continually studied particularly in regard to the kind of assistance that is needed. I believe that clear-cut mental disorders should have attention, if possible, of persons highly trained in psychiatric skills, and general programs, such as counseling and group therapy work for all wards, cannot progress beyond a certain point unless the leaders have a good training background and unless adequate personal attention is given to each individual in addition to the group work. Otherwise, the group therapy program will lose its effectiveness before long.
5. The field of corrections needs, in my opinion and I hope that I am wrong, a strong organization behind it, probably a professional organization or perhaps a combination of professionals and non-professionals that have strength in numbers of members, in financial resources, in planning, training, and research brains to lead this entire effort in the direction of manpower for corrections.

The field of mental health has both a strong professional organization and a strong citizens' organization, and, between the two, a strong position is maintained nationally and in each state. The field of corrections, in my opinion, does not have this type of support.

A Possible Model for a Manpower Commission

The American Psychiatric Association has created, after a number of years of consideration, a "Manpower Commission," to move towards action along the lines of much-repeated factual information and general statements that have been spread before us for a number of years.

The organization of this commission, its purposes and general plan of action, are presented as a model which the field of corrections might be able to use in some part, or perhaps to suggest ways in which the American Psychiatric Association and its resources can be brought to the assistance of the field of corrections.

The Manpower Situation in Mental Health—Assets

1. The field of mental health has in the medical specialty of psychiatry a professional group, 100 percent involved in the psychiatric needs of the nation. The group has competency, leadership ability, interest, and willingness to take responsibility for the total situation. Its members have both authority and responsibility by virtue of their positions as State Directors of Mental Hygiene, institutional superintendents, clinic heads, Directors of Professional Education, professors and chairmen of Departments of Psychiatry in medical schools, and as practitioners of psychiatry and community leaders. This adds up to strong influence and power which are now being harnessed toward the objectives under discussion.

2. The field has the advantage of a citizens' organization, namely, the National Association of Mental Health and the National Association of Retarded Children and Adults, which provide strong public backing for mental health programs in a number of ways.

3. The American Psychiatric Association has the strength of 12,000 members, all of whom have M.D. degrees and the minimum of eight years beyond college graduation; thirty-eight standing committees and commissions; strong state branches; about fifty full-time employees, and an operating budget of about $1,000,000 a year.

State and local programs under the leadership of psychiatrists have the advantage of this national and state organization which has strength and dedication. It has, in varying but increasing degrees, the strength of organized medicine behind it.

Does the field of corrections have comparably organized professional and citizens' backing?

The Manpower Commission of the APA is composed of a chairman, who is about to become president of the association, and fifteen other members. These represent a number of specialized fields, such as the Assembly of District Branches so that all the states are represented, a

Commissioner of Mental Hygiene from one of the large states, a professor of psychiatry in one of the medical schools, someone who has taken a special interest in the possibilities of the recruitment of women, two others who have a special interest in the better utilization of Negroes in medicine and psychiatry, people closely associated with the studies of medical schools carried on by the medical school deans of the country, by the American Medical Association and its program, by one specially interested in college dropouts, others operating programs in summer employment for high school and college students as a recruiting device, and it also has a professional statistician who will spend his time studying the manpower problems of the nation and of the association.

No large sum of money has been obtained to operate this commission. It is not expected to be tremendously expensive, and probably will not have more than one or two meetings a year of the complete commission. On the other hand, two or three at a time will compose sub-committees for special purposes, and these will meet frequently in addition to the Executive Committee, composed of five, who will also meet frequently.

The problem of manpower is so diffuse and can be attacked in so many areas that it was decided that the APA would give first priority to psychiatrists, and its second priority to the recruitment and utilization of physicians, these two being strongly linked because psychiatrists are only drawn from the pool of physicians.

It will at the same time join with others to see that work is done and leadership developed to push for meeting demands of all other needed personnel. It will do all it can to stimulate all professional and citizen groups to action, and along this line it has called a meeting of some twelve professional groups involved in full-time employees in the mental health field. This is merely to exchange information, let them know what we're doing, find out what they're doing, and create some sort of communication between us.

The commission has adopted a general plan which was worked out by some members of the commission for the benefit of the AMA, National Congress on Mental Health, Section on Personnel, which is as follows:

The major elements in the program are:

1. Development and exercise of leadership
2. Increasing the number of available psychiatrists by
   a. Recruitment
   b. Better distribution

Recruitment will include (1) recruitment into medicine, especially for those who will be likely to enter psychiatry (as these are identified; (2)

recruitment into psychiatry from graduate physicians; (3) recruitment into subspecialties of psychiatry (including forensic or correctional); (4) recruitment into programs and areas where psychiatrists are in short supply including correctional programs; (5) utilization of current efforts with general practitioners and other physicians to get the medical profession to give more and more service to mental patients.

3. Better utilization of existing personnel, including revision of function, use of time, additional assistance to the physicians, more delegation of authority and responsibility under supervision, organizationally to place operations in areas where part-time workers are available, greater use of more less-trained persons and volunteers, and the creation of better inducement for employment in various programs.

4. Increased training programs, both professional, i.e., residency training, and in-service, both for physicians and other mental health personnel, and with training more and more suited, we hope, to the most important needs of the nation.

5. Research into personnel practice and patient needs, operational research toward better administration, more efficient treatment, and other research leading towards etiological agents and methods of attack.

6. The reduction of the psychiatric load to better use available short supply by more primary prevention where these techniques are proven useful. The relief of intolerable stress before mental illness develops (for corrections, before trouble with the law develops), and by analysis of load and distribution of segments of the load to others than high-priced and personnel-short hospital situations.

7. The utilization of a plan of scrutiny and division of services as illustrated in the "Zonal Classification of People" (see chart on page 187 opposite).

These various efforts, which cover the situation as completely as can be envisioned at this time, can also be carried on at levels of action.

These levels of action are:

1. National, including the utilization of experiences of other nations when available, and here one would work with the appropriate national organization, the federal government, national foundations, business groups, etc.

2. At the state level with state government, state Departments of Mental Hygiene, state medical societies and other professional groups, psychiatric societies, citizens' groups, etc.

3. County or city level with state local programs, county hospitals, and tax-supported programs, county medical societies and other professional groups, local citizens' groups interested in mental disorders and retardation.

4. In institutions where persons are living, where training can be

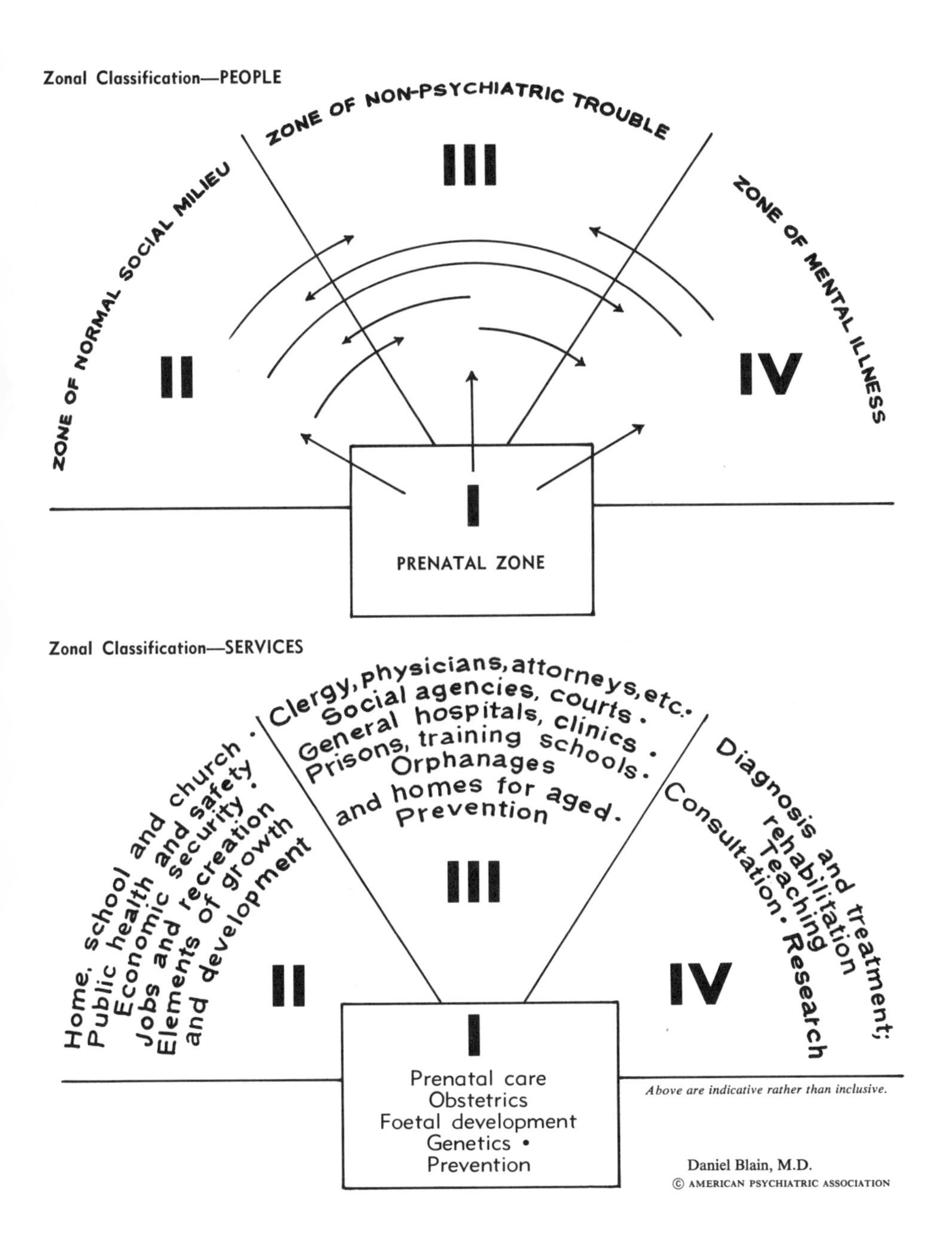
Zonal Classification—PEOPLE
ZONE OF NON-PSYCHIATRIC TROUBLE
III
ZONE OF NORMAL SOCIAL MILIEU
II
ZONE OF MENTAL ILLNESS
IV
I
PRENATAL ZONE
Zonal Classification—SERVICES
Clergy, physicians, attorneys, etc.
Social agencies, courts.
General hospitals, clinics.
Prisons, training schools.
Orphanages
and homes for aged.
Prevention
III
Home, school and church.
Public health and safety
Economic security.
Jobs and recreation
Elements of growth
and development
II
Diagnosis and treatment;
rehabilitation
Teaching
Consultation. Research
IV
I
Prenatal care
Obstetrics
Foetal development
Genetics •
Prevention
Above are indicative rather than inclusive.
Daniel Blain, M.D.
© AMERICAN PSYCHIATRIC ASSOCIATION

developed, and utilization of clinical facilities for research and training to provide better manpower and utilize manpower that is available in the best possible way.

For the time being, the APA Commission on Manpower will devote itself:

1. To psychiatrists
2. To other physicians

It will emphasize the recruitment by studying and improving the image of psychiatry for the public, by working with guidance and counseling personnel toward placing before high school and college students an understanding of the profession of medicine and the specialty of psychiatry, and pushing for national coverage a program of summer employment for high school and college students working in mental hospitals, clinics, and research programs, as this has been proven the best possible device for recruitment, and produce material on psychiatry as a career for recruitment purposes.

3. To develop a medium of communications with other organizations to stimulate broad effort and action in the whole mental health field.

Elements in the " 'New Look' in American Psychiatry and Mental Health Operations"

This list has been presented to a number of groups. It may be that some of the general principles underlying these elements of the "new look" could be of some use to the field of corrections.

These elements of the "new look" are:

1. Adequate treatment will be made available (McNeels' Ideal) as early as possible, as continuously as possible, with as little dislocation as possible, with as much social restoration as possible.
2. Dislocation will be specifically avoided with treatment on the job, at home, in the community to the extent that these are possible.
3. Less hospitalization will be needed.
4. Patients will be classified from the point of view of their need for supervision, relationship to others, and social needs, and large hospital populations will be distributed in smaller, more appropriate, groups for each segment.
5. Social forces will be utilized far more than now.
6. The continuity of treatment will be the rule, not the continuity of residence.
7. Services for indigent and less fortunate financially will be improved with more money in the hands of individuals who seek their own place of treatment which will produce, in turn, demands for more low-cost private facilities.
8. Payment for services will come from multiple sources.

9. More dependency on the volunteer and non-governmental sector of society will develop.

10. Many more general medical and non-medical facilities will be utilized in the mental health program.

11. The entire medical profession will accept more responsibility for mental conditions.

12. Professional training for all mental health personnel will be a part of all service units.

13. Closer association with public and private welfare personnel; public health officers and nurses will emerge as a pattern of cooperation.

14. There will be greater utilization of non-medical personnel.

15. There will be more and more less trained personnel made useful.

16. Programs emphasizing certain services would also be alert to opportunities for clinical and operational research.

17. More private and semi-private patients will be utilized for teaching and research.

18. Mental health services of various kinds will be constructed in a single campus, in an area organized in such a way as to overcome the disadvantages of distance while avoiding the unnecessary replacement or relocation of already existing services.

19. Constant attention to the extra-curricular, that is carried out by others, in the field of primary prevention, must be part of the conscious efforts and framework of all mental health programs, with particular emphasis on suitable conditions in the pre-natal period, the normal social milieu, and those subject to unusual stress.

It is apparent in psychiatry that the conditions under which treatment is carried out are sometimes even more important than the treatment itself. There exists in classical literature (Dickens' *Christmas Carol*) a classic example of the theme that one's technical operations are sometimes the least important of the "businesses" of an individual.

" 'But you were always a good man of business, Jacob,' faltered Scrooge who now began to apply this to himself.

" 'Business,' replied the ghost, wringing his hands, 'Mankind was my business, charity, mercy, forbearance, and benevolence were all my business. The dealings of my trade were but a drop of water in the comprehensive ocean of my business.' "

In mental health and in corrections, these sentiments of Charles Dickens are perhaps even more important than technical, therapeutic procedures.

Persons with these characteristics will become more and more useful in our technical programs.

What Is the Role of the Correctional Policy-Maker in Resolving Manpower and Training Problems?

by LLOYD W. MCCORKLE AND ALBERT C. WAGNER

FOR THE PURPOSES of this paper, the term "correctional policy-maker" refers to correctional institution superintendents and the heads of correctional departments. These are selected because they can make decisions for their organization and because the government structure places responsibility for a total operation at these two points. The words "role" and "resolving" in the title of this paper suggest action and imply that the policy-maker can do something about manpower and training problems. This assumption will be explored, and some external and internal factors which either limit or facilitate the power of the administrative role to mobilize personnel for achieving objectives will be described.

We might begin by enumerating the issues which arise from operating difficulties caused by insufficient funds, burdens of recruitment, and organizational inflexibility. These are important, especially as they are related to the administrator's inability to influence key areas of decisions regarding personnel. Issues in these areas, however, are symptomatic of problems in two interrelated and interdependent areas: the structure of the society within which the organization provides service, and the degree of public support available for its program.

The correctional administrator confronts a rapidly changing social scene from an institution described as having "so many conflicting attitudes, contradictory motives, and intellectual uncertainties . . . grafted on to each other in steel and concrete."[1] Although the physical structure represents social improvisation and expediency within which the administrator must accommodate conflicting attitudes toward the offender by

[1] R. Korn and L. W. McCorkle, *Criminology and Penology* (New York: Henry Holt and Company, 1959), p. 458.

a moody and unpredictable public, he must meet certain standards of performance; e. g., the going minimum for inmates in the areas of food, clothing, and shelter, and at least the semblance of control of the institution. The larger social structure limits his action at all levels of service. Just as institutional performance cannot fall below a certain minimum of humanitarian safekeeping, the program cannot make life too soft for offenders. Between these extremes, there are alternative lines of action available to the administrator to achieve limited or generalized goals. The selection of any alternative between these extremes is critically dependent upon the manpower available and the administrator's estimate of the quality of personnel.

The impact of several factors, which either shrink or expand alternatives within these extremes, is suggested in a brief study of employee turnover rates for New Jersey correctional personnel during a four-year period. This study indicates that correctional officer salary ranges, population density, and institutional overcrowding are related to employee turnover. For instance, during the three-year period 1959-62, salary ranges for New Jersey correctional officers were $3,909-$5,079, $4,104-$5,334, and $4,309-$5,599. Personnel turnover during this period for all correctional institutions was 24.5 percent, 25.3 percent and 25.5 percent. In 1963, the salary range for correctional officer moved up sharply to $4,988-$6,482, and employee turnover dropped to 18 percent. The New Jersey State Prison has two branches, one located in the most densely populated, and the other in the most sparsely populated, area of the state. During this four-year period, the institution located in the highly populated area had employee turnover rates of 33.6 percent, 38.6 percent, 40 percent, and 20 percent, while the institution located in the sparsely populated area had no percent, 7.7 percent, no percent, and 7 percent during the same period. During this four-year period, the state's two reformatories were chronically overcrowded, and both had high rates of employee turnover. One overcrowded reformatory located within ten miles of an adult institution operating only slightly in excess of its capacity had almost double the turnover rate.

First and foremost among the factors which significantly limit or facilitate the administrator's ability to mobilize personnel is the budget, the device by which taxpayers, through their elected representatives, allocate financial resources to the correctional organization to carry out its mission. It is, on the one hand, the implementation of society's values of corrections and, on the other, the legitimatizing of its goals.[2]

---

[2] Talcott Parsons, "Suggestions for a Sociological Approach to the Theory of Organizations," *Administrative Science Quarterly* (June, 1956).

The number of authorized budgeted positions limits the manpower available to the organization for carrying out its assignment. Consequently, to the extent that the personnel or funds available for training limit the attainment of the organization's goals, the administrator must look to the political power structure for the resolution of his problem.[3] The moment the administrator does more than look, however, he enters an area where he will need more than good intentions, slogans, and cliches. If he attempts to deal with power realities in politics by making the issue public, he commits both himself and his organization, as Ohlin points out, to a hazardous undertaking.[4]

When the administrator perceives the solution of his manpower problems are being exclusively dependent upon the realignment of political power realities, he is caught on the horns of a cruel dilemma.[5] To influence this power structure he must pursue a course of action potentially dangerous not only to himself but also his organization. But not to act frustrates both him and his organization. This dilemma may explain the enthusiasm of corrections for good public relations. Programs of "good public relations" enable the organization to abandon efforts to solve the problem in favor of a pretense at efforts.[6]

A central problem for corrections is to resolve this dilemma in a way that will promote not only a public awareness and acceptance of correctional programs, but also the conviction that corrections serves the general public directly and that program defects will not be tolerated. When the general climate of public opinion is intolerant of serious deficiencies in corrections, it will be both politically expedient and administratively necessary to eliminate them. What makes all this relevant to manpower and training is the hard fact that operating budgets and employee salary structures most often reflect the extent of public support. Before the administrator concludes that his manpower problems can be solved only by the manipulation of power realities in the larger structure, he would do well to subject his organization to close and careful scrutiny. He might ask himself questions such as "Has the

---

[3] This is also true, although less obviously so, for salary ranges, salary adjustments and personnel reclassifications. Space does not allow an attempt to trace the subtle relationships between, at one level, budget and civil service regulations and, at the other, program administration and business management.

[4] Lloyd Ohlin, "Conflicting Interests in Correctional Objectives" in *Theoretical Studies in Social Organization of the Prison* (Social Science Research Council Pamphlet 15).

[5] The alternatives available to the administrator to avoid this perception range from preoccupation with routine trivia to pontifical observations about the sad state of society.

[6] Most "good public relations" programs in corrections seem to be aimed at the imagination of people and, consequently, frustrate, rather than contribute to, a public dialogue on the significant issues in the field.

important function of budget preparation received the attention it deserves?" "Does the organization have adequate formal procedures to review and control personnel operations?" and "Do the budget justifications for new personnel contain more than an expression of administrative interest in resolving poorly formulated problems?" In short, does the budget request for the organization reflect the interest, hard work, administrative skill, and knowledge of the chief executive and his staff? If it does, it is likely to command respect and a sympathetic hearing; if not, it may very well be one more casualty of efforts to hold down the rising cost of governmental service.

One or two additional points in the area of budgeting need at least brief mention. Elected public officials frequently find themselves caught between accelerating costs of providing government service and the average citizen's interest in holding the tax line. In this situation, the smaller the total budget, the larger the proportion of correctional costs to the total; the more restricted the tax base, the greater the pressures to curtail correctional services. Since personnel represents approximately 70 percent of the total operating budget, the pressure is likely to be against the immediate hiring of additional personnel. Correctional services compete with all other governmental services when a budget is being developed. Corrections often finds itself in competition with other welfare services for that portion of the tax dollar available for these services, and it not only has less broad appeal than most of these services, but it frequently has less well formulated goals, programs, and budget justifications. The recent population explosion has raised all welfare costs, and this also has had a serious impact on the availability of funds for corrections. In the relationship of corrections to other welfare services in competing for financial resources, the role of the federal government is significant. By making it mandatory that states meet certain requirements if they are to receive federal matching funds, the federal government has a lever to force standards upward in welfare services. This is true not only for welfare programs of financial assistance, but for capital construction in mental health and mental retardation since matching funds are now available for this purpose. (Federal appropriations to the Department of Health, Education, and Welfare also make possible the hospital improvement grant programs.) The objective is to demonstrate new and improved methods of care and treatment in public institutions for the mentally ill and retarded. Grants are made directly to mental hospitals and institutions for the retarded to demonstrate new or improved programs without any matching by the state or local government responsible for the main support of that institution. They are expected to lead to better standards of care and ultimately become part of the operating fabric of the institution with state support.

Less crucial than budgeting but of basic significance to the solution of manpower and training problems in corrections are relationships with departments of civil service. Civil service policy decisions, regulations, and procedures determine the type and quality of personnel brought into the correctional organization. Severe restrictions are placed on alternative lines of administrative action by the fact that government, not the correctional administrator, is the employer; in this relationship, civil service is the personnel officer. Although correctional organizations may collaborate in developing qualifications and specifications for positions, in the inclusion of standards or material for competitive examinations, the central and primary responsibility for executing the public employment statutory mandate rests with civil service. The implications of this for some sectors of public employment where character traits of employees are of paramount importance have resulted in a point of view that the wide acceptance of civil service as an alternative to political patronage has not been an unmixed blessing. Many correctional administrators share the sense of frustration expressed by O. W. Wilson:

> "The best-qualified man is not invariably made available for appointment or promotion. This results in part from a failure of the civil service agency to adopt suitable standards, and in part from a failure to appraise or to permit the appraisal of less easily measured intangible personal qualities such as character and personality. In their eagerness to prevent favoritism they rule out the appraisal of all qualities that are not susceptible of exact measurement. For example, the character requirement is sometimes restricted to absence of felony conviction; less serious conduct which may, nevertheless, indicate unsuitability for service is then ignored. In consequence of these failures, eligible lists are sometimes headed by men who are completely unsuited for police service or lacking in essential leadership qualities. And the police chief usually has no choice but to make appointments and promotions that he knows are unwise.
>
> "Punishment and dismissal under civil service are not undertaken in many instances where such action is desirable. This results from the unwillingness of the police chief to undertake the long-drawn-out and redtaped procedure that frequently is more nearly a trial of him than of his delinquent subordinate. When punishment is meted out, its measure is influenced by the personal background and feelings of the board members, and consequently, in nearly all instances, it is too lenient. Their lack of intimate knowledge of police work renders them unqualified to establish sound behavior standards for policemen. For example, it is not uncommon for civil service boards to deal more leniently with a policeman who has stolen than would the criminal court. Evil, of course, results from his return to police service, which frequently happens. Civil service machinery usually serves to protect the unqualified policeman rather than to assure his removal."[7]

---

[7] O. W. Wilson, "Toward a Better Merit System," *The Annals of the American Academy of Political and Social Science* (January, 1954).

These comments by an outstanding distinguished police administrator raise the issue of departmental versus state personnel standards for employees. We can only refer to this problem. The basic arguments of the proponents on each side can be quickly summarized: Those who want departmental standards or wish to enlarge the department's power in determining personnel standards base their case on the administrator's lack of authority to manage personnel in the pursuit of organizational objectives; those who argue for state standards contend that this limit on administrative power is highly desirable when viewed in the context of a larger value system. The degree to which the correctional administrator can collaborate with civil service on examinations, selection, and enforcement is dependent upon local policies and regulations. This is also true of his flexibility in developing, within basic civil service policies and regulations, departmental or institutional standard-setting and enforcement.

Whatever the degree of collaboration, the administrator still has some areas of leverage which allow him to contribute to the solution of manpower problems. The most significant of these is the probationary period for all new employees certified by civil service. This work-test period provides the correctional administrator with an opportunity to observe the on-the-job performance of employees. Although the employees are generally unusually circumspect during this time, it is still possible for the organization to determine whether or not they have the potential to become satisfactory correctional employees. To make this determination with the objectivity likely to impress review boards is the problem. If the administrator is to come to grips with it, his total organization must be committed to formal procedures for reviewing the individual's job performance. This is counter to a tendency on the part of organizations to avoid a decisive test of the employee's fitness after he has been certified to the organization. The reasons for this tendency are varied and easy to understand. During the work-test period, patterns of friendship, mutual concern, and interest are established, and practically everybody wants to be nice. It is easier, especially for the supervisor in immediate contact with the employee-probationer, to want to believe that he will do better in the future. The total organization often develops rationalizations for individual deficiencies in seeking to avoid a decisive test. Some individuals are placed in less demanding assignments, the institution's need for "good tower guards," is asserted and other things are done. If the administrator is to avoid future personnel problems, he needs formal, objective, institutionalized procedures for the probationary period which will make sure that the individual being tested gets a fair opportunity in a work situation, in which his performance is balanced against an objective estimate of his potential for contributing to the achievement of the institution's goals. Establishing such procedures must be a major concern of the administrator if his organization is not to be limited by having inadequate permanently appointed personnel. What has been said about the probationary period is also true for performance ratings of personnel, the employment of temporary employees, and the use of negative sanctions.[8]

The administrative role in corrections must be responsive not only to the aspirations of the larger social system and the structure of government but also to correctional employees and inmates.[9] The correctional institution previously was seen as essentially a symbol of improvising and expediency. It can now be defined as

> "a physical structure in a geographical location where a number of people, living under highly specialized conditions, utilize the resources and adjust to the alternatives presented to them by a unique kind of social environment. The people creating and enmeshed in this environment include administrative, custodial, and professional employees, habitual petty thieves, one-time offenders, gangsters, professional racketeers, psychotics, pre-psychotics, neurotics, and psychopaths, all living under extreme conditions of physical and psychological compression. The formal administrative structure of the prison may be comprehended in a brief glance at its table of organization. This table reveals a series of bureaucratically arranged positions with the warden at the top, and formal flow of power downward from his position. A more penetrating glance at the social structure of the prison reveals an on-going complex of processes that can neither be described nor anticipated by a static enumeration of formal powers and functions. For interacting with this formal administrative structure—and in many ways independent of it—is another social structure, the inmate social system, which has evolved a complex of adaptational processes with which inmates attempt to cope with the major problems of institutional living."[10]

The administrative process must seek not only to balance the delicate and powerful forces suggested above but also do this within a program that accommodates custodial safeguards, production goals, and treatment objectives. One persistent and basic problem confronted is related to the unresolved issues inherent in the conceptions of the criminal by the

---

[8] The implications of accepting the above as administrative objectives for correctional treatment are obvious. In effect, almost everything stated suggests that the solution of manpower problems is dependent on the development of a good bureaucracy. Questions can be and have been raised about the effectiveness of good bureaucracy for the rehabilitation of offenders. (Cf. L. W. McCorkle and R. Korn, "Resocialization Within Walls," *The Annals of the American Academy of Political and Social Science* [May, 1954]).

[9] Space and the complexity of the problem require that, for the most part, we ignore the interaction between the world of officials and the world of inmates.

[10] L. W. McCorkle and R. Korn, "Resocialization Within Walls," *The Annals* (May, 1954), *op. cit.*

classical and positivist schools of criminology. When Lombroso cut corrections loose from the firm intellectual justifications of Beccaria and Bentham, the scientific treatment of the criminal was ushered in on an ideological level. There was, however, a basic difference between eighteenth and nineteenth century criminologists. In the case of the former, a practical alternative was available to implement their recommendations. The nineteenth and twentieth century criminologists have yet to match their ideological and educational success with a comparable technical achievement. From the famous Declaration of Principles of 1870 until today, the chronicle of corrections is the effort to adapt itself to the new demands of science.

Whatever conflicts and intellectual uncertainties corrections must accommodate the forces already mentioned in a program for personnel and inmates. How it accommodates these forces is reflected at the ideological level by the official pronouncements of the correctional institution and at the action level by the behavior of personnel.

Earlier, the budget was defined as the concrete implementation of society's values of corrections and the legitimatizing of its goals. In this context, the correctional program is the framework within which these goals are attained. Consideration must be given to the central problem of goals. Basically, the administrative dilemma can be quickly stated: Unless goals are specifically defined, personnel do not understand what the objectives are, and their behavior becomes random and aimless, while the attempt to define specific goals raises issues for which there seems to be no readily available solution. It is essential from the point of view of manpower and training that the dilemma somehow be resolved. It is important to the utilization of manpower and its training that the goals of the institution be communicated to all personnel. In fact, the communication of organizational goals is probably more important than the precise substance of the goals. If utilization and training of personnel are goal-oriented, they make sense to individuals in the organization. This perception by personnel shapes their attitudes toward one another and the work situation and makes possible concerted lines of action for implementing policy. This requires not only that there be goals but also that these goals have two interrelated characteristics: feasibility and consistency in implementation.

It would be impossible to exhaust the reasons for the importance of having feasible goals to guide the operations of the organization. For our purposes, a feasible goal is one the organization has the resources to achieve. Feasible goals, therefore, have to be defined in terms of specific criteria and administrative operations. When defined in this way, they are likely to seem puny and pedestrian compared to the sweeping objectives of corrections. However, the efforts of corrections to organize itself around idealistic and non-operationally defined aspirations have had more important consequences than the commonly observed disillusionment and cynicism of personnel and inmates. Their most pernicious result has been the defensive posture of corrections in relation to critical questions that probe the gap between aspiration and reality.

A review of available literature in corrections reveals little factual information pertaining to the vital issues upon which society's plans for the operation and management of its correctional program should depend. More unfortunate, still, is the relative absence of research directed toward assembling relevant facts. This situation is both paradoxical and incredible, since the social and economic consequences of correctional programs are vast and far-reaching. Why, in view of their recognized importance, has there been so little inquiry into their operations? The answer, no doubt, is many-sided. We do not claim to have it. Certain conditions which contribute to this lack of inquiry can be discerned, however, and warrant consideration.

Correctional programs are related to subjects which reach deep into human emotions. There is no lack of public interest in correctional programs nor any shortage of opinion about what is wrong with them. On most of the basic and historic questions in corrections, there are strong but conflicting opinions. For instance, in discussing the punishment of delinquents or criminals or effective treatment for the sex offender or narcotics addict and similar correctional questions, the emotions evoked are conflicting, inconsistent, contradictory, and carry strong personal convictions. Such feelings do not promote attitudes of self-doubt nor the awareness that information is lacking and they are not congenial to the kind of detached curiosity about the subject which is the essence of scientific inquiry. The disposition of persons approaching correctional problems conflicts with an attitude of intellectual curiosity so necessary for the psychological experience leading to the feeling of "I don't know." Since most persons approaching correctional problems are unaware or not concerned that their conclusions may be incorrect, they do not experience the "hitches" in thinking which provide the stimulation for meaningful investigations. Since lay and professional persons approaching these problems are also unaware that they may be in error, they see little or no need to investigate further. One has only to contrast this state of mind with that of the scientist who is disciplined to become aware of his conceptual inadequacies and who tries to get at the bottom of them to understand a part of contemporary confusion in corrections.

Of lesser importance is the fact that research techniques in the social sciences develop within university departments which, to a considerable extent, have been isolated from the subject matter of corrections. While academic social scientists have lacked intimate and immediate contact with correctional operations, personnel working in corrections have not formulated their difficulties so that they can be readily translated into research problems. Consequently, while the vision of scientific corrections is not new, the field has not done much toward taking the first step in developing a science, which is assembling relevant data. There are some integrative efforts being made to bridge this gap between universities and corrections, but much remains to be accomplished.

When goals are feasible, the problem of their consistent application throughout the organization makes it a function of management to develop internal administrative measures that will insure desired responses by personnel to organizational goals. To accomplish this, the organization must relate to both procedural and motivational problems. At the procedural level, the administrative task is to translate organizational goals into a series of specific objectives at each operational level. To illustrate: The institution's industrial training program goals must be translated for wing officers into the objectives of getting inmates out of their cells and into the shops on time, keeping inmates engaged in industrial training by shop officers, scheduling sick calls by physicians at times other than when inmates are in the shop, and having the counseling service cope with the problem of malingering. There is always a danger that as feasible goals are redefined at each operational level, they may seem unrelated or trivial to the personnel who must implement them if the organization is to achieve its objectives. Also, the subgoals for particular roles become relatively meaningless when they have to compete with other pressures that may be unrelated or antagonistic to the organization's goals. The administration must be constantly sensitive to the motivational problems of employees and willing to use both inducements and negative sanctions to insure conformity to role requirements. In addition to establishing procedures, the administrator must be prepared to put his prestige on the line to facilitate cooperation between various parts of the organization.

The device available to the administrator to achieve objectives is the administrative process described by Litchfield[11] as a cycle of action which includes the following specific elements: decision-making, programming, communication, controlling and reappraisal. From this point of view, a correctional institution is an organization where people are enmeshed in the administrative process. The prison thus becomes a series of administrative wheels within wheels, the totality of which is action. The responsibility for the coordination of the wheels and the

---

[11] Edward H. Litchfield, "Notes on a General Theory of Administration," *Administrative Science Quarterly* (June, 1956).

elements described by Litchfield within a particular wheel is a function of the executive.

What are some general conditions in corrections which facilitate or hinder the administrator in discharging this responsibility? Mention has already been made that elements within the correctional structure have different purposes. Cressey describes the structure of a prison as "providing for three principal hierarchies—devoted respectively to keeping, using, and serving inmates—but not for the integration of their divergent purposes."[12] He points to the different and contradictory purposes of the elements concerned with these functions and the different objectives of the hierarchies. The professional roles in the correctional structure reflect this, and persons in these roles come with attitudes and expectations shaped by their academic and professional experience. Thus, when the educator views the prison, he not only sees a school, but his view of himself in relation to inmates is shaped by, let us say, the philosophy of progressive education. The social worker not only sees an agency, and the psychiatrist, a mental hospital, but they also see it through values and attitudes which reflect their professional training. Frequently, persons in professional roles do not think of themselves as correctional workers but rather as specialists who are practitioners of a professional discipline. In most instances, the work situation of professionals is fluid and uncertain, and their functions are defined in ambiguous and uncertain terms. Two writers summarized this problem as follows: "one looks in vain for the unified body of theory and practice which is to guide their (professionals) operations, for the traditions that will unify expectations around their efforts and provide standards protecting the quality and continuity of their work from the disruption of individual idiosyncrasy."[13]

Since the correctional structure as a bureaucracy requires personal loyalty and discipline, the potential for conflict between professionals and the structure is considerable. Clashes between the professional's conception of his role and the obligations imposed by the structure do much to explain the relatively low status of corrections as a vocational choice among many professionals. They explain, in part, the rapid turnover of professionals during times of full employment and the considerable number of books and articles on the deficiencies of the correctional environment. Organizational adjustments to these clashes range from allowing professionals to do anything so long as they do

---

[12] D. R. Cressey, "Limitations on Organization of Treatment" in *Theoretical Studies in Social Organization of the Prison* (Social Science Research Council Pamphlet 15).

[13] Korn and McCorkle, *The Annals, op. cit.*

not get in the way to limiting their role so severely as to make certain they will never get in the way. Reactions on the part of professional personnel range from resignation to enthusiastic and uncritical adoption of the real or imagined values of the correctional structure. It has been asserted that the way to resolve this problem is to make corrections more inviting to professionals, and that only by this method can qualified professionals be recruited and retained in the system. This argument overlooks another possibility: The development of professionals who can maintain their integrity and accept the discipline required to function within the correctional organization. Probably both approaches are needed and should operate simultaneously if this problem is to be resolved satisfactorily.

The use of formalized procedures for selecting public employees, combined with anti-discrimination statutes, have provided fresh employment opportunities for socially mobile non-whites. The employment of non-whites in corrections which, for most practical purposes, started not more than twenty-five years ago, has moved steadily upward. In some states the number of non-white correctional employees is far greater than the percentage of non-whites in the general population. In the past decade not only has the number of non-white correctional employees increased, but they have moved to positions of leadership, responsibility, and prestige. The non-white in corrections, whether custodial officer or professional, is also a member of a minority group currently engaged in a concerted effort to secure for its members the privileges and responsibilities of full citizenship. He finds himself in an environment in which many of the people he must supervise are also minority group members who often feel that their incarceration is due to the disadvantaged position their group has in society. The unique problems of the non-white correctional employee and the special tensions and strains on him have not received the serious attention they deserve.

The problems and issues raised in the general struggle of non-whites to achieve equality will also be felt by a sensitive correctional administration. For instance, the administrator may find overt or covert patterns of racial discrimination in the institution. These patterns will intrude in the administrative process and may complicate such a basic matter as administrative discretion in making post or shift assignments. As long as any discrimination exists, what may very well have been a purely administrative decision can be misinterpreted by not only staff but also significant community leaders as an act of discrimination. This problem is often highlighted when it becomes necessary to apply negative sanctions to non-white employees. When an employee is disciplined, there is an almost inevitable human tendency to look for reasons beyond job performance. In this, non-white employees are no exception. And if any pattern of discrimination exists, it is convenient for them to use it as a rationalization for their failure to perform satisfactorily on the job. One result may be a reverse type of discrimination whereby non-white employees are dealt with more leniently because of administrative anxiety about being charged with discrimination. Apart from moral and ethical values, it is an administrative imperative that discrimination be eliminated simply because it lowers the efficiency, as well as the morale, of the organization.

In some institutions, a considerable number of non-white employees occupy relatively low-status, cottage-life positions, overseeing the operation of a correctional program where the majority of inmates are non-white but where all supervisory positions are filled with middle-class whites. If the administrative process depends upon good communication and if it is true that middle-class whites do not fully understand the psychology of the lower-class minority groups, the relevancy of this for study and serious discussion by correctional personnel is obvious.

There are other areas where the employee's outside roles may conflict with administrative expectations regarding his behavior. As a father, the correctional employee may be expected home Christmas Day and he may feel this obligation to be greater than the responsibility of working the second shift. As town clerk, he may be more interested in the tax rate in Smithville than in the control he exercises over his wing. As the past master of a lodge, he may be more concerned with the outcome of a fraternal picnic than with the production of the textile shop. As a good neighbor, he may be more interested in helping a friend than in reporting a serious infraction of rules by a fellow employee. Put another way, those relationships which define him as a person may impose on him obligations and objectives which conflict with correctional goals. In addition, the correctional worker frequently finds himself in situations which bring moral courage into play. These crisis situations are usually highly-charged emotional interactions between employees and inmates. When they occur, they put the organization to its most crucial tests, the responses to which are shaped not only by the administrative process but also by the personal characteristics of the participants. It is impossible to design administrative or operational procedures which anticipate all eventualities. When procedures do not anticipate the situation, the organizational response depends on discriminating judgments exercised by personnel. For the administrator and the institution, it is important that these crisis situations be continuously scrutinized with a view to either improving procedures, personnel, or both.

There are always some who argue that the inability of personnel to carry out one set of procedures can be counteracted by adopting new and better sets of procedures. They reason that the indifference or carelessness which resulted in the neglect of one set of rules might somehow be neutralized by changing the plan instead of improving the executors of the plan. The difficulty with this argument is that no one has yet devised a plan which does not require attention to detail, diligence, and care. Given a certain level of ability and interest, any employee or group of employees have a point beyond which new and improved procedures fail to produce results. When this point is reached, the administrator must either get new employees or train the ones he has if he is to get better results. In most instances, the only practical alternative available to the administrator is training.

When training is viewed as the communication of skills, knowledge, and attitudes to employees in order to improve job performance, the administrator must be constantly involved in the process. His major responsibility in training is to establish lines of communication between himself and others, and among the various parts of the organization. After these channels of communication have been opened, the administrator must see to it that they remain open and that they are used by personnel. Unless this is done, the training will not be meaningful, and whatever formal program the organization does attempt in this area will be an empty ritual.

The training of managerial personnel for corrections has not received the attention it urgently needs. As the field of corrections matures and the administrative task becomes more complex, the pressure to recruit or develop more sophisticated talent will become greater. Since career patterns in corrections limit possibilities for recruitment outside the system, increased attention will have to be given to methods of identifying and developing potential administrative talent within the organization. To do this will require policies, procedures, and personnel at the correctional department level related to this area. The process of identifying and developing talent will have to be built around a long-range program for the department that, on the one hand, anticipates future organizational personnel needs and, on the other, develops individuals to meet these needs. The organization, of course, must be large enough to permit mobility of personnel and flexible enough to provide new experiences for them.

Individuals identified as potential institutional superintendents should be given educational leave to pursue graduate or professional training at a recognized school of public or business administration. The reluctance of most governmental units to support such programs and the hesitation of correctional organizations to make the personnel adjustments necessary for their success reflect lack of vision. Although industry and certain sectors of government recognize the need to develop executive personnel and are prepared to expend tremendous resources to do so, state, county, and municipal services have not been stimulated to make the necessary investments for the success of such personnel development programs. Related to these programs, but not a substitute for them, is participation by correctional organizations in intensive "top or middle management" training programs. When these are carefully developed, usually in conjunction with a university or university personnel, they encourage organizational personnel to redefine their problems and raise the general level of administrative practice.

If there are unique characteristics that shape the roles of professional practitioners, the field will have to examine the uncritical assumption that individuals are adequately trained to fill these roles without formal indoctrination. As correctional institutions participate more fully in graduate or professional training which includes internships in corrections, a part of the problem of recruiting professionals into the correctional organization will disappear. We can hope for the day when there will be more correctional institutions certified for field placement by schools of social work and for clinical internships by university training programs in clinical psychology. Even after this is achieved, there will still be individuals who enter the system as teachers, counselors, classification specialists, and the like. Most of these will probably have limited training beyond the bachelor's degree. Well-conceived, formal indoctrination periods for these individuals would save the organization false starts and lost motions. Two ways to approach this problem suggest themselves: The development of regionalized facilities used by several correctional systems, or the development of a specialized training sequence at a university for one correctional system. The training, while developed in close collaboration between the university and the correctional system or systems, should be ultimately the responsibility of the university.

Any discussion of the development of professional personnel for corrections should recognize the various attempts to develop specialized university training courses, either at the undergraduate or graduate level. The major problem confronting this development has been the inability to relate the completion of the program to either civil service requirements for correctional positions or career patterns in corrections. Persons completing such courses frequently present themselves to the correctional organization prepared to do little more than run the system. Superintendents are not selected in this fashion, and the correctional organizations do not have entrance positions acceptable to the graduates. When non-specific titles such as "instructor-counsellor" are used as a technique for bringing such people into the organization, these people are frequently frustrated by the nature of their assignments and their "subprofessional status." Since it seems likely that present career patterns in corrections, which follow either the custodial hierarchy or recognized professional disciplines, will persist, specialized training programs for persons entering corrections will have a limited impact. Specialized corrections training at the university or professional school level for persons already in the field—training that they can pursue on a part-time basis—is needed and should be encouraged.

The training of line or uniform personnel has, for some time, been a standard operating procedure in most correctional organizations. This training varies from school sessions established for custodial personnel to informal brief periods where neophyte officers "soak up" experience in association with older officers. The pre-service training of corrections officers varies from the communication of highly specific skills —searching, handling locks and keys, counting inmates—to generalized and vague courses on the history of progressive penology or the rehabilitation of inmates. Both pre-service and in-service training are indispensable adjuncts to any operating correctional system. Certainly more time and attention need to be given to determining the most efficient and economical method of communicating necessary information and essential skills in these training programs.

A maximum-security prison approached its in-service training needs by developing a questionnaire and circulating it among custodial personnel to determine the type of training corrections officers felt they needed most. The questionnaire contained a number of items listed under the following headings: (a) paper work; (b) routine duties; (c) how to treat or deal with inmates; (d) keynotes on various assignments; (e) duties of the correctional officer; (f) personal requirements of the correctional officer; (g) relationship with inmates. The officers were asked to check whether or not they felt training in these areas was needed (1) immediately; (2) eventually; (3) not at all, or (4) would like. After they checked all of the items, the officers were requested to list, in order of rank, the ten most important areas in which they felt training was needed. They were also asked to indicate those situations they felt could best be handled on a man-to-man basis rather than through in-service training. Approximately 97 percent of the questionnaires were returned. The results were tabulated and the areas in which the officers felt they needed training in the order of rank of their importance were as follows:

a. What to do in the event of trouble—98.5 percent
b. Importance of duties—96.6 percent

c. Safeguarding information—96 percent
d. How to search an inmate—96 percent
e. How to count—94.3 percent
f. Graft and bribery—93.7 percent
g. Responsibility to superiors—93.1 percent
h. Personal appearance—92.6 percent
i. Significance of oath of office—91.4 percent
j. Safety precautions—90 percent

If this is an accurate reflection of what officers are most concerned about and where they feel the need for assistance and training, both pre-service and in-service training at the correctional officer level should be primarily geared to the operational realities that confront the officer as he carries out his assignments.

In the training of uniformed personnel, an area frequently overlooked is the category of positions in the custodial hierarchy just above corrections officer. Just as pre-service and in-service training programs for corrections officers need to recognize that the officer is also a manager of individuals, and should include material relevant to his responsibilities as an employer of inmates, the training of superior officers should emphasize these officers' important management responsibilities. The supervisory positions immediately above corrections officer are the ones through which the broad policies of the institution are filtered into operational realities. If it is assumed that institutional policies, as they relate to inmates, ultimately depend on the relationships of officers to inmates, it is the responsibility of persons in these supervisory positions to control and review the officers' behavior. It would, therefore, appear that great emphasis should be placed on the training of these individuals. When an officer is promoted, he should undergo a formal training period during which he receives, among other things, intensive training in management techniques, problem solving, and executive procedures, prior to assuming his supervisory duties. Since in any given organization, it probably will not be possible to implement all the training devices which have been only briefly described, this group should receive priority as far as training is concerned.

The Role of the Private Charitable Foundation in Resolving Manpower and Training Problems in Corrections

by Clyde E. Sullivan

Introduction

What is the role of the private charitable foundation in resolving manpower and training problems in corrections? A variety of responses could be given to that question. Each response would be both satisfying and dissatisfying, depending on who receives it. The response I choose to make is based on what seems to me to be one of the most fundamental concerns of a socially responsible, modern, charitable foundation—that is, how to give money wisely.

What I say will probably be somewhat distressing to those who feel that intervention in correctional problems and decisions about corrections should be left to "experts" identified with the correctional field. It will also be dissatisfying to anyone believing that satisfying answers to correctional manpower and training problems have already been found and that the only real need is for money to demonstrate their efficacy.

This paper does not attempt to prescribe a standard role for a foundation to follow in dealing with corrections. Nor does it provide a list of projects to be undertaken. Instead, it is an effort to create a perspective for guiding and developing a fruitful interaction between money-granting agencies, such as foundations and the people, professions, and agencies which make up the correctional field. To be effective, collaboration between foundations and corrections in resolving manpower and training problems should be built on a sound evaluation of the current status of the field. Further, each partner should know something about the other, and both must share a common perspective of underlying issues and reasons for problems. This paper is an attempt to develop such a frame of reference and perspective for interaction.

Some General Observations About Foundations

The private charitable foundation now plays an increasingly significant role in modern America. In fact, "foundation" has gained such stature in the public mind that it tends to be a "magic" word. For many scientists, educators, and public administrators, modern foundations have come to be almost synonymous with the opportunity to undertake innovative action in study, demonstration, or research. Such an aura of respectability and substance surrounds the term that it is regularly used by confidence-men to provide a "cover" in hoodwinking victims.

An organization for giving large sums of money to philanthropy dates back to at least Middle Roman times. For the most part, such organizations were designed to provide a protected way for donors to distribute temporary, direct relief to unfortunate victims of circumstances. But in the last fifty years, and particularly in the United States, a somewhat different concept has emerged. During the last quarter of the nineteenth century and the early years of the twentieth century, huge industrial fortunes were accumulated in the United States. This period saw the end of a laissez-faire economic philosophy which emphasized a rugged individualism and large-scale organization of business and industry. The major channels for expending surplus wealth were conspicuous consumption, reinvestment, and speculation. There were inevitable limitations to using these channels for managing surplus. Conspicuous consumption, reinvestment, and speculation created almost as many problems as they resolved. Reinvestment, for example, would result in greater production—but, unless consumption was also increased, production would simply depress prices. Similarly, speculation in the stock market provided a solution more apparent than real. Since large-scale trading and speculation were confined to a relatively small group, it was frequently a matter of exchanging one surplus for another. As the threat of government intervention, control, and income tax increased, large-scale philanthropy became a popular way of releasing surplus wealth. As a result, charity began to wear a new look. Large-scale philanthropy on a long-term basis began to develop an organizational character, reflecting many of the organizational attitudes and management patterns of that time. This trend, coupled with individualism and the desire of the philanthropist to determine and direct the ways in which his money was spent, created a core for what has become a unique type of philanthropic unit.

At first, these organizations were somewhat circumscribed in their activities and strongly reflected the individuals and the special interests establishing them. There was little to distinguish the philanthropy of many of these newcomers from the philanthropy that had gone before. But in the establishment of these new organizations, some comprehensive moral concerns had been publicly expressed and some significant principles had been incorporated in their charters dedicating their resources to meeting deep human needs and the general human welfare. Because of these explicitly stated principles and purposes, sweeping freedom of action was granted by law and confirmed by public acceptance.

Gradually, as the result of subsequent experiences in seeking to implement these charter principles, and in coping with internal requirements for developing a rationally consistent philosophy and practice of giving, a larger concept of the role of foundations took form. Where the classical idea of philanthropy was built on providing temporary relief for victims of fate, the modern trend is increasingly founded on the notion that foundation support of research, development, demonstration, and exploration into underlying causes may bring long-term relief from human misery. Not all foundations have followed this trend, but it seems characteristic of most of the major foundations, and their influence on smaller foundations has been considerable.

The funds in the control of private charitable foundations in the United States have been aptly described as the "venture capital" of philanthropy. Some foundations have assumed a relatively passive and somewhat isolated role in disbursing this capital, first receiving appeals for funds, then withdrawing to judge the merits and appropriateness of each appeal, and emerging after a time to approve those appeals that seem most worthy at the moment. Other foundations have taken an active role in developing requests and deliberately create situations, opportunities, and institutions to which they give their financial support.

In the introduction to the comprehensive study of foundations published by the Russell Sage Foundation, Andrews groups foundations into five broad categories. He comments ". . . foundations present an almost infinite variety. Generalizations are unsafe, but to understand foundations at all it is probably necessary to consider them under certain broad classifications. Division is not sharp; a particular foundation may change in character and program through the years, and at a given period exhibit characteristics of several types."[1] His general groupings and descriptions follow:

General Research Foundations

This classification includes nearly all the larger, well-known foundations, which operate under broad charters. They support research projects in

[1] F. Emerson Andrews, Introduction to *The Foundation Directory,* Edition 2, Prepared by the Foundation Library Center, Ann D. Walton and Marianna O. Lewis, Editors (New York: Russell Sage Foundation, 1964), p. 27.

education, health, and welfare which characterize foundation work in the public mind. Usually they have large endowments, but some smaller foundations also support programs of national significance and fall properly into this category of general research. There are a board of trustees (directors, managers) with broad interests; and a trained professional staff to serve as the "eyes" of the foundation, seeking out promising new ventures, evaluating projects offered, handling details of grants—or actual operation if the foundation is of the operating type—and following through on results so that future programs may be built on past experience. Only 190 foundations are believed to fall into this category, but these control 64 percent of the assets of all foundations and are the ones most in the public eye. To a large degree, they are the leaders and standard-setters.

Special Purpose Foundations

These foundations are created—many of them by wills or trusts rather than by incorporation—to serve a charitable purpose, usually in the charter or in a letter of gift. . . . The special purpose may be as narrow as that of the Prairie Chicken Foundation of Illinois . . . which is devoted to preserving remnants of prairie chicken flocks, or as broad as the whole field of education, in which case there is hardly any danger of the purpose becoming outmoded. Special foundations are the butt of much of the humor directed at foundations, but many restricted funds are managed efficiently and serve useful ends. The danger does not lie in concentrating on particular needs or projects, which is also the policy of the general research foundation, but in rigid restrictions which prohibit the foundations from concentrating on other needs as they arise.
Many special purpose funds are small, but a few have large endowments . . . they control about 9 percent of the total foundation endowment.

Community Foundations

These are composite foundations, usually set up as trusts rather than corporations, which function under community control in a sense seldom found in other philanthropic endowments. Capital gifts or bequests are received and the principal administered by the trust departments of qualified local banks and trust companies. The income is distributed together with such portions of the principal as may be authorized in any trust, under supervision and control of a distribution committee selected for its representative character and knowledge of charitable affairs. Power is reserved to transfer to similar purposes any funds which can no longer be effectively used for the ends originally designated. The donors may be numerous, and each donor may either specify how his gift is to be used or leave it to the discretion of the distribution committee, but usually with the proviso that the gift be used within the city or county where the community foundation is located.
. . . The National Council on Community Foundations, tabulating all community foundations without size restriction, reported total active capital for 170 such foundations at $430 million at the end of 1962. The Directory, applying its size restrictions, listed 102 such foundations with active capital of $425 million . . . (this) represents only 3 percent of the assets of all foundations in the Directory.

Company-Sponsored Foundations

A wave of foundations of a new type has crested in the past decade. The "company-sponsored" foundations are tax-exempt, non-profit legal entities separate from the parent company but with trustee boards consisting wholly or principally of corporation officers and directors, and having for their purpose an easy way of corporation giving.
. . . While the total of 1,716 represents more than 28 percent of all foundations, some states and regions have few or none; the concentration is chiefly in the industrial areas.
. . . Obviously, company-sponsored foundations are conduit foundations to a much greater extent than any other group. They spend not only their investment income, as do nearly all foundations, but they also receive substantial new funds each year, or at least each year of good profits, and spend a large portion of this new money.

Family Foundations

Typically, family or personal foundations are set up by a living person or persons rather than by a bequest.

Generally, they are initially small and may have no administrative organization or headquarters other than the office of the donor or that of a law firm. The trustees are likely to be the donor or donors, his immediate family and possibly his lawyer, banker, or business associate.

At the beginning, many family foundations serve simply as the channel for the current giving of the living donor. Assets are often no adequate measure of their present potential; they may make grants out of current gifts of the donor far out of proportion to income from assets.

Programs often differ little from donations by wealthy men and women who have not incorporated their charity. . . .

Many of these initially small foundations may become the recipients of very large bequests upon the deaths of donors, and some of them build substantial assets through yearly accretions. As funds increase and experience lengthens, programs may change, the trustee board may grow in breadth and perhaps in size, and the foundation may support projects of national importance. Nearly all of the present large general research foundations began as family foundations with limited funds, oriented to the personal charities of their donors. In the family foundations of today and those to be created lie possibilities for further large foundations.

With the exception of some special purpose funds, foundations have wide latitude in setting goals for themselves, choosing areas for activity, and means for accomplishing objectives. In recent years, some legal restrictions have been imposed, which limit the extent to which a foundation may hold investment income, but no restrictions have been set on disbursements. Most foundations are free to dip into capital and to spend as much of their resources deemed desirable in any period of time. The freedom to select recipients of gifts is similarly broad. Grants may be given to individuals, groups, universities, research institutions, survey and research councils, social and government agencies, or corporations established for the specific purpose of receiving and administering a grant. Some foundations also have programs and projects supervised directly by foundation staff.

In modern society, this freedom of action in determining foundation functions and roles is tied to a level of responsibility for objective decision and considered action that was not required of charitable organizations previously.

By law as well as by charter, a foundation ". . . is dedicated to public welfare. Its responsibility is to the public as a whole. In political and social issues it cannot be partisan. This very non-partisanship and objectivity gives to the foundation a great positive force, and enables it to play a unique and effective role in the difficult and sometimes controversial task of helping to realize democracy's goals."[2]

But needs and problems of human welfare far exceed the combined capacity of all available foundation funds. Thus, one of the first concerns of a foundation must be to find a sound basis for choosing among a variety of requests and alternative ways of spending money. What criteria should be used in making such decisions?

It has been suggested that the proper role for a modern foundation is to be a "risk-taker on man's intellectual, humanitarian, scientific, and cultural frontiers; its gifts . . . catalytic agents to inspire and aid people, communities, institutions, and agencies to solve their problems. . . ."[3] This distills the essence of the general philosophy that seems to motivate a majority of foundations in the United States.

Being a catalyst and stimulus to pioneering is a difficult assignment. How can the officers and staff of a foundation make sure that the activities they choose to support will truly contribute to advances in practice and knowledge? What elements must be considered? How does one decide what is an important idea? What makes one idea more important than another? For example, since corrections deals with a highly dangerous area of social deviance, is a mediocre idea in corrections more important than an exceptional idea in a less dangerous sector of human problems? To what extent does the significance of a problem field add to or detract from the significance and quality of the questions being asked? Simply because we in corrections are faced by important problems does not mean that we are asking significant questions, nor that we are meeting problems with important ideas. Are we in a position to urge that our projects and proposals be supported and given preference over other problem areas?

There are also other difficulties. What information and understanding are needed to obtain funds when and where they are needed?

---

[2] *Report of the Study for the Ford Foundation on Policy and Program* (Detroit, Michigan, November, 1949).

[3] W. K. Kellogg Foundation, *Annual Report* (Battle Creek, Michigan, 1963).

Experience teaches that the best way of solving some of these problems is to find people who are likely to make significant contributions to society and to strongly support them. There is no reason to assume that the field of corrections will be different from other fields of human endeavor. It seems probable that major insights and innovations will come only through the actions and contributions of a comparatively small number of original and gifted men and women. What are these people like? How are they to be found, and what kind of training is required to foster their growth and maturation? In what ways do conditions of work affect their development and performance . . . and do the circumstances and atmosphere of contemporary correctional settings establish a stimulating, creative environment, or do they contribute to an inhibiting, vitiating cycle of activity?

If we are going to propose that charitable foundations and other funding agencies become partners in resolving manpower and training problems, and if we ask them to make investments in activities concerned with corrections, it is imperative that we be clear-eyed and frank in assessing ourselves as candidates for such support. It may be uncomfortable at the outset, but it will provide the base for a sound partnership and collaboration.

Foundations can bring a great deal more than just money to such a relationship. One of the most important things foundations have to share comes from their experience in trying to answer some of the questions posed earlier and from their interaction with a variety of groups and individuals who have been successful in their search for better ways of meeting human problems.

There should be an informed and balanced appreciation of the strengths and biases of both sides of such a partnership. Thus, if the officers and staff of a foundation do not avail themselves of mature advice and counsel from knowledgeable sources in the field, they are likely to support many naive and fruitless activities. On the other hand, if they draw too extensively from the advice and observations of established scholars, experts, and institutions in the field, they may unwittingly relinquish their catalytic role and may tend to perpetuate the status quo.

A foundation can easily slip into a pattern of giving money in a way which is approved instead of giving in a way which will bear significantly on critical issues. It may seem to be more stable and solid to support conventional ideas rather than unusual ideas, and innovations and novel ideas with real value for the future may fail to get support. It is very difficult mentally to rearrange a familiar network of information and ideas, adopt a new perspective, and escape from a prevailing frame of reference. As the "outsider" and review agent in the working relationship with corrections, the foundation should bear much of the responsibility for maintaining a critical perspective.

There is need at the same time to be sensitive to some of the subtle, seductive qualities of power and authority and to the danger of assuming responsibilities beyond one's true competence. "By the way in which it decides to give money to one research project and refuses it to another, a foundation may in effect become the manager of research, determining the employment of staff and the interpretation of results."[4]

Such a pattern should be avoided. It is reasonable, however, to urge a foundation to take action in developing a field and to accept responsibility for the kind of influence exerted and the direction of subsequent movement. Eventually, the field itself must have the ultimate responsibility for decisions and action. This suggests the rudiments of a working principle for selecting those people and programs most likely to yield results. Important innovations are most likely to come from people and programs with a commitment to self-evaluation and review, and where efforts have already been made to gather an extensive reservoir of information upon which decision and action may be based and to develop an able and informed group of decision-makers.

The proliferation of foundations, increased federal support, and the greater availability during the last two decades of money for supporting scientific research and development have had a profound effect on the organization of scientific studies. Many feel that the greater availability of money is a mixed blessing. There is an increasing tendency by many scientists to use the amount of money going into a research activity as an index of the value of the work being done.

A variety of administrative functions have mushroomed . . . there is a preoccupation with how to design research to get support, and in some situations some of our best scientists are enmeshed in a kind of "scientific politics," campaigning for the next grant. Alvin M. Weinberg, Director of the Oak Ridge National Laboratory, has called this "Big Science" and criticizes this trend in the following words:

> . . . since Big Science needs great public support, it thrives on publicity. The inevitable result is the injection of a journalistic flavor into Big Science which is fundamentally in conflict with the scientific method. If the serious writings about Big Science were carefully separated from the journalistic writings, little harm would be done. But they are not. Issues of scientific or technical merit tend to get argued in the popular, not the scientific, press, or in the congressional committee room, rather than in the technical society lecture hall; the spectacular, rather than the perceptive, becomes the scientific standard. . . .
>
> In the second place, one sees evidence of scientists spending money in-

---

[4] *Report of the Study for the Ford Foundation on Policy and Program* (Detroit, Michigan, November, 1949).

stead of thought. This is one of the most insidious effects of large-scale support of science. In the past the two commodities, thought and money, have both been hard to come by. Now that money is relatively plentiful but thought is still scarce, there is a natural rush to spend dollars rather than thought—to order a $\$10^7$ nuclear reactor instead of devising a crucial experiment with the reactors at hand, or to make additional large-scale computations instead of reducing the problem to tractable dimensions by perceptive physical approximation. The line between spending money and spending thought is blurring.

Finally, the huge growth of Big Science has greatly increased the number of scientific administrators. Where large sums of public money are being spent, there must be many administrators who see to it that the money is spent wisely. Just as it is easier to spend money than to spend thought, so it is easier to tell other scientists how and what to do than to do it oneself. The big scientific community tends to acquire more and more bosses. The Indians with bellies to the bench are hard to discern for all the chiefs with bellies to the mahogany desks. Unfortunately, science dominated by administrators is science understood by administrators, and such science quickly becomes attenuated if not meaningless. . . .

What really bothers me is the evidence that Big Science is invading the universities. . . . A professor of science is chosen because he is extremely well qualified as a scientist, as a thinker, or as a teacher. If he becomes too involved with Big Science he will have to become a publicist, if not a journalist, an administrator, and a spender of big money. I do not for a moment suggest that college professors are less able big-time administrators than are professional administrators. I merely point out that the proper function of a professor is to be a professor; that once Big Science has invaded his precincts and he becomes an operator (even though a very effective one), his students and his intellectual eminence and proficiency are bound to suffer. . . . Big Science can ruin our universities by diverting the universities from their primary purpose and by converting university professors into administrators, housekeepers, and publicists.[5]

The Nature of the Correctional Field

A candid appraisal of the extent to which corrections currently is effective in making significant contributions to the store of human knowledge and to general human welfare reveals that it is falling short of its potential in many ways. Viewed as a whole, the "modern" correctional setting is still primarily a "holding" operation, which needs more help from society than it is able to give in return. Certainly, it is a highly significant area of concern for all mankind, but the fact that a problem area is important does not mean that it is organized in a way that will be productive, nor that the questions and issues available for study and evaluation are significant. If we are going to urge foundations to participate in resolving correctional problems, we should be

---

[5] Alvin M. Weinberg, "Impact of Large-Scale Science on the United States," *Science* (July 21, 1961).

prepared to take a long careful look at the current state of the field and its value as an "investment."

Corrections has been given a conflicted social assignment. Workers are expected to manage a socially explosive collection of handicapped, inadequate, larcenous, and violent people at minimum expense and with maximum security for society. In this task, they are expected to operate within a framework of democratic ideals and to provide ways of changing a majority of these unfit and unwilling clients into relatively able and self-disciplined members of the community. Because of the contradictions involved, short-term security and managerial controls are emphasized, and the programs of many agencies and institutions become static, rule-ridden, and inflexible.

Corrections tries to avoid crises, but it is controlled by them and by the fear that they may occur. At the same time, correctional administrators try to walk on both sides of the street and use a crisis philosophy to control others as they themselves feel controlled. For example, at the time of submitting an annual budget to the legislature, it is common that correctional administrators "view with alarm" rising trends of crime and delinquency in headlines. Later, when the budget crisis has passed, similar headlines are deplored and rationalized by the same administrators. Staff members, offenders and the general public are differentially subjected to similar stress and control through threat and are disciplined through fear of crises. This reflects a real dilemma, and neither social scientist nor reformer should be hasty to criticize. Due attention should be given to all aspects of the situation. Any program of education or analysis in corrections should be sensitive to conflicting pressures impinging on the correctional worker.

Public indifference, public sentimentality, and public vengeance reinforce elements of conflict. A public service forced to operate in a climate of indifference and contradiction develops an internal climate of conservatism. In such a climate, resistance to change becomes a virtue. Motivation and anticipation in work are dulled and blunted. The guiding theme becomes one of "no untimely headlines." The prevailing expectation is that only a minimum service level can be expected or maintained. A correctional agency operating with such a philosophy becomes little more than a processing agency, operating with assembly-line methods, dominated by rules rather than by principles, and giving little more than lip service to the idea that it is possible to function as an effective force for change and social restoration of clients. Unfortunately, this is what has happened in many parts of the correctional field, and much of the actual current practice of corrections is a compromise of these conflicts.

One of the most frustrating and morale-reducing factors in correctional agencies today is a pattern of "split-level" decision-making that has developed. Ideally, the responsibility for decision and the power to make decisions should be as integrated as possible. In corrections, there is a frequent separation between policy-making levels and management and treatment levels. Many decisions which are critical in determining programs and operations in correctional settings are made outside the settings in which the decisions are implemented. Frequently, the basis of the decision and the requirements which it makes necessary are not even central to correctional concerns. The most obvious example of such a separation is that between a committing court and a state prison. The same kind of discrepancy can be seen in a single correctional agency. Investigation and supervision are sometimes widely separated in probation services, discipline and treatment are sometimes established as separate, uncommunicating activities within the institutions . . . and because of the ever-present anxiety about criticism from newspapers, legislators, and local politicians, correctional personnel working directly in contact with offenders are often unable to make important decisions at the right time, but instead have to delay the decisions and pass the question to a higher supervisory level. By repeating the procedure many times, the processing agency pattern is reinforced. The process most likely to be corrective is one which is based on consistent, effective communication and smoothly articulated services that can operate in timely ways. Management objectives may differ at different levels; conflicts are inevitable. However, conflicts should be resolved in ways which recognize the inter-relationships between levels. Decisions at every level of the process should be related and aimed at providing the best long-term public service. In practice, legislative, judicial, and administrative decisions about correctional matters often reflect the special interests of particular groups rather than the long-term welfare of society as a whole.

Decisions sometimes are arbitrary and stereotyped because personnel are incompetent or inefficient. If correctional manpower is of inferior quality, the problem may be a matter of replacement and recruitment. On the other hand, if ineffectiveness and stereotypy are due to inexperience or lack of knowledge, then study, research, and training may be indicated.

A processing agency, however, is not likely to produce new knowledge, and a working setting of hamstrung decisions and perpetual compromise is not likely to attract the kind of manpower corrections needs. Successful management and treatment of offenders require that those who manage and those who treat be people with a broad perspective and knowledge of society, people of high principle and integrity with a deep understanding of the principles of living which spark and preserve spontaneity and vitality. Ideally, the entire staff of a correctional agency should be of this quality. Hopefully, at least supervisory and administrative positions will be staffed by such persons. Practically, we should take steps to nourish and maintain this kind of leadership where it already exists and seek to increase the supply. As a guideline for action by foundations, programs which are moving away from processing and holding orientations and those which are actively promoting development of personnel are the most likely prospects for the future.

The question of training and support for this training opens up an area of inquiry outside the practical setting.

The need for university-level coursework and training directly applicable to corrections is largely ignored by most colleges and universities. Academic colleagues may protest that this is an extreme statement. There are a few exceptions. For the most part, however, those college programs offered as "preparation for correctional work" are usually only general courses, as applicable to many other areas of work as to crime and delinquency.

There is much to be said for developing broad integrating principles for the novice or beginning student to organize and relate diverse ideas and new information to the broad spectrum of human behavior. Even at advanced levels of practice and training, it is recognized that theories, hypotheses, and practical techniques must be tested and fitted into a framework of what is generally known. Such an integration is one of the marks of a maturing professional. But between being a novice and becoming professional, there are critical stages of intensive, focused study. Universities and professional schools generally reject claims that a need exists in corrections for specialization and dedicated attention.

Schools of law, social welfare, medicine, and psychiatry, and departments of psychology seem to handle correctional issues in an irregular, off-hand fashion, almost as an "after-thought." When attention is focused on an issue for any length of time, it is usually more related to the enthusiasm of a single professional than to support or stimulation from one of the university schools, departments, or disciplines.

Sociology has been the most persistent and systematic academic discipline in defining concepts, developing theory, testing hypotheses, and organizing an increasing pool of knowledge with an immediate implication for correctional problems. It, however, has tended to emphasize etiological factors and is rarely concerned with clinical issues. Moreover, the rugged empiricism of many sociological studies has sometimes alienated correctional workers. Antagonisms have developed as scientific values have been pushed without apparent consideration for practical pressures impinging on the correctional system. On the other hand, correctional workers have been careless in evaluating correctional programs and casual in continued reliance on established patterns of practice. Some of the most influential concepts and beliefs affecting practice have been "validated" only impressionistically in the accumulation of clinical experience.

As a result, most sociological studies are overwhelmingly pessimistic and bitingly critical of current correctional practice. Unfortunately, many critics have taken little responsibility for showing how one might move from the present situation to a new standard. They leave the impression that the entire system should be abandoned and started anew. This is not realistic. Even if the substitution of a totally new system was accepted as the solution, an intervening period of conversion and social change should be planned. But immediately there looms a complex question: "Change to what?" For this, we have only a sketchy answer. Bridging concepts, guiding principles, and well-articulated programs of research and practice are sorely needed. Critics willing to extend themselves to help develop these and to involve themselves deeply enough to supply substance and detail in their recommendations are few in number.

There are many paradoxes in corrections, one of the most interesting of which is a result of extended, thoughtful observation by correctional administrators and workers engaged in daily routine contacts, decisions, and interactions. Corrections contains a relatively rich and varied clinical experience with considerable versatility and skill developed as a kind of intuitive art among a few practitioners. At the same time, there is a paucity of explicit principles for practice and only a meager store of tested teachable knowledge related to a body of theory and principles directly applicable to corrections.

Theory is used by correctional administrators and correctional workers. Out of their daily experience they develop a private store of hunches, intuitions, hypotheses and inter-correlations upon which they base their decisions and actions. Consciously or unconsciously, every worker makes assumptions about the nature of his clients and the ways in which their problems can be eliminated or alleviated. To adapt his actions in practice, a serious worker must develop functional answers to many questions. For example, he must ask himself and be able to answer such questions as: What kind of person is my client? How did he get into trouble? What could cause him to change? If it is important for him to react in a specific way, how can the causes of his reaction be manipulated to facilitate and to gain a particular desired effect? Gradually these working answers are "tested" and integrated into a kind of rule-of-thumb theory. A personalized set of intervention premises which guide decision and action is established.

Rule-of-thumb theory is important because it is fashioned in the reality of experience. However, because it is so close to other personal elements in experience, rule-of-thumb theory sometimes makes us feel too deeply that our convictions have been completely substantiated. To support such convictions, a mass of folklore and anecdote is frequently developed to give a self-evident quality of truth which brooks no real evaluation. These personal convictions must be made explicit and subjected to evaluation by empirical methods. It is important, both from the standpoint of learning and of helping the field in its attempts toward greater professionalization. One of the most significant assists that might be given would be to support programs and approaches that were seriously engaged in such self-evaluation.

There is much discussion about whether corrections is an occupation which should be professionalized or whether it is a setting which should be professionalized so that a number of occupations and professions may function together with maximum efficiency. This is a rather useless argument, since, at the present level of development, the major developmental problems and principles underlying either choice are essentially the same.

However, the problems of developing a new profession or of moving a field toward greater professionalization may be larger and more permanently demanding than a foundation may like. If this is one of our objectives, then, again, we must be sure of what we are asking.

One of the distinguishing features of a profession as opposed to an occupation ". . . is the basing of its techniques of operation upon principles rather than rule-of-thumb procedures or simple routine skills. For an occupation to be a profession, it should involve complex tasks which are performed by artistic application of major principles and concepts rather than by routine operations or skills. This is an important differentiating feature. A skilled trade, obviously, involves some fairly complex tasks, but the members of the trade are able to perform these tasks through acquiring certain routine skills and through following certain specified rules. Many problems encountered by a member of a profession are, in a certain sense, unique. To solve such a problem, he must draw upon certain basic principles. However, the application of these principles necessitates an analysis of the particular problem to see what are its unique aspects which require adaptation of the principles. This adaptation is an artistic task; that is, it involves individual judgment and imagination as well as skill. A skilled trade does not demand this type of intellectual operation.

"A profession not only utilizes basic principles rather than depending on rule-of-thumb procedures, but as it becomes more mature it recognizes that the principles used in the profession must be viewed in an increasingly larger context and that, correspondingly, the science needed by the profession must be continually extended to more basic content rather than restricted only to the obvious applied science."[6]

A second distinguishing characteristic of a profession is that it has a code of ethics that commits the members of the profession to base decisions made in their work on a set of social values rather than on personal or local interests such as income, power, or loyalty to one's own group. Moreover, some form of group discipline supporting these values is established and invoked for violations.

In some ways, corrections measures up to these requirements. For example, corrections has the rudiments of a code of ethics in such documents as the *Manual of Correctional Standards* published by the American Correctional Association. However, many compromises and contradictions are scattered through its pages. In addition, in many quarters of the correctional community, there is real anxiety that this document may be used as a base from which to launch a nationwide assessment and comparison of correctional personnel and practices. Instead of dedication to its objectives and standards, there are efforts to forestall any such general usage. Finally, the aspirations of the National Council on Crime and Delinquency and the American Correctional Association notwithstanding, there is no generally accepted instrument of group discipline to enforce the values to which corrections has given lip service. A lack of understanding and agreement about basic principles and goals leaves no standard by which to judge the efficiency and effect of the typical ways and means by which we operate. Without such a yardstick, no one can sensibly predict whether a given plan, policy, or practice will facilitate or inhibit progress to correctional goals. The problem is further complicated in some quarters because of conflict and controversy about goals.

A related problem arises out of a tendency for individuals already identified as "professionals" (e.g., psychiatrists, clinical psychologists, social workers, and scientists from academic settings) to act in ways which are reasonably ethical in the context of their own discipline and yet to be ignorant of other social values that are being violated in a new setting. A correctional agency is likely to produce this sort of interaction. There is a need for an integrating ethic to help everyone see and understand the social implications of professional interaction in the correctional setting against the general background of human and social problems. Finally, there is a need to define the principles and goals of total correctional networks and systems and to promote a widespread and broadly based understanding of them.

---

[6] Ralph W. Tyler, "Scholarship and Career Education for the Correctional Service," *California Youth Authority Quarterly*, Vol. X, No. 3, pp. 4-5.

Corrections needs master plans. If correctional actions are to be effective, then interaction and change must be examined in the light of the best information about man, society, and social deviation. To fulfill its responsibilities, corrections must be provided with intellectual and institutional resources appropriate to the task.

Specific attention should be given to improving sources of information relevant to the planning and execution of policies and programs. Without sound information, decisions are hampered. Currently, much policy is set and actions are taken in ignorance of important facts. Many failures and frustrations plaguing correctional endeavors today result less from lack of capacity and effort than from the inadequate information on which decisions are based.

A search of the literature directly identified with corrections reveals little more than a mass of relatively sterile descriptions, speculations, wishful thinking, criticisms, and anecdotes. Depending on the breadth and depth of a reader's experience, this material may provide an excellent opportunity to compare personal experiences and beliefs, but it is not worth much more; most of it is merely descriptive. Sober evaluation reveals too many recommendations for techniques and tactics and too few suggestions and fewer principles which are helpful in formulating strategy for either research or practice.

This criticism applies not only to the evaluation of theories, but also to the evaluation of reported clinical applications. Professionals in several disciplines are inclined to base practice in corrections on what is essentially unverified theory. In some cases, theories which have not been verified in other settings have been adapted to the correctional setting without attempting to verify basic assumptions and applicability to offenders.

A typical article about diagnosis and treatment describes procedures and mechanics of a program in careful detail and uses anecdotes and experiences to demonstrate "success" or "failure." This has value, but it is no more than a beginning. Such material provides only the raw material for action; the facts should be related to one another, hypotheses formed, tested, and rendered significant with reference to an underlying theory of cause and effect, before the raw material is translated into action programs. Facts are most meaningful when they are related to a theory which can explain the why as well as the what of a situation. Unfortunately, the organization of experience and facts in corrections remains largely uncommunicated. Sharing in depth takes time and structure, which are rarely provided in a correctional agency. As a result, knowledge in the field as a whole remains fragmented and provincial in character.

One of the most significant steps that could be taken in developing knowledge for correctional use could be to provide assistance directed at developing more integrated theory. There is a serious need to discover how tested theory and research findings can be woven together and then translated into prescriptions for action at various levels of policy development and action.

There must be proper conditions and opportunities for correctional scientists and administrators of unusual intellect and objectivity to develop and test ideas in a setting where they can give constant attention to major points of social interaction. They should be free to follow shifts in conditions and attitudes in clients, staff, and social structure, and to analyze the flow and sequence of crises and decisions. Finally, they must be able to observe the effects of new perceptions and alternatives as they are introduced. In brief, if knowledge and theory are to be used effectively, they must be tested and studied under conditions of careful coordination and controlled observation.

Unlike those sciences in which hypotheses may be tested by experimental application to physical materials, behavioral scientists in corrections operate in life situations. We have customarily thought that basic research must be limited in normal life situations. However, the closed situation provided by correctional institutions offers a real-life situation that is a natural for basic studies as well as demonstration and project research. In addition, there is a potential in such activity for decreasing the service problems while adding to the store of verified knowledge.

There is no inherent structural opposition between science and corrections. There are obviously differences in the ways in which each has sought and achieved its goals and thought must be given to planned interaction. Difficulties may arise when the "search for facts" is pressed too vigorously without due regard for human and social needs, or when a clinical or correctional worker feels that all that matters is that something works for the client. However, as points of contact are planned and anticipated, and as a planned policy of interaction is developed, many of these difficulties can be eliminated.

Close, long-term, cooperative participation is indicated. By joining forces in organized, continuous study to widen and deepen the area of experience from which hypotheses are developed, both the scientist and worker contribute to effective action and the development of a store of verified, tested, and usable knowledge. There is very little collaboration of this sort in corrections today.

On the contrary, most research now being conducted is the work of projects individually initiated and operated, and scattered among numerous agencies and universities and several disciplines. Many administrators talk about "hit and run" researchers. The field is suffering from "projectitis," having too many small, isolated projects, while starving for integrated, long-term programs of research large enough and coordinated sufficiently to develop significant information and answers to basic problems. The policy of giving money which some foundations follow has fostered this situation.

A service orientation can be antithetical to research, since the worker is inclined to place the welfare of his client and his responsibility to the community foremost. It is frequently true that he has little time or energy left for the kind of evaluation, contemplation, and systematic clarification required. On the other hand, researchers studying case material in an academic or non-service setting frequently seem unaware of the clinical urgency of service problems. In addition, the theories and findings of research are not usually formulated in ways meaningful and maximally useful to the practitioner.

It seems unreasonable to assume that either of these approaches must exclude the other. Both well-tested techniques and knowledge which can be applied with clinical ingenuity are needed. Practice without theory is like an unguided missile. "Theory without practice is pure speculation. Practice is needed to identify problems and to specify the conditions under which they must be solved. Theory is needed to give unity and meaning to possible ways of attacking the problems. Theory suggests alternative solutions. Practice provides a check on the validity of these solutions and thus on the adequacy of theory."[7]

Needed are experimental institutions and "field laboratories" with built-in potential for self-study and with freedom to modify programs so that significant tests can be made. In such a setting, both research and practice should have clearly established aims, and should be directed, coordinated, and professional. If adequate consideration can be given to the design of the conceptual framework within which applied aspects of the program and research aspects of the program may operate, an easy and mutually productive collaboration can be established.

If concepts and hypotheses have been clearly specified and explicitly shared, there can be an effective working relationship. In any case, the most useful theory is one which is built around concepts having a specific relationship to what can be observed and measured. Most theory in corrections has not been of this type.

The problems of manpower and training in corrections are also embedded in larger social problems. First-rate minds and talents are in generally short supply in social welfare and government service. Any move to bring about more professional attitudes and sophisticated pat-

---

[7] Tyler, *op. cit.*

terns of knowledge must acknowledge the fact that corrections does not attract and hold enough competent, imaginative workers. In many ways corrections seems to be "low man" in competing for personnel. Granted that there is no strong tradition in the United States to draw people into public service, corrections still is not getting a proportionate share of the talent that does come into public service. It has been suggested that the situation would be improved if salaries were increased substantially. There is undoubtedly some merit in this recommendation, particularly as it might apply to top levels of administration. However, financial considerations are only part of the problem. Many middle-range positions in corrections have salaries quite comparable to the salaries of similar levels and positions in other areas of public service. Other things being equal, a person choosing to work in public service is likely to rate corrections as one of the least desirable of possible alternatives. In general, the crucial determinants of this negative attitude are associated with: (1) Loss of prestige and respect in the community, (2) conflicts and barriers in developing initiative and personal potential, and (3) insufficient opportunity for stimulating, challenging work.

Despite the fact that the average correctional setting can be a mean and unrewarding sector of life in which to work, there are some outstanding exceptions. In these places, correctional workers, administrators, social scientists, educators, and therapists, working in closely knit programs, find the correctional setting challenging and worthwhile. Much depends on the personal attitudes and preparation of the worker, and on the way the correctional assignment is defined and implemented by administrators, fellow workers, and the community. These "pockets" of optimism and high morale should be encouraged and supported. These are the settings in which critics and students should be involved so that criticism and education relating to corrections can lead to progress.

Implications for Interaction

Foundations are in a good position to help resolve a number of manpower and training problems in corrections. Moreover, an active partnership is likely to be mutually rewarding since correctional interests overlap with so many other phases of human welfare. Study and clarification of issues and problems in corrections can cast new light on many beliefs and social institutions that appear only peripherally related to corrections, but which are matters of central concern in other areas of human welfare.

At the same time, corrections needs a "balance-wheel"—i.e., an objective influence having a real commitment and investment in the field, but with a critical perspective that can generate an uncompromising inner need for self-evaluation and review of cherished patterns and procedures. Foundations can partially fulfill such a function. Important as financial support is, if a request for help is appropriately directed to a foundation, the foundation generally has related experience and information that often can be of more importance than the dollars which it might give.

In the past, corrections has not distinguished itself in spending money wisely. In fact, it is only as political patronage in appointing wardens and others has diminished that one can say with any assurance that money has even been spent honestly. It is not unreasonable, then, to insist that ideas, projects, demonstrations, and programs seeking financial support be submitted to a searching analysis and require systematic documentation. Further, criticisms implied or expressed in the rejection of certain proposals conceived by corrections should not be minimized or rationalized but instead should be used as a focal point for developing better proposals. On the other side of the coin, the acceptance of proposals should not be taken as a final index of their value.

An effort was made earlier to identify some underlying causes of the low quality of personnel and ideas in corrections. This was not conceived as a comprehensive survey of problems or causes but was rather a selection of sub-problems in areas where the potentials of the correctional field lie in six basic ways. They can be organized to:

1. Help develop people to work in the field.
2. Help develop knowledge to be used in the field.
3. Help resolve conflicts destructive to effective performance in the field.
4. Help stimulate development of standards and ethics for the field.
5. Help in developing a strongly supportive and informed external climate in the community.
6. Help develop an internal climate of optimism and growth, and settings and field laboratories where the failure to work a total "cure" does not become so oppressive that the staff retreats to a complacent acceptance of the status quo and the simple ritual of "processing" delinquents.

Developing People to Work in the Field

The need to attract, develop, and retain quality personnel is important at every level of correctional practice. Change and development, however, are most rapid and effective when they are initiated and supported by top levels in an organization and passed down to lower echelons. Junior staff training and personnel requirements flow from needs and programs of administration. The development of key career personnel and leadership is, therefore, a matter of prime importance.

In other fields, foundations have helped in this task of developing key personnel. It is probably one of the most likely areas in corrections where assistance could be given.

Many highly competent people have worked in correctional settings for brief periods of time. The field has served as a "port of entry" for a variety of social service and public administration careers. Many young administrators, young lawyers, and other young professionals have had some experience in corrections. Many of these people have made outstanding contributions in other fields after they have left corrections. If they had been persuaded to remain in the correctional field, the creative potential expended so fruitfully elsewhere might have been equally effective in modifying the correctional setting. Great administrators and scientists with an enduring commitment to corrections are needed to develop advanced ideas and designs for the future. Real advances and real understanding are most likely to come where there is a continuous thread of reason and courage, and vision and experimentation and self-evaluation. Such attitudes and activities result in a productive review of familiar patterns and develop the kind of understanding that moves men from one conceptual level to another.

How is it possible to persuade people capable of such insights and innovation to stay? Long-term involvement is based largely on the degree of personal satisfaction attained—on the needs in the person's life satisfied by the work setting, by related self-development, and by a sense of progress and participation.

For young persons, work-study programs, traineeships, internships, and other plans which combine correctional experience with professional development are available to be explored.

For older people, the problem is more complex. At the least, it should be remembered that time and opportunity for creative and prestigeful work are certainly as important as financial rewards.

In addition, decisions and actions in corrections should be timely and logical, and responsibility should be placed where it can be most effective and give satisfaction.

Despite the primarily negative tone in this paper regarding correctional personnel, there are some outstanding leaders whose mature insights and wisdom should be shared more widely than is currently possible. Several of these men have demonstrated a capacity for trenchant exposition and vital detail in writing and speaking. Some of them, recognizing the need and trying to respond to it, have made notes for books that may never be written simply because of lack of time.

Sabbatical years, as well as time to think, organize, and write, are recognized essentials for academic and scientific development. Perhaps a similar kind of program on a selected basis could be evolved and tried in corrections.

Teaching and personnel development are also satisfying activities sometimes limited in correctional settings because of the pressure of work. It would be valuable for both older and younger people if top-quality leaders could be provided with enough time to try to increase the number of promising young men with whom they may work in a close fashion. At the present time, they are unable to do much more than work closely with the one man who may replace them.

There are other problems for mature workers in the field. Merton, for example, has outlined some stresses and conflicts experienced by intellectuals in public service.[8] He describes two kinds of intellectuals, the bureaucratic intellectual (who identifies himself with the policy makers of the organization) and the unattached intellectual (who identifies himself with the public). The unattached intellectual may view his bureaucratic colleague as a "sell-out." He can hold fast to his formulations since they are not translated into action, and he may have little appreciation for the action problems of the bureaucratic intellectual.

On the other hand, the bureaucratic intellectual has limited altenatives for adjusting his position: 1) He may accommodate his social values and special knowledge to the values of the policy makers. This may result in an incorporation of the bureaucracy's values and a shift in his own perceptions and outlook; 2) he may try to change the policy makers; with failure he may leave the field; or 3) he may rationalize his functions as being purely technical and without value implications; in so doing, he separates a large part of himself from his work.

In this connection, the observations of Gouldner[9] are pertinent. He distinguishes between two types of professionals. One type is low on loyalty to an employing organization, high on commitment to specialized role skills, and is likely to use an outside reference group. The other type is high on loyalty to the employing organization, low on commitment to specialized role skills, and likely to be oriented to an inner reference group. Either pattern is likely to produce stress because of the organization's needs for expertise and loyalty. Conflict will occur whenever there is a demand for quality performance. Where quality can be ignored, as sometimes occurs in corrections, the stress will be diminished within the organization, but the individual with quality strivings may be frustrated enough so that he will leave.

I have no real solution to these problems, but it occurs to me that the private foundation might profitably support studies aimed at clarifying some of these conflicts and ambiguities in corrections.

---

[8] Robert K. Merton, "Role of the Intellectual in Public Bureaucracy," *Social Theory and Social Structure* (New York: The Free Press, rev. 1957).

[9] Alvin Gouldner, "Cosmopolitans and Locals: Toward an Analysis of Latent Social Roles," *Administrative Quarterly,* Vol. 2 (December 1957-March 1958), pp. 281-306, 444-480.

The Development of Knowledge

The development of knowledge for use in corrections is very much tied up with the development of people and the development of training and study centers of field laboratories in corrections. These things have already been discussed extensively.

From the standpoint of interim training, however, the organization and integration of available knowledge bearing directly on correctional problems must have high priority. There is need to discover how theories, research, and experience can be blended, woven together, and translated into prescriptions for action effective at various levels of practice and policy development.

Training materials designed specifically for use in corrections are sorely needed. At the same time, corrections must also use books and manuals, films, and supplemental training aids developed in other settings. Some of these materials can be adapted readily; others are barely applicable. A careful listing and review of what is available and an assessment of what is pertinent and adaptable to correctional use would be helpful.

While there is general agreement on the kind of broad educational background and general knowledge that should be provided, there is no consensus on the skills and detailed information which should be emphasized in advanced training. Moreover, there is strong disagreement on the discipline or school or cluster of disciplines responsible for a program of training. If a program of education and training for correctional work is to be successful, it must be managed and directed. Therefore, there is a pressing need to decide who is to be responsible so that the continuous attention and effort required can be organized, planned, and budgeted.

If differences about who should teach and what information should be given cannot be reconciled, perhaps some additional facts and new perspectives are needed. A foundation might help in this, not by taking one side or the other of the controversy, but by helping to create conditions and opportunities for objective, coordinated, cross-disciplinary study and evaluation. Work and research situations can be set up so that controversial issues may be examined and tested. Since the selection of knowledge to be taught and the interpretation of information are affected by the teacher's frame of reference, time should be spent to develop well-rounded frames of reference. This requires unified, interdisciplinary thought and action, without which the current fragmentation of knowledge about crime and corrections is likely to continue.

It was suggested earlier that much correctional practice is based on unverified theory. Unfortunately, this is likely to be the case in any primitive field of endeavor. For some time to come, corrections will undoubtedly have to operate with a network of loosely related, small conceptual systems. Nevertheless, the attempt to tie practice, demonstration, and research to fundamental concepts should be made so that our fund of knowledge will be cumulative.

In addition, we should try wherever possible to utilize concepts from many disciplines and within a single design. Finally, both practice and research should try to operate with a long-term programmatic orientation, linking activities and studies in a planned sequence of related actions and observations.

RESOLUTION OF CONFLICTS

Foundations are in a good position to help resolve some of the conflicts between differing groups and agencies, and between competing philosophies and traditional loyalties. The independent status of a foundation makes it adaptable to direct or support inquiries which cut across group boundaries and interdisciplinary rivalries. In situations where official agencies or professional organizations may be inhibited by political consideration or self-interest, "outside" consultation, supported by foundations, may lead to reformulations and reorganization of issues so that new alternatives are visualized and efforts can be better coordinated.

It requires a special social commitment and a large amount of immediately available cash to finance a thoroughly competent and comprehensive short-term consultative force of this sort. This is particularly true when large issues and large organizations are involved. Foundations have this kind of financial flexibility and social commitment.

This capacity for generating consultative forces may be used in direct and indirect ways.

Correctional agencies operate under tremendous pressure to produce a huge volume of daily decisions. Frequently, there is not enough time to anticipate problems well enough in advance to plan for them or to undertake a long-term analysis of them. In the pressure of work, it may be difficult to have enough objectivity to come to unambiguous conclusions. Only a few correctional agencies have been able to convince governing and legislative groups that they need permanent staff to develop and up-date long-term master plans. Finally, even where some planning staffs have been allowed, the staffing pattern cannot be made sufficiently broad nor flexible enough to cover the range and variety of expertise required. Consultative resources that are accessible and of high caliber are needed.

A foundation might help to meet such needs by making it possible to develop consultative resources which could provide single agencies, groups, or individuals with direct, impartial aid in developing master plans and in formulating, assessing, and designing policy. In addition, materials, observations, experience, and evaluative data gathered in such interaction could be studied and generalized for distribution to the field as a whole. This last, of course, is a more indirect approach to strengthening and changing the field and is like a more familiar pattern. A few model plans, codes, and the like have already been developed and widely shared.

The Development of Standards and Ethics

Standards and ethics are a sensitive subject and sometimes difficult to discuss. Nevertheless, the subject cannot be avoided. Professional competence, professional attitudes, and a stabilized program of professional training must have a substantial base of principles, standards, and ethics. Both society and corrections need a more unequivocal set of standards and ethics so that realistic, uncluttered evaluations can be made of correctional objectives and services. The social assignment given corrections needs to be pruned and made consistent. Such clarification is a first step toward establishing an improved working relationship between society and correctional agencies and institutions. In addition, realistic expectations and criteria for measuring the quality and level of work performance can be established—the kind of skills, the kind of direction, and the competencies required can also be specified. And finally, such expectations and specifications can then be meaningfully linked to relative and actual costs.

Development of a Strongly Supportive and Informed External Climate

This section might have been discussed as a type of consultative service rendering indirect aid to corrections. It is important enough, however, to justify a separate emphasis.

Any final resolution of manpower and training problems must involve enlightened public support. Ideally, a public education program should anticipate progress and be slightly in advance of current programs. That is, public awareness should be developed today for understanding the intentions and programs of tomorrow. Unfortunately, we are still struggling with the last century!

The average citizen still engages in a kind of psychological "transportation and exile" of offenders. He rationalizes his own delinquencies and behaves as if crime were something foisted on an otherwise innocent and law-abiding community. Friends, neighbors, and the mass media reinforce this attitude.

Here again, facts must be gathered, interpreted, and made public, preferably under independent and non-partisan auspices. It would be also helpful if critical issues could be anticipated (e.g., as in this conference) and public understanding could be developed in advance of official actions. Such advance planning and intervention should be guided by the recognition that public agencies have a need to explain themselves to a variety of publics. They must deal with a "public" of administrators, legislators and taxpayers, a "public" of offenders, a "public" of the injured, a "public" of behavioral and social scientists, and other "publics."

Under modern conditions, the distribution of facts requires an ability to compete with well organized and powerful elements for television and radio time and magazine and newspaper space. In the face of this competition a correctional service has a great deal of trouble promoting its own program and telling its own story.

Moreover, perhaps because of the barrage of ideas, information, and appeals from so many sources, an increasingly suspicious public requires more and more documentation and "scientific" fact to establish a basis for change of opinion and belief. Unfortunately, corrections is handicapped in developing such documentation and presents even that which it does have amateurishly. As a result, the inclination is to slide into the well worn "crisis appeal" as the only reliable stimulus to change.

Finally, part of a strongly supportive external climate requires some structure in society such as a foundation to seek deliberately to create a prestigeful acceptance of the people who choose to work in correctional settings.

Development of Correctional Field-Laboratories—An Internal Climate of Learning, Growth, and Optimism

Reference has been made to ways in which the present internal climate may be contributing to manpower problems. It has also been suggested that a way out of some of these troubles would be to change that climate by developing correctional agencies and institutions as kinds of field-laboratories in which service, research, and training are established as integral functions and co-partners in the overall correctional enterprise.

This is not proposed as a panacea, but is urged as an approach having many values and a potential for developing the unified body of knowledge, skill, experience, and understanding required to establish correctional practice on a truly professional base.

In such a setting, foundations would function much as they have in the past, underwriting the risk of exploration and failure by supporting promising people and untested but promising demonstrations and research. It would be extremely useful if a few full-scale field laboratories could be planned and established. There is no reason, however, why any agency or institution should not adopt the philosophy and orientation of a field-laboratory and seek to move toward the final objective by stages. Again, foundations might help in this process by providing consultation and/or support for some studies and projects in this area. Relatively small amounts of money strategically spent could generate the kind of interaction and experience that is self-sustaining.

For example, suppose a grant has been given to a university to do research on the basic personality patterns of offenders in a state prison. The university would be expected to establish the kind of working relationship with the institution that would insure a valid and reliable study and minimize disruption and interference with the ongoing service program.

It is unlikely, however, that time or money would be budgeted to either initiate or maintain such activities. It probably would be taken for granted that time would be somehow found to take care of whatever has to be done. As a result, the activity becomes residual.

Provision should be made explicitly for teaching, explanation, and interpretation to all levels of correctional staff. To do away with "hit and run" research and its negative effects in correctional settings, some money should be budgeted to provide time, personnel, and follow-up materials. The research itself would be benefited and the experience of participation and its value would be enhanced.

As another example, a few years ago it would have seemed strange to hire an anthropologist to work in a mental hospital. Today, as the result of some initial superficial involvement of a few anthropologists, several mental hospitals have hired full-time anthropologists and regard them important staff personnel. Perhaps it would likewise be useful to support a few competent professionals from disciplines not usually found in corrections to simply explore the field and its potentialities from their point of view.

Two cautions should be voiced in urging the development of field laboratories for practice and research. The first is that such an institution could easily get enmeshed in a deadly round of developing projects and negotiating for supporting grants, and fail to develop a true programmatic emphasis. The second caution is not to become so enmeshed in data collection that sight of the fact that major insights inevitably must come from integration of data in the minds of gifted men is lost. Here again, as in the case of the administrator, such minds must be found and increased support provided for them. Moreover, in designing a "field laboratory" for observation and work, time should be planned for thought and exploration.

Teaching can also be important to this kind of development. Obviously, a variety of research assistantships and fellowships might be developed in conjunction with established university programs. Qualified people from many disciplines and activities are needed to associate themselves with corrections, people who can communicate with one another at complex levels of thought and programming, and who are involved enough with the field to devote a major portion of their time to the definition of critical problems and to the search for solutions.

In a complex field, significant, concise, operationally-defined questions are not likely to be formulated without a long period of preparation, study, and observation. In corrections, this requires considerable familiarity with the theory, systematic thought, and expertise of several disciplines, and must also involve considerable seasoning and testing of thought in the field laboratory of correctional experience.

There is precedent for foundations to become involved in the development of such a concept as a field laboratory as a focal point of change in corrections. Public health is an example of a field in which the initial effort of the foundation was to support demonstration and rigorous application of basic medical and biological science findings. Groups supported by foundations developed new forms of management and procedure to facilitate and control these applications. Subsequently, both technical applications and standards were taken over and eventually incorporated in government and professional practice.

Remarks

by LEONARD S. COTTRELL, JR.

IT IS DIFFICULT to comment on a paper with which one finds himself in close agreement.

Dr. Sullivan gives an excellent review of the different types of foundations and their patterns of operation. He also gives a serviceable overview of the institutional complex known as corrections. He then discusses the processes and problems of productive interaction between foundations and corrections, and provides an admirable survey of the ways foundations might contribute to the general upgrading of personnel, knowledge, and the quality of operations in corrections.

While foundations can undoubtedly be helpful to the field in ways suggested by Dr. Sullivan, they can probably be even more helpful if those associated with corrections could come forward with some bold new ideas that need testing. Further, it is likely that foundations could be even more helpful if corrections could somehow be more creative and imaginative in integrating its efforts with other community activities directed toward prevention, treatment, and rehabilitation of offenders.

In watching the development and growth of community demonstration programs in the fields of juvenile delinquency and youth crime, I have been struck by the difficulties of integrating correctional activities with these comprehensive efforts. I am not sure where the difficulties lie, but I have seen very little creativity and boldness on this front.

It has occurred to me that these programs and others that will be projected under the broader Economic Opportunity Program might provide exciting opportunities for attempting new things in corrections itself and new ways of relating efforts in education and welfare to coordinated efforts in the correctional processes.

For example, the major thrust of the demonstration programs is to open up increasing opportunities for deprived youth in education, employment, recreation, and other essential areas of life. Parallel with this is the effort to upgrade the capabilities of youth and their families to take advantage of these opportunities as well as to become more competent in coping with the world in which they live. It should not be impossible to have a closely coordinated program of corrections which provides a greater system of increasingly stringent disciplinary programs with intensive reconstructive and rehabilitative activities.

Such a parallel system could make it possible to take youth who are not making satisfactory use of the new opportunities or the programs designed to enhance their competence in making use of these opportunities and place them in a disciplinary setting which provides, in addition to the needed discipline, a continuation of intensive upgrading activities. When such youth so treated appear ready to enter the comprehensive programs of the community, there could then be a well-worked-out plan for their reinduction. Should they fail again somewhere along the line of upgrading, they could then be moved back into a more stringent disciplinary setting, but one which also has a program that continues the upgrading activities preparatory to reintroducing them again in the community.

This is certainly not an easy operation to design, and it will take highly skilled correctional manpower and superior planning and coordination. But I suspect that a well-worked-out plan would receive generous support from governmental as well as from private sources.

Such an operation should also be a source of a new kind of training for correctional theory and practice and be highly stimulating to new, bold, and imaginative approaches to a field so frequently plagued with pessimism and apathy.

What Is the Role of Government in Resolving Manpower and Training Problems in Corrections?

by MERRITT GILMAN

IN THE FIELD OF CORRECTIONS, the government is the consumer, the employer, the critic, and the leader. Obviously, the role of government has many facets, and therefore it is necessary for us to define our particular interest—the role of leadership. Before turning to the role of leadership, it is necessary to sketch in some background material so that we all begin from the same reference points.

The definition of government, "the authoritative direction and restraint exercised over the actions of men in communities, societies, and states," can be used to accent the responsibility that municipalities, counties, states, and the federal government have in the field of corrections. Each subdivision has a responsibility. One of the things that we need to keep in mind is the relationship among these units of government which offers the greatest benefit to our clientele and to society.

The American College Dictionary defines "correction" as "that which is substituted or proposed for what is wrong." The term has also been defined as punishment, chastisement, discipline, or reproof. The dictionary, our practice, and the public image of corrections all reflect a strong component of punishment in the understanding of the word "correction." Persons working in the field of corrections, and particularly those attending such a conference as this one, see corrections as rehabilitation or treatment rather than punishment. We are seeking to control anti-social behavior. To be both truthful and facetious, we might say we are for law and order and against crime. We are for health and against illness. We are for constructive and creative people and against deviance. With such acceptable values, it would seem that we should have higher status. The fact is that our clientele comes from those who are criminals, mentally disturbed, or deviants, and this affects the way in which the public views us and the programs we administer.

The stereotype of the correctional worker is the guard—a hostile, club-wielding brute who checks to see that the prisoners are where they should be and that they are behaving docilely. He keeps the lid on; he carries out orders. He is not seen as a decision-maker or as an agent of change. This distorted perspective may determine how correctional programs should be supported.

When the tax dollar is allocated, city councilmen, county commissioners, state legislators, and congressmen are inclined to give more to health measures, for example, than to correctional programs. Fighting germs is a positive measure; fighting crime and delinquency is different. You can kill germs because they are destructive; you cannot, in most cases, kill the criminal or the delinquent for his destructiveness. What you can do costs money, and controllers of the budget are reluctant to spend money for offenders. The field of corrections might well take a leaf from mental health to achieve a change in status.

To serve offenders requires personnel. Corrections has not had adequate staff, either in quantity or quality. Our complaints have echoed over the years about the problem of manpower and training. How does the problem develop in a new unit created to control and help the offender?

In the first place, each new unit such as a specialized court, a detention home, or an institution, has been created to serve specific purposes and to perform stated functions—and these the staff strive to fulfill. As the unit develops, the strain and stress of everyday operation call for changes. In many situations, the pressure of the numbers of people to be served makes it necessary for staff to ignore standards set by the very organization responsible for the operation of the unit. While the job grows larger, and its nature more complex, additional facilities and additional personnel are not made available to handle the situation. Adjustments in service are necessary, and the original purposes and functions no longer serve as the guidelines of the organization. Each person here knows of cases in which an organization, created to serve both society and the offender, has deteriorated over a period to the point that its philosophy and practice are quite different than they were at the beginning.

The leadership role of government is to correct such deterioration—to evaluate service given, to inform the public of the problem, and to help it find an adequate solution. You can show where government has given such leadership. However, let me offer two recent examples, one from a county and the other from a state:

(1) In April 1963, Kent County in Grand Rapids, Michigan, opened a new million-dollar juvenile court center which included modern detention facilities. To accomplish this took sustained effort over a

number of years. It involved the Citizens Advisory Council, the League of Women Voters, the National Probation and Parole Association, the *Grand Rapids Herald,* and the Kent County Board of Supervisors. For a time, it seemed that the county would not have sufficient funds to engage necessary personnel. Faced with this problem, the judge, staff, and strong advisory committee decided not to move into the much-needed new facility until there was enough money to secure staff. When it was made clear that the need for staff was as great as the need for a building, the budget was met.

(2) In North Carolina, the Director of Probation, the Director of Prisons, and the Chairman of the Board of Paroles, working together and with the aid of the University of North Carolina's Institute of Government, prepared proposals which reflected a coordinated correctional effort and an increased emphasis on community treatment in preference to imprisonment of the convicted offender. The Governor strongly supported the requests for funds to expand probation and parole services. The General Assembly of 1963 was persuaded that the proposals would effect overall economies, help rehabilitate selected offenders, and improve the welfare of their dependents. Accordingly, funds were appropriated for sixty-one additional probation officers and thirty additional parole officers to be engaged for a two-year period. This represented a 50 percent expansion of probation and parole staffs.

Basic training for the new officers is provided by the Training Center on Delinquency and Youth Crime, which is financed by funds from the state and from the President's Committee on Juvenile Delinquency and Youth Crime. The Training Center has also developed and conducted courses for experienced probation officers and has scheduled similar courses for experienced parole officers with a view to raising the level of performance.

I would also like to cite an example of leadership on the federal level. In October 1954, the Secretary of Health, Education, and Welfare, acting on the strong recommendation made at the National Conference on Juvenile Delinquency, authorized the creation of a Division of Juvenile Delinquency Service in the Children's Bureau, whose interest in delinquent youth dates back to its inception in 1912.[1] The formation of this unit was also urged in a subcommittee report of the Senate Judiciary Committee, which said: "A large number of persons, either in testimony before or in communications to the subcommittee, felt that there was a lack of adequate national leadership in the battle against juvenile delinquency."[2] It recommended that funds be made available to

---

[1] Report of the National Conference on Juvenile Delinquency, Children's Bureau, U.S. Department of Health, Education, and Welfare (1954).

[2] *The Children's Bureau and Juvenile Delinquency Facts & Facets #1,* U.S. Department of Health, Education & Welfare. (Washington, D.C.: U.S. Government Printing Office, 1960), p. 21.

enlarge the consultation services of the Children's Bureau in relation to problems of juvenile delinquency. The new Division of Juvenile Delinquency Service was set up to provide technical assistance to public and voluntary agencies and to develop standards, guides, and methods relating to various types of services and care for delinquent children. Included in the fields covered was that of training programs for professional and non-professional personnel working with delinquent youth.

In creating this Division, the responsibility for leadership on a national level for training and for the development of standards and guides was recognized. By April 1955, the Director of the Division had listed ten long-range goals for the nation in improving its method of dealing with juvenile delinquents.[3]

By September 1958, the Division listed its goals for prevention, treatment, and control, based on the requests for consultation received from states, local communities, and national organizations.

The goals for prevention were:

1. Adequate training for present child welfare personnel, and recruitment and training of additional personnel;
2. Extension and improvement of basic child welfare services;
3. Helping communities carry out preventive programs;
4. Further research on the nature and extent of problem conditions contributing to delinquency.

The goals for treatment and control were:

1. Adequate training for personnel working with juvenile delinquents;
2. Learning the extent to which existing facilities conform to accepted standards;
3. Working to bring existing facilities and services into line with current standards;
4. Stimulating efforts to develop more effective treatment methods.[4]

To accomplish these goals, legislation providing federal funds for grants to states for extending and strengthening state and local services in the treatment and control of juvenile delinquency was recommended. Grants would be specifically used for training, demonstration projects, research studies, and jointly-arranged cooperative ventures with state and public and non-profit organizations were recommended.

For a number of years, Congress considered various bills on juvenile delinquency that incorporated the training of personnel. Finally, in Sep-

---

[3] Statement of Philip Gordon Green on taking office as the Director of the Division of Juvenile Delinquency Service in Children's Bureau, U.S. Department of Health, Education & Welfare, April 8, 1955.

[4] *The Role of the Federal Government in Meeting the Problems of Juvenile Delinquency* (Department of Health, Education & Welfare, Children's Bureau, September 1958).

tember 1961, it passed Public Law 87-274, which provided for short-term training of personnel in the prevention or control of juvenile delinquency or youth offenses, for grants for demonstration and evaluation projects, and for technical assistance service.[5] This action of Congress, coupled with the earlier establishment of the President's Committee on Juvenile Delinquency and Youth Crime, firmly established the fact that the federal government has a leadership role in the field of corrections and also indicated that the federal government would accept greater responsibility in its work with local communities to find effective solutions to the problems of juvenile delinquency.

A similar history of leadership in this field might be developed by those in other organizations, such as the Bureau of Prisons or the National Institute of Mental Health. In each of the examples cited, the leadership role of government has been linked to training, adequate staff, and the financial support of an adequate program. Leadership and support necessarily go hand in hand. Ample evidence of this is documented in the Health, Education and Welfare publication, *Grants in Aid and Other Financial Assistance Programs Administered by the U.S. Department of Health, Education and Welfare.*

The Goal of Leadership

The goal of leadership is to improve the service to the public and the offender. To do this, it is necessary to turn to education and research. Dr. Milton Wittman of the National Institute of Mental Health has referred to the trial of service, education, and research, with education and research being subordinate to service. The problem of providing for research and education is a major one.

What are the problems related to education? Cost is one. Various levels of government have provided scholarships, stipends, or work-study plans to help workers or recruits obtain graduate training. Not only have individuals received assistance in obtaining their professional training, but schools of higher education have also been aided by agencies which provide field instructors for students placed with them. Where this plan of financing education has been arranged, the service to the public and the offender has improved.

Another problem related to education is the question of what discipline prepares one best for corrections. What jobs require graduate preparation? While there may be different answers to these questions, it is clear that the scientific approach of each discipline is needed. The

---

[5] The Federal Delinquency Program, Objectives and Operation Under the President's Committee on Juvenile Delinquency and Youth Crime, and the Juvenile Delinquency and Youth Offenses Control Act of 1961 (November 1962). Mimeographed.

field of delinquency and crime has benefited through the contributions of many professions; none of their efforts should be lost by narrowing the approach. The battle for supremacy would be a losing one. Corrections, just as the health field, needs the combined efforts of the interdisciplinary approach.

What are the problems regarding research? Again, cost is a major item. Why spend money on research when you already know that poor service is often the result of insufficient or untrained personnel? Why not put money into staff, thus improving service?

The answers to such questions are involved. Staff for service and research are both needed. Without the findings of research to enrich knowledge, new techniques would not develop, and the effectiveness of current practice would not be measured. While service has the first priority, the contribution of education and research is essential to progress.

Another problem is that of communication. How do the findings from research get into the practice of the probation officer or the institutional worker? In working on a case-to-case basis, there is a strong tendency to focus on the psychodynamics of the individuals in the caseload and to overlook the influence of the social environment. To guard against an imbalance, the staff member needs to aid in the preparation for research. He does this by recording social information accurately and adequately and by posing questions for study. But the research problem is larger than this. Full-time attention of qualified personnel is needed to analyze and select from the tremendous volume of material available in the correctional field.

The need for sound in-service training programs and for studying the practice of one's own agency must be underscored. Responsibility for in-service training should be assigned to a qualified staff member. In larger courts and institutions, this should be a full-time job. Similarly, the research function requires special attention. When the time factor is considered, since research is time-consuming, it is well to question whether it is time that is lacking, or conviction. Not until there is conviction of the value of research will it gain the attention it deserves.

Service, education, and research are the triad. In the words of a popular song, "you can't have one without the other."

The Manpower Problem

The problem of recruiting and training able personnel is shared by all professions. What has the government done to study this problem? Following are some actions which it has taken:

1. In 1958, the Surgeon General of the Public Health Service established a Consultant Group on Medical Education to whom he posed

the question: "How shall the nation be supplied with adequate numbers of well-qualified physicians?"[6]

The Consultant Group's well-documented ninety-five-page report, published in October 1959, contained specific recommendations for action by many different groups, including foundations, states, and the federal government.

2. In the spring of 1961, the Surgeon General of the Public Health Service appointed a Consultant Group on Nursing to advise him on nursing needs and to identify the appropriate role of the federal government in assuring adequate nursing services.[7] Throughout its deliberations, the group recognized that federal action alone would not solve the many problems of nursing, and that private initiative and local government have a share of the responsibility. Their seventy-three-page statement described the present situation, predicted the needs for 1970, and included recommendations for governmental support.

3. In March 1963, the Public Health Service published a document (No. 1027) entitled *A Mental Health Manpower Studies Program.* The introduction points out that the National Institute of Mental Health has tried during the past several years to develop comprehensive programs in the general area of mental health manpower statistics and studies. It also states that "the administrative and technical vehicle for implementing the acquisition of mental health manpower information is the National Institute of Mental Health's Mental Health Manpower Studies Program. A major objective of the program is to collect and analyze statistical data concerning a number of general characteristics of psychologists, psychiatric social workers, psychiatric nurses, and psychiatrists, as well as other professional and subprofessional personnel working in mental health settings."[8]

This last reference is of special interest because it concerns manpower data covering several disciplines and both professional and subprofessional services. In addition, it reaffirms the role of governmental responsibility in defining manpower needs and goals.

4. In January 1963, the Assistant Secretary for Legislation of Health, Education and Welfare established a Departmental Task Force on Social Work Education and Manpower. Its specific responsibilities were

---

[6] "Physicians for a Growing America," *Report of the Surgeon General's Consultant Group on Medical Education* (Public Health Service Publication No. 709, October, 1957, U.S. Department of Health, Education & Welfare).

[7] "Toward Quality in Nursing: Needs and Goals." *Report of the Surgeon General's Consultant Group on Nursing* (Public Health Service Publication No. 992, February 1963, Department of Health, Education & Welfare).

[8] *A Mental Health Manpower Studies Program,* U.S. Department of Health, Education and Welfare, Public Health Service, National Institutes of Health, Bethesda, Maryland (March, 1963).

delineated, and it was requested to make such reports and recommendations as were deemed necessary. The Task Force was composed of persons from all units of the department concerned with the scope of the Task Force's work.

There is ample precedent for the government to be the leader in determining the manpower and training problems of a profession. It has accepted this responsibility and should be expected to help serve the needs of corrections.

PUBLIC SUPPORT

For the government to lead, it must have public support and understanding. Can we tell the story of corrections in such a way that funds will be appropriated willingly rather than grudgingly? Do we have success stories that we can tell? The rehabilitated criminal or reformed delinquent gives us pride, but we protect him from exposure. Success stories are needed, however, since the public is interested in achievements. A wealth of material should be available to us, and we should be able to find ways of presenting it.

In our zeal to explain our programs, we must be realists. Not until the public trusts us to reveal the failures will it credit the successes. Not until people know the extent and nature of the problems we face can they be expected to follow our leadership. Recidivism, for instance, is a problem we can either talk about or try to hide. It offers evidence of the failure of our programs. How we interpret this can determine how the public offers its support.

How do we explain that juvenile arrests for major felonies are increasing?[9] How do we cope with serious delinquent or criminal activity? How do we make these serious problems ones that the public tries to help us solve?

One method used to gain public support has been to set up an Advisory Board or an Ad Hoc Committee. The interested and capable people drawn into the program bring a wealth of knowledge and background to bear on the problems considered. They communicate to the community and to the agency they are serving. Such a citizen group, attuned to the tempo and mood of the community and informed about the problems of the agency, will not move faster than the community can tolerate. It will be able to recognize that there are many things the community will accept if presented to it in stages. Then, when the community does see the benefit of some improvement, the readiness for change will increase.

---

[9] The President's Committee on Juvenile Delinquency and Youth Crime, *Report to the President* (May 31, 1962), p. 5.

Leadership, whether it comes from the citizen group or from a professional, exerts pressure on the community with a force of facts; it appeals to the community conscience; it does not let the community forget its responsibilities. Leadership probes the nerve continually and keeps working toward needed solutions.

There is an art to getting others excited about what concerns you. People get excited for a variety of reasons. Whatever the reason—love of fellowman, concern with taxes, desire for status—the citizen whose nerve is touched is a potent social force. When he knows what the problems are, and what resources are needed, and when he understands that treatment is really less costly than custodial care, then he will work to provide the necessary resources. When people know, people care. Citizen groups can arouse public interest in the work being done and can push for needed change.

But there is often resistance to citizen participation programs. They require time and energy for current problems, lest they get out of hand. A working committee requires competent staffing; members need to learn the depth of the problems, for them to deal with them knowledgeably rather than superficially. At the same time, the staff needs to be able to hear the valued comments and proposals for solutions.

Government officials can also exercise leadership in correctional agencies by taking a prominent part in the Welfare Council of the community. These councils are often dominated by private agencies, not because public agencies are not welcome, but because they have developed this means of working together to define social problems and gain community support. Their financial support is often tied to their relationship to the council and the community chest. The private agencies interpret their activities and views through the council; the correctional agency has an equal opportunity to submit its views and seek public attention for its problems. The correctional agency needs to be a part of the total community's concern for the welfare of people; it can not afford to be left out of comprehensive planning, particularly if it is a municipal or county agency.

The leadership responsibilities of the different levels of government have not been delineated, although delineation is in order. For years, our experience and belief have been that the local community is in the best position to control the individual and to plan for and with him and his family. Both state and federal designs for action in corrections have taken this into account. The guides to communities and the setting of standards have often been the province of states and the federal government.

The problem of governmental intervention into the affairs of a community or a state remains one of controversy, or perhaps of balance.

On the one hand, the cry is that we have settled for a grant-in-aid system that finances local leadership but does not provide for state or national leadership; on the other hand, the cry is that control follows the dollar and that local leadership is stifled by the eligibility requirements attached to the aid.

Still other questions are posed: Do state and local funds dry up because of funding from foundation and federal sources? Does the long look for the dollar outside the community have a deleterious effect?

Recognizing that planning and development are essential functions of government should make it easier to determine the balance required to reach the goals of the various levels of government. Leadership is not restricted to any one level but is essential at each.

In summary, what is the role of government in meeting the manpower and training needs? Tautological? It is to provide enough well trained manpower to do the job of control and rehabilitation. To accomplish this, it must provide the opportunity for training and for upgrading present personnel. Its responsibility is to set and maintain standards of service, performance, and facilities, and to inform the public so that the issues are as well known and of as great concern as are other vital issues of the day.

Epilogue

by Charles S. Prigmore

On September 10, 1965, President Lyndon B. Johnson signed the Correctional Rehabilitation Study Act. In one sense, this was a culmination of plans and activities launched by the Arden House Conference on Manpower and Training for Corrections held in June 1964 and described in this book.

The Arden House Conference ended at noon on June 26, 1964. Within two hours of the adjournment of the Conference, an Interim Committee, which had been unanimously voted upon by the delegates, was set up. The Conference had charged this committee to plan the establishment of the three-year non-governmental Joint Commission on Correctional Manpower and Training.

The Interim Committee, initially comprising the five chief sponsoring organizations of the Conference (the American Correctional Association, the American Sociological Association, the Council on Social Work Education, the National Council on Crime and Delinquency, and the Western Interstate Commission for Higher Education), came quickly to the following decisions: (1) The Committee voted to request a one-year grant from the Vocational Rehabilitation Administration of the U. S. Department of Health, Education, and Welfare, to be used in the organization of the Commission. (2) Dr. Charles S. Prigmore, who had served as Secretary of the Conference, was appointed to assume a full-time planning role if the grant were to become available. Later, the American Bar Association and the American Psychiatric Association were added to the Interim Committee and became very active.

Immediately following the Arden House Conference on Manpower and Training for Corrections and the establishment of the Interim Committee, the Decisions of the Conference were printed and distributed. The 10,000 copies of the first printing were exhausted within three or four months after the Conference.

On December 1, 1964, a one-year planning grant was received from the Vocational Rehabilitation Administration, which made it possible to begin the preparatory work. The Interim Committee met almost monthly after June to discuss plans for fund-raising, for developing the research design for the studies, and for the involvement of representation from labor, business, industry, and other key national bodies.

Several meetings were held with Representative Edith Green, Chairman of the Special Sub-Committee on Education in the U. S. House of Representatives, as well as with her staff, and on January 11, 1965, she introduced H. R. 2263, the Correctional Rehabilitation Study Act of 1965, to provide a part of the funds for the Joint Commission. The remarks in the *Congressional Record* at the time she introduced the bill were reprinted and widely distributed. Demands for copies were still coming in through September 1965. Shortly after Representative Green's introduction of H. R. 2263, Representative Albert Quie of Minnesota introduced an identical bill, making the measure one of bipartisan sponsorship.

To the sixty-one original organizations sending delegates to the Arden House Conference were added such national groups as the American Legion, the Adult Education Association of the U. S. A., the American Association of Colleges for Teacher Education, the American Council on Education, the American Federation of Labor and the Congress of Industrial Organizations, the American Personnel and Guidance Association, the U. S. Chamber of Commerce (informal), the International Association of Chiefs of Police, the National Association of Manufacturers, the National Association of Citizen Crime Commissions, the National Conference of Superintendents of Correctional Institutions for Girls and Women, the National Council of the Churches of Christ in the U. S. A., the National Council of Women of the United States, the National Recreation and Parks Association, the National Rehabilitation Association, the Public Personnel Association, the U. S. Department of Defense, the U. S. Office of Economic Opportunity, and the U. S. Public Health Service. The sixty-one affiliated groups grew to eighty. Others were still considering affiliation after exploratory invitations from the Commission.

In the meantime, offers to support H. R. 2263 came in daily from adult and juvenile correctional administrators on state and local levels in every part of the nation, from state parole board chairmen, from youth commissions, from chief probation officers, from judges, and from private correctional agencies. The eighty affiliated bodies pushed for Congressional action.

The legislation also had vigorous support from state governors. The Western Governors Conference passed a unanimous resolution in June 1965, supporting the establishment of a Joint Commission on Correctional Manpower and Training. By September 1965, forty-five of the fifty governors had publicly announced their support of the act, or the Commission, or both.

In the Senate, Senator Joseph Clark, Chairman of the Sub-Committee on Employment and Manpower, became interested in the critical shortage of skilled correctional manpower as an aspect of his already strong concern with the pressing need for professional personnel in all the social service fields. On April 22, 1965, Senator Jacob K. Javits and Senator Clark introduced a companion bill, S. 1807, as a bipartisan measure. Eventually, eleven co-sponsors joined in the active support of the bill.

The hearings in both the House and the Senate revealed a strong and growing awareness on the part of individual witnesses, organizations, the Federal Administration, and the Congress itself that the Correctional Rehabilitation Study Act of 1965 was urgently needed to provide an objective, systematic study of manpower needs and resources, to gain consensus regarding educational and in-service training curriculum content, and to launch an action program to meet needs in personnel recruitment, education, training, utilization, and retention.

As with the Mental Health Study Act of 1955, upon which the bill was very closely patterned, no specific commission was named in the bill. The bill simply required that the organization which would conduct the program of research and study must be a non-governmental agency, organization, or commission, composed of representatives of leading professional associations, organizations, or agencies active in the field of corrections. A Senate amendment, agreed to later in the House without a formal conference, provided for the establishment of a National Advisory Council on Correctional Manpower and Training in the Department of Health, Education, and Welfare, to consider applications for grants and to make recommendations to the Secretary for approval of grants.

On June 21, 1965, the House of Representatives passed H. R. 2263 under suspension of the rules. On August 11, 1965, the Senate passed the amended H. R. 2263, and within a few weeks the House approved the amended version. The bill provides for $500,000 for the first fiscal year and $800,000 for each of the two succeeding years.

President Lyndon B. Johnson signed the Correctional Rehabilitation Study Act of 1965 into law on September 10, 1965, as Public Law 89-178.

Since the Arden House Conference had stressed that the Joint Commission on Correctional Manpower and Training should be a non-governmental body, funds were also sought from private foundations. By the fall of 1965, grants had been received from the Smith, Kline, and

French Foundation, and the Child Welfare Foundation of the American Legion. A number of other foundations were considering grants of various amounts in early October 1965.

The appropriation bill for Public Law 89-178 was signed shortly afterwards, and the Joint Commission on Correctional Manpower and Training is expected to be named by the National Advisory Council in January, 1966, as the group best equipped to carry out the purposes and objectives of the law.

Quarters for the Commission were located at 1522 K Street, N. W., Washington, D. C., and the actual work was planned to begin as of January 1, 1966.

A listing of the officers and members of the Board of Directors as of October 1, 1965, may help to complete this brief recapitulation of the events from June 1964 to October 1965. It is due to the efforts of these men and women, as well as the individual members of the 89th Congress, the affiliates, the fifty state correctional administrators of adult corrections, the state administrators of adult corrections, the state administrators of juvenile corrections, the state parole board chairmen, the judges and various interested citizens that Public Law 89-178 became a reality and the Joint Commission on Correctional Manpower and Training the vehicle to translate its potentialities into action.

President
James V. Bennett, *Consultant*
Bureau of Prisons
U. S. Department of Justice
HOLC Bldg., Room 332
Washington, D. C.

Vice-President
Warren Olney, III, *Director*
Administrative Office of the U. S. Courts
Supreme Court Building
Washington, D. C.

Chairman
Milton G. Rector, *Director*
National Council on Crime and Delinquency
44 East 23rd Street
New York, New York

Vice-Chairman
Dr. Peter P. Lejins
Department of Sociology
University of Maryland
College Park, Maryland

Secretary-Treasurer
Richard A. Chappell, *Chairman*
United State Board of Parole
U. S. Department of Justice
Washington, D. C.

William T. Adams, *Director*
Juvenile Delinquency Programs
Western Interstate Commission for Higher Education
University East Campus
30th Street
Boulder, Colorado 80303

Dr. Daniel Glaser, *Head*
Department of Sociology
342 Lincoln Hall
University of Illinois
Urbana, Illinois

Dr. Daniel Blain, *Chairman*
Manpower Commission, American Psychiatric Association
2100 Clarkson Avenue
Philadelphia, Pa.

ROGER CUMMING, *Chief*
Community Resources Section
Welfare Branch
Division of Claims Policy
Room 752
Social Security Administration
Baltimore, Maryland

DR. WALTER RECKLESS
Department of Sociology
Ohio State University
1775 South College Dr.
Columbus, Ohio

DR. HOWARD P. ROME
Senior Consultant
Section of Psychiatry
The Mayo Clinic
Rochester, Minnesota

RUSSELL G. OSWALD, *Chairman*
New York State Board of Parole
162 Washington Avenue
Albany, New York

DR. ARNULF M. PINS
Associate Executive Director
Council on Social Work Education
345 East 46th Street
New York, New York

MRS. THOMAS SCALES
1205 S. W. Cardinell Drive
Apt. 621
Portland, Oregon

DR. CLYDE E. SULLIVAN
Co-Principal Investigator, SERVE Program
Social Restoration Research Center
New York, New York

HONORABLE LUTHER YOUNGDAHL
Judge, U. S. District Court
4101 Cathedral Avenue, N. W.
Washington, D. C.

A final, and special, word of appreciation is due to the Board of Directors, the staff, and the constituent bodies of the Council on Social Work Education for identifying the need for joint action, for the success of the advance planning leading up to the Arden House Conference, for the remarkable achievements of the Conference itself, and for the results following the Conference. Seldom before has an organization established to advance the interests of a single profession been so farsighted and responsible as to take leadership for unifying and strengthening an entire multi-professional field of human and social service.

There seems to be little doubt that the groundwork has been laid for a revolution in the field of corrections—a revolution to be directed initially at the key target of manpower, for it is the professional and skilled personnel who hold the answer to any program of behavioral change. But the revolution is certain to be extended later to buildings, programs, administrative patterns, laws, and all other aspects of corrections.

I am personally certain that the poor working conditions, low salaries, ill-defined tasks, confusion of goals, conflict between punitive and rehabilitative philosophies, public apathy, inadequate budgets, and grossly ineffective rehabilitative programs for juvenile and adult offenders will soon be past history. It is my belief and prayer that the Correctional Rehabilitation Study Act of 1965, through the Joint Commission on Correctional Manpower and Training, will usher in a new era in the correctional field. Soon offenders really will be seen as human beings entitled to rights and responsibilities. The same level of treatment and rehabilitation will be extended to the Negro, the poor, the Indian, and the Mexican as is now available to the wealthy person able to afford a private psychiatrist, medical specialist, able attorney, remedial teacher, or any other highly qualified professional, when he or his children violate the law.

Only then will the real culmination of plans developed at the Arden House Conference on Manpower and Training be achieved.

APPENDIXES

Appendix I

COUNCIL ON SOCIAL WORK EDUCATION

ADVISORY COMMITTEE TO THE CORRECTIONS PROJECT*

1964-1965

Chairman: MILTON G. RECTOR

WILLIAM T. ADAMS
Project Coordinator
Demonstration Education Programs for Juvenile Correctional Workers
Western Interstate Commission for Higher Education
University East Campus
30th Street
Boulder, Colorado 80304

BENJAMIN F. BAER
942 W. 34th Street
Los Angeles, California 90007

MRS. BEULAH COMPTON
Associate Professor
School of Social Work
University of Minnesota
Minneapolis, Minnesota 55455

DR. VERNON FOX
Chairman, Criminology and Corrections
School of Social Welfare
Florida State University
Tallahassee, Florida

DOROTHY M. FRITZ
Executive Director
Youth Services
410 North 34th Street
Philadelphia 4, Pennsylvania

JOHN R. HARTNETT
Acting Dean
School of Social Work
Syracuse University
926 South Crouse Avenue
Syracuse, New York 13210

PAUL W. KEVE
Director
Department of Court Services
22 Courthouse
Minneapolis 15, Minnesota

A. M. KIRKPATRICK
Executive Director
John Howard Society of Ontario
168 Isabella Street
Toronto 5, Canada

TULLY MCCREA
Western Regional Director
National Council on Crime and Delinquency
821 Market Street
San Francisco, California

GEORGE F. MCGRATH
Commissioner
Department of Correction
120 Tremont Street
Boston, Massachusetts

* Agency designation as of October 1964.

MILTON G. RECTOR
Executive Director
National Council on Crime and Delinquency
44 East 23rd Street
New York, New York 10010

CHARLES H. SHIREMAN
Assistant Professor
School of Social Service Administration
University of Chicago
Chicago, Illinois 60637

DR. REX A. SKIDMORE
Dean, Graduate School of Social Work
University of Utah
Salt Lake City, Utah 84112

DR. CLYDE E. SULLIVAN
Director of Research
The American Foundation
Studies in Corrections
1638 Philadelphia National Bank Building
Philadelphia 7, Pennsylvania

JOHN WALL
Assistant Professor
School of Social Work
Tulane University
New Orleans, Louisiana 70118

JOHN A. WALLACE
Director of Probation
Office of Probation for the Courts of New York City
2 Lafayette Street
New York, New York 10007

Ex-Officio Members

JOSEPH P. ANDERSON
Executive Director
National Association of Social Workers
2 Park Avenue
New York, New York 10016

DR. DONALD CLEMMER
President, American Correctional Association
Department of Corrections
300 Indiana Avenue, N. W.
Washington 1, D. C.

MERRITT C. GILMAN
Chief, Training Branch
Division of Juvenile Delinquency Service
Children's Bureau
Department of Health, Education, and Welfare
Washington, D. C. 20201

H. G. MOELLER
Assistant Director
Bureau of Prisons
U. S. Department of Justice
Washington, D. C. 20201

DR. DAVID C. TWAIN
Chief, Crime and Delinquency Section
Community Research and Services Branch
National Institute of Mental Health
Bethesda 14, Maryland

Appendix II

PUBLIC LAW 89-178

89TH CONGRESS, H. R. 2263

SEPTEMBER 10, 1965

AN ACT

79 STAT. 676

To provide for an objective, thorough, and nationwide analysis and reevaluation of the extent and means of resolving the critical shortage of qualified manpower in the field of correctional rehabilitation.

Be it enacted by the Senate and House of Representatives of the United States of America in Congress assembled, That this Act may be cited as the "Correctional Rehabilitation Study Act of 1965".

Correctional Rehabilitation Study Act of 1965.

SEC. 2. Section 12 of the Vocational Rehabilitation Act (29 U.S.C. ch. 4) is amended to read as follows:

68 Stat. 662.
29 USC 42.

"GRANTS FOR SPECIAL PROJECTS IN CORRECTIONAL REHABILITATION

"SEC. 12. (a) (1) The Secretary is authorized, with the advice of the National Advisory Council on Correctional Manpower and Training, established by subsection (b) of this section, to make grants to pay part of the cost of carrying out a program of research and study of the personnel practices and current and projected personnel needs in the field of correctional rehabilitation and of the availability and adequacy of the educational and training resources for persons in, or preparing to enter such field, including but not limited to the availability of educational opportunities for persons in, or preparing to enter, such field, the adequacy of the existing curriculum and teaching methods and practices involved in the preparation of persons to work in such field, the effectiveness of present methods of recruiting personnel for such field and the extent to which personnel in the field are utilized in the manner which makes the best use of their qualifications. Such a program of research and study is to be on a scale commensurate with the problem.

"(2) Such grants may be made to one or more organizations, but only on condition that the organization will undertake and conduct, or if more than one organization is to receive such grants, only on condition that such organizations have agreed among themselves to undertake and conduct, a coordinated program of research into and study of all aspects of the resources, needs, and practices referred to in paragraph (1).

"Organization."

"(3) As used in paragraph (2), the term 'organization' means a nongovernmental agency, organization, or commission, composed of representatives of leading professional associations, organizations, or agencies active in the field of corrections.

National Advisory Council on Correctional Manpower and Training.

Establishment.

"(b) (1) There is hereby established in the Department of Health, Education, and Welfare a National Advisory Council on Correctional Manpower and Training, consisting of the Secretary, or his designee, who shall be Chairman, and twelve members, not otherwise in the regular full-time employ of the United States, appointed without regard to the civil service laws by the Secretary after consultation with the Attorney General of the United States. The twelve appointed members shall be selected from among leaders in fields concerned with correctional rehabilitation or in public affairs, four of whom shall be selected from among State or local correctional services. In selecting persons for appointment to the Council, consideration shall be given to such factors, among others, as (1) familiarity with correctional manpower problems, and

(2) particular concern with the training of persons in or preparing to enter the field of correctional rehabilitation.

"(2) The Council shall consider all applications for grants under this section and shall make recommendations to the Secretary with respect to approval of applications for and the amounts of grants under this section.

Council members, compensation.

"(3) Appointed members of the Council, while attending meetings or conferences thereof or otherwise serving on business of the Council, shall be entitled to receive compensation at rates fixed by the Secretary, but not exceeding $100 per day, including travel time, and while so serving away from their homes or regular places of business they may be allowed travel expenses, including per diem in lieu of subsistence, as authorized by section 5 of the Administrative Expenses Act of 1946 (5 U.S.C. 73b-2) for persons in the Government service employed intermittently.

60 Stat. 808; 75 Stat. 339, 340.

Appropriation.

"(c) For carrying out the purposes of this section there is hereby authorized to be appropriated for the fiscal year ending June 30, 1966, the sum of $500,000 to be used for a grant or grants to help initiate the research and study provided for in this section; and the sum of $800,000 for each of the two succeeding fiscal years for the making of such grants as may be necessary to carry the research and study to completion. The terms of any such grant shall provide that the research and study shall be completed not later than three years from the date it is inaugurated; that the grantee shall file annual reports with the Secretary, the Congress, the Governors of the several States and the President, among others the grantee may select; and that the final report shall be similarly filed.

Report to President and Congress, etc.

"(d) Any grantee agency, organization, or commission is authorized to accept additional financial support from private or other public sources to assist in carrying on the project authorized by this section."

Approved September 10, 1965.

LEGISLATIVE HISTORY:

HOUSE REPORT No. 381 (Comm. on Education & Labor).
SENATE REPORT No. 543 (Comm. on Labor & Public Welfare).
CONGRESSIONAL RECORD, Vol. 111 (1965):
June 21: Considered and passed House.
Aug. 11: Considered and passed Senate, amended.
Aug. 26: House concurred in Senate amendments.

Other Publications on Corrections Which May Be Ordered from the Council on Social Work Education

---

Casebook in Correctional Casework. Committee on Corrections for the Committee on Teaching Materials. 1958. (#8-51-1)

Concepts of Prevention and Control: Their Use in the Social Work Curriculum. Special Workshop Report, New York. 1961. (#61-95-6)

A Conceptual Approach to Teaching Materials: Illustrations from the Field of Corrections. Elliot Studt. 1965. (#65-96-6)

Education for Social Workers in the Correctional Field. Elliot Studt. A Project Report of the *Social Work Curriculum Study,* Volume V. 1959. (#9-87-1)

The Expansion of Correctional Field Placements and Internships. Report of a Mountain States Institute, Brighton, Utah. 1964. (#65-96-4)

Perspectives and Guides in the Expansion of Social Work Education for the Correctional Field. Committee on Corrections. 1958. (#8-34-6)

Report on a Survey of Social Work in the Field of Corrections. Eileen L. Younghusband. Reprinted from August 1960 issue of *Social Work Education.* (#63-96-23)

COUNCIL ON SOCIAL WORK EDUCATION

DATE DUE
